The Unconscious

The Unconscious explores the critical interdisciplinary dialogue between psychoanalysis and contemporary cognitive neuroscience. Characterised by Freud as 'the science of the unconscious mind', psychoanalysis has traditionally been viewed as a solely psychological discipline. However, recent developments in neuroscience, such as the use of neuroimaging techniques to investigate the working brain, have stimulated and intensified the dialogue between psychoanalysis and these related mental sciences. This book explores the relevance of these discussions for our understanding of unconscious mental processes.

Chapters present clinical case studies of unconscious dynamics, alongside theoretical and scientific papers in key areas of current debate and development. These include discussions of the differences between conceptualisations of 'the unconscious' in psychoanalysis and cognitive science, whether the core concepts of psychoanalysis are still plausible in light of recent findings, and how such understandings of the unconscious are still relevant to treating patients in psychotherapy today. These questions are explored by leading interdisciplinary researchers as well as practising psychoanalysts and psychotherapists.

This book aims to bridge the gap between psychoanalysis and cognitive neuroscience, to enable a better understanding of researchers' and clinicians' engagements with the key topic of the unconscious. It will be of key interest to researchers, academics and postgraduate students in the fields of psychoanalysis, cognitive science, neuroscience and traumatology. It will also appeal to practising psychoanalysts, psychotherapists and clinicians.

Marianne Leuzinger-Bohleber is Professor of Psychoanalysis at the University of Kassel, Germany, Head Director of the Sigmund Freud Institute, Frankfurt/Main, Germany, training analyst of the German Psychoanalytical Association (DPV) and Vice-Chair for Europe of the Research Committee of the International Psychoanalytical Association (IPA).

Simon E. Arnold, Dipl.-Psych., is research associate at the Sigmund Freud Institute, Frankfurt a.M. He studied psychology, literary studies, art history and philosophy in Konstanz, Paris and Beer Sheva.

Mark Solms is Professor of Neuropsychology at the University of Cape Town, South Africa, President of the South African Psychoanalytical Association, Director of the Science Department of the American Psychoanalytic Association, Co-Chair of the International Neuropsychoanalysis Society and Chair of the Research Committee of the International Psychoanalytical Association.

Psychoanalytic Explorations Series

Books in this series:

The Unconscious

A bridge between psychoanalysis
and cognitive neuroscience

Edited by
Marianne Leuzinger-Bohleber,
Simon Arnold, and Mark Solms

 Routledge
Taylor & Francis Group

LONDON AND NEW YORK

First published 2017
by Routledge
2 Park Square, Milton Park, Abingdon, Oxon OX14 4RN

and by Routledge
711 Third Avenue, New York, NY 10017

First issued in paperback 2018

*Routledge is an imprint of the Taylor & Francis Group,
an informa business*

British Library Cataloguing in Publication Data
A catalogue record for this book is available from the British
Library

Library of Congress Cataloging-in-Publication Data
CIP data has been applied for.

ISBN 13: 978-1-138-57965-1 (pbk)
ISBN 13: 978-1-138-92044-6 (hbk)

Typeset in Bembo
by Apex CoVantage, LLC

Contents

Figures

Tables

Contributors

Simon E. Arnold, Dipl.-Psych., is research associate at the Sigmund Freud Institute, Frankfurt a.M. He studied psychology, literary studies, art history and philosophy in Konstanz, Paris, and Beer Sheva. His research interests include clinical psychoanalysis and the history of science – especially neurology, forensics and psychiatry – social psychology and critical theory. Within this field he worked on a study on mentally ill arsonists and the history of pathological firesetting. He is member of the *Gesellschaft für psychoanalytische Sozialpsychologie*, and writes a column on the quotidianity of myths. He is part of a research group on the aftermath of the Holocaust, in which they try to understand the transmission of trauma and anti-Semitism.

Werner Bohleber, Dr. phil., psychoanalyst in private practice in Frankfurt a.M., Germany. Training and supervising analyst, former president of the German Psychoanalytical Association (DPV). Member of the Board of Representatives of the International Psychoanalytical Association (IPA) (2003–2007). Co-Chair for Europe of the IPA Research Advisory Board (2000–2008). Member of the EPF Working Party on Theoretical Issues. Editor of the German psychoanalytic journal *Psyche*. Author of several books and numerous articles. His latest book is *Destructiveness, Intersubjectivity, and Trauma. The Identity Crisis of Modern Psychoanalysis.* London, Karnac, 2010.

Tamara Fischmann, Prof. Dr. rer. med., psychoanalyst DPV/IPA. Professor for Clinical Psychology at the International Psychoanalytic University Berlin. Staff member and scientific researcher at the Sigmund Freud Institute, Frankfurt. Chief methodologist in psychoanalytic empirical research, dream researcher. Publications on interdisciplinary research in bioethics, dream research, attachment and ADHD, as well as imaging technique studies in neurosciences.

Karl Friston is a theoretical neuroscientist and authority on brain imaging. He invented statistical parametric mapping (SPM), voxel-based morphometry (VBM) and dynamic causal modelling (DCM). Friston received the first Young Investigators Award in Human Brain Mapping (1996) and was elected a fellow of the Academy of Medical Sciences (1999). In 2000, he was president of the international Organization of Human Brain Mapping. In 2003, he was awarded the Minerva Golden Brain Award and was elected a fellow of the Royal Society in 2006. In 2008, he received a medal, Collège de France, and an honorary doctorate from the University of York in 2011. He became a fellow of the Society of Biology in 2012, received the Weldon memorial prize and medal in 2013 for contributions to mathematical biology and was elected as a member of EMBO (excellence in the life sciences) in 2014.

Theodore J. Gaensbauer, MD, is, in addition to his work as a private practitioner, a Clinical Professor of Psychiatry at the University of Colorado Health Sciences Center and also on the faculty of the Irving Harris Program in Child Development and Infant Mental Health within the Division of Child Psychiatry. He is a distinguished fellow of both the American Academy of Child and Adolescent Psychiatry and the American Psychiatric Association and a graduate of the Denver Institute for Psychoanalysis. His particular areas of clinical and research interest have been emotional regulation and attachment in infancy, the impact of trauma on young children's social/emotional development, the nature of early traumatic memories, and the treatment of early trauma.

Robert M. Galatzer-Levy, M.S., M.D., is Clinical Professor of Psychiatry and Behavioral Neurosciences at the University of Chicago and a Training, Supervising, and Child and Adolescent Supervising Analyst at the Chicago Institute for Psychoanalysis, where he is a faculty member. In addition to the clinical practice of psychoanalysis, Dr. Galatzer-Levy's interests include the integration of nonlinear dynamic systems theory into psychoanalysis, the relationship between law and psychiatry and the critical study of psychoanalytic texts.

Juan Pablo Jiménez is Professor of Psychiatry and Director of the Department of Psychiatry and Mental Health East at University of Chile (Santiago) and Visiting Professor at the University College London. He is a training and supervising analyst in the Chilean Psychoanalytical Association. He has held an important number of positions, including president of the Chilean Psychoanalytical Association (1995–1998), member of the House of Delegates of the International Psychoanalytical Association (IPA) and representative at the Council (1994–1996), president of the Latin-American Psychoanalytic Federation, FEPAL (2007–2008). He is a member of the International Research Board and of the Conceptual Integration Committee of the IPA. His research interest focuses on issues of clinical epistemology and integration between clinical psychoanalysis and empirical research.

Marianne Leuzinger-Bohleber, Ph.D., is professor of psychoanalysis at the University of Kassel and director of the Sigmund Freud Institute, Frankfurt, a. M., Germany. She is a training analyst of the German Psychoanalytical Association (DPV) and completed her psychoanalytical training at the Swiss

Psychoanalytic Society. She is the chair of the Research Committee of the DPV and was the chair for the Committee for Clinical, Conceptual, Historical and Epistemological Research Committee (2002–2010). Since 2010, she has been Vice Chair of the Research Committee of the IPA. She is on the editorial board of several journals. She has published over 300 chapters and articles and authored or edited many books. She has been and still is responsible for several large research projects in the field of psychoanalytic psychotherapy research and early prevention. Contact: *leuzinger-bohleber@ sigmund-freud-institut.de*

Rolf Pfeifer is Professor of Computer Science and Director of the Artificial Intelligence Laboratory in the Department of Informatics at the University of Zurich. He is the author of *Understanding Intelligence* (MIT Press, 1999).

Michael Russ, Dr. rer. med., is a clinical neuropsychologist. His fields of professional experience and research are cognitive neurology, neuropsychology, and fMRI. He is affiliated with the Sigmund Freud Institute, Frankfurt am Main, Germany, as a scientist conducting the fMRI investigations of the LAC depression study.

Dominique Scarfone is Professor of Psychology at the University of Montréal and Training and Supervising Analyst at the Montréal Psychoanalytic Institute and Society. His work integrates the thought of Jean Laplanche, D. W. Winnicott, Piera Aulagnier, Michel de M'Uzan and others. He is author of many books and numerous journal articles. These include recently: *Laplanche: An Introduction* (New York 2015) and *Oublier Freud? Mémoire pour la psychanalyse* (Montréal 1999), as well as the articles "A Matter of Time: Actual Time and the Production of the Past" (2006, *Psychoanalytic Quarterly*, 75:807–834); and "The Three Essays and The Meaning of the Infantile Sexual in Psychoanalysis" (2014, *Psychoanalytic Quarterly*, 83: 327–344). Until recently, he was co-editor of the *International Journal of Psychoanalysis*. He is a member of the *Conceptual Integration Project Group* of the IPA.

Margerete Schött, Dipl.-Psych., is research associate and Ph.D. student at the Sigmund Freud Institute, Frankfurt (Mentor: Prof. Leuzinger-Bohleber). Current involvement in fMRI research on attachment. Further research interests in neural mechanisms of dream, depression and borderline personality disorder.

Carlo Semenza graduated in Medicine and specialized in Psychiatry. He is presently Full Professor of Neuropsychology in the Department of Neurosciences at the University of Padova. He has been Director of the Department of Psychology at the University of Trieste. He has been visiting professor at Boston University, Melbourne University, University of Athens and at the Basque Centre for Cognition, Brain and Language in S. Sebastian. He is the founder and organizer of the yearly European Workshop on Cognitive Neuropsychology. He has published extensively about neuropsychological disorders, in particular in the domains of language and mathematical cognition. He also shares an interest in, and has published articles and book chapters on, the relation between psychoanalysis and neurosciences.

Riccardo Steiner, Ph.D., is a retired academic and a psychoanalyst in private practice in London. He is a full member of the British Psychoanalytic Society. He is the author of several papers on the linguistic, cultural, sociopolitical and theoretical clinical issues in psychoanalysis and has published several books. In 2001, he was awarded the Sigourny prize for his contributions to psychoanalysis. Amongst other distinguished contributions to psychoanalysis, he edited, together with Pearl King, *The Freud-Klein Controversies.* The book was awarded the prize of the American Psychoanalytic Association in 1994, and nominated 'Le livre de l' année" by the Paris Psychoanalytic Society in 1995. His other books, *'It's a New Kind of Diaspora': Explorations in the Sociopolitical and Cultural Context of Psychoanalysis; Tradition, Change, Creativity: Repercussions of the New Diaspora on Aspects of British Psychoanalysis; Unconscious Phantasy; and Within Time and Beyond Time: A Festschrift for Pearl King,* are published by Karnac Books.

Mark Solms is Chair of Neuropsychology at the University of Cape Town and Groote Schuur Hospital (Departments of Psychology and Neurology), President of the South African Psychoanalytical Association, Director of the Science Department of the American Psychoanalytic Association, and Research Chair of the International Psychoanalytical Association. He was awarded an honorary membership in the New York Psychoanalytic Society in 1998 and the American College of Psychoanalysis in 2004 and will be named Honorary Fellow of the American College of Psychiatrists in 2016. He is best known for his discovery of the forebrain mechanisms of dreaming, and for his integration of psychoanalytic theories and methods with those of modern neuroscience. He founded the International Neuropsychoanalysis Society in 2000 and was founding editor of the journal *Neuropsychoanalysis.* He has published widely in both neuroscientific and psychoanalytic journals, as well as in general-interest publications such as *Scientific American.* He has published more than 250 articles and book chapters and five books. His second book, *The Neuropsychology of Dreams* (1997), was a landmark contribution to the field. Together with Oliver Turnbull, he wrote *The Brain and the Inner World* (2002), which is a bestseller and has been translated into 12 languages. He is authorized editor and translator of the forthcoming *Revised Standard Edition of the Complete Psychological Works of Sigmund Freud* (24 vols.) and the *Complete Neuroscientific Works of Sigmund Freud* (4 vols.).

Sverre Varvin, MD, Ph.D., is a training and supervising analyst and a past president of the Norwegian Psychoanalytic Society. He is Professor at Oslo and Akershus University College, and his main research areas are the traumatization and treatment of traumatized patients, refugees and their exile experience, traumatic dreams, and psychoanalytic training. He has held several positions in the IPA (e.g., Vice-president, Board representative, member of research committees, chair of program committee for 2013 IPAC) and is currently chair of the China Committee.

Heinz Weiß, Prof. MD, Psychoanalyst (DPV, DGPT, Guest member Brit. Psychoanal. Soc.), is Director of the Department of Psychosomatic Medicine, Robert-Bosch-Krankenhaus, Stuttgart, Germany. He worked as a visiting scientist in the Adult Department of the Tavistock Clinic, London (1992/1993) and is a Member of the Editorial Board of *Psychoanalytic Psychotherapy*. As author and (co)editor, he has published several books: *Der Andere in der Übertragung* [The Other in the Transference] (1988*), Ödipuskomplex und Symbolbildung* [Oedipus Complex and Symbol-Formation], a Festschrift for Hanna Segal (1999), *Perspektiven Kleinianischer Psychoanalyse* [Perspectives of Kleinian Psychoanalysis], Vols. 1–12 (1997–2004), and *Projektive Identifizierung. Ein Schlüsselkonzept der psychoanalytischen Therapie* [Projective Identification, A Key-Concept of Psychoanalytic Psychotherapy] (2007).

Samuel Zysman, MD. After practicing as a pediatrician, he moved into child psychiatry and completed psychoanalytical training at the Argentine Psychoanalytical Association. Currently, he is a training analyst and professor at the Buenos Aires Psychoanalytical Association. He has written many papers on psychoanalytic technique, child analysis, ethics and psychoanalysis, literature and psychoanalysis, etc. His current focus is on the psychoanalytic study of actions, cognitive processes, and the meta-psychological status of scientific theories.

Preface

It gives us pleasure to publish some of the main papers from the 15th Joseph Sandler Research Conference, which took place in March 2014 in Frankfurt, Germany. This conference was organised in cooperation with the Sigmund Freud Institute (SFI), the IDeA Center of the State of Hesse, the Universities of Frankfurt and Kassel and the Research Committee of the International Psychoanalytical Association (IPA). We want to thank the organizing teams of all these institutions as well as the outstanding speakers and discussants who made it such a success. And we hope that the enthusiasm and the sense of excitement which filled the meeting some time ago is still noticeable for the reader today. We were especially grateful for the professional support provided by the administrative director of the Sigmund Freud Institute, Panja Schweder, and by Paula Barkay, the administrative director of the International Neuropsychoanalysis Centre, London. Many thanks also to the team of the SFI: Renate Stebahne, Dirk Schildt, Elke Weyrach and to the many young scientists and psychoanalysts who helped organize the conference. We should also not forget the incredible translators of the talks and the articles. The conference was generously funded by the German Research Foundation (DFG).

We hope that readers of this volume will enjoy the spirit of the conference as they engage afresh with the curiosity, openness and intellectual challenges presented by the speakers, discussants and participants. The pages of this book abound with new insights into the core research topic of psychoanalysis: the unconscious.

Marianne Leuzinger-Bohleber, Frankfurt
Simon Arnold, Frankfurt
Mark Solms, Cape Town

Introduction

Chapter 1

The unconscious

A contemporary interdisciplinary dialogue: some introductory remarks[1]

Marianne Leuzinger-Bohleber

FRANKFURT

and

Mark Solms

CAPE TOWN

This publication is devoted to a central topic of the interdisciplinary dialogue between contemporary psychoanalysis and other scientific disciplines: the unconscious. As is well-known, in Freud´s time, psychoanalysis was characterised as "the science of the unconscious mind". In the last hundred years, many other disciplines, among them cognitive science, have studied non-conscious mental functions. What are the differences´ between the conceptualisation of "the unconscious" in psychoanalysis and cognitive science? Is the core thesis of psychoanalysis still plausible, namely that unbearable impulses and fantasies from the past and present are banished into the unconscious, from where they continue to determine feelings, thoughts and behaviours in unknown ways? And is such an understanding of the unconscious still central for helping patients in contemporary psychotherapy?

Throughout his entire life, Freud had hoped that new developments in the neurosciences would contribute to exploring psychoanalytic processes from a natural scientific point of view. In many of his historical and theoretical papers it has been substantiated that Freud – due to the standard of neuroscientific methods during his times – turned his back on this vision and defined psychoanalysis as a solely psychological science of the unconscious (Solms, 1997/2003). Over the past few years, recent developments in the neurosciences, e.g. investigating the living brain with the help of neuroimaging techniques, as well as the neuro-anatomic method, as described by Solms and other psychoanalytic researchers, have stimulated and intensified the interdisciplinary dialogue between psychoanalysis and the neurosciences. Thus it has been a kind of a gift to the 150th birthday of Sigmund Freud in Germany, that even the widely read journal "Der Spiegel" talked of a "Renaissance of psychoanalysis". A main contributor to this new attention devoted to psychoanalysis was the Nobel laureate neuro-biologist Eric Kandel. His twin papers published more than a decade ago in the American Journal of Psychiatry, *"A new intellectual framework for psychiatry"* (1998) and *"Biology and the future of psychoanalysis: a new intellectual framework for psychiatry revisited"* (1999) created a large interest in the dialogue between psychoanalysis and the neurosciences, initiating an internationally challenging, broad discussion of fascinating new interdisciplinary research perspectives.

For many authors, as for Kandel (e.g. 2009), a vision of Sigmund Freud turned into reality in the last decades: Freud never gave up his hope that developments in the neurosciences might someday contribute to a "scientific foundation" of psychoanalysis. He abandoned this attempt, his "Project for a Scientific Psychology" (1895), due the obvious limitations of the neurosciences' methodology at that time (see Kaplan-Solms & Solms, 2000), subsequently defining psychoanalysis as a "pure psychology of the unconscious". As Kandel points out in his twin papers, the developments in the neurosciences and in neuroimaging techniques (as the MEG, EKP, PET, fMRI) open a new window for psychoanalysis to "prove" its concepts and findings by applying the methodologies of current "hard natural sciences". Kandel is passionate about this vision: his unique, spirited speeches claim that the future of psychoanalysis mainly depends on its taking up this challenge.

The necessity to investigate psychoanalytic treatments by neuroscientific methods?

For Kandel, psychoanalytic treatments must show effectiveness also in studies applying methods of contemporary neurosciences. His vision is connected with challenging epistemological and methodological questions, as will shortly be discussed below. But seen from a perspective of the sociology of science, of course, Kandel is right: if psychoanalysis could show that psychoanalytic treatments influence the brain's functioning, this would tremendously heighten its acceptance as a treatment method in medicine and the Mental Health systems. Several groups of researchers presently engage in such studies. To mention some in the field of depression research: the Hanse Neuro-Psychoanalysis Study by Buchheim, Viviani, Kessler, Kächele, Cierpka, Roth et al. (2012) investigates the changes of depressive patients during psychoanalytic treatments, e.g. by fMRI. The research group of Northoff, and Boeker (2006) at the Psychiatric University Clinic in Zürich compares different treatments of severely depressed patients by neuroimaging methods. The Sigmund-Freud-Institute (Tamara Fischmann, Leuzinger-Bohleber et al.) – in cooperation with the Max Planck Institute for Brain Research (Wolf Singer) and the Psychiatric University Clinic Frankfurt (Aglaja Stirn, Michael Russ et al.) – is realizing a substudy of the large LAC depression study comparing psychoanalytic and cognitive behavioural long-term treatment with chronically depressed patients using fMRI and EEG (in the sleep laboratory of the Freud Institute (see Fischmann, Russ, Baehr & Leuzinger-Bohleber, 2012; Fischmann, Russ &

Leuzinger-Bohleber, 2013; Leuzinger-Bohleber, 2015, p. 161ff). Other psychoanalytical research groups are also engaged in similar studies: e.g. the Mainz Psychosomatic Department (Manfred Beutel et al.), researchers at Yale University (e.g. Linda Mayes et al.), at Columbia University in New York (e.g. Bradley Peterson et al., Andrew Gerber et al., Steven Roose), at the University College London (Peter Fonagy and his team) and at the University of Cape Town (Mark Solms et al.), to mention just a few. Thus many international research groups are taking up Kandel's demand.

Neuropsychoanalysis

Kaplan-Solms and Solms (2000) have developed neuro-anatomical research methods to investigate patients with brain lesions with clinical psychoanalytical research methods. In different countries, interdisciplinary research groups work systematically with patients with precisely localised brain lesions, seeking specific psychoanalytic treatment techniques enabling us to help them (see Leuzinger-Bohleber et al., 2003; Leuzinger-Bohleber, Röckerath & Strauss, 2009). Their findings are broadly relevant for studying the old mind-body problem in new and fascinating ways (see e.g. Damasio, 1999; Sacks, 2007 and many others).

The first volume of the international journal "Neuropsychoanalysis" was published in 1999; leading psychoanalysts and neuroscientists presented studies on emotion and affect, memory, sleep and dreams, conflict and trauma, conscious and unconscious problem solving etc. The International Society for Neuropsychoanalysis, founded in 2000 by Mark Solms and others, organizes interesting annual international conferences.

Thus, nowadays it seems undeniable that an exchange between psychoanalysis and neuroscience is most promising for both parties. The neurosciences have obtained objective and exact methods to verify complex hypothesis on human behaviour, while psychoanalysis can contribute the necessary concretion and rich knowledge concerning the meanings and motivations of psychic processes and can therefore direct interesting questions at the neurosciences.

Psychoanalytical conceptual research and some epistemological remarks

Another field of research, mentioned by Eric Kandel, is psychoanalytical conceptual research, a specific and genuine psychoanalytical research field. As we have discussed in several papers, the interdisciplinary dialogue fertilises the clinical psychoanalytical work not in a direct way. Results from neuroscientific studies will never be able to tell a clinical psychoanalyst how to cope with a certain analysand in a certain psychoanalytical situation. The psychoanalytical treatment technique – and intuition – is something fundamentally different than the further development of concepts and theories. Therefore, the exchange between the knowledge base of psychoanalysis and the neurosciences always takes place on the level of concepts and theories, never on the level of the concrete clinical interactions (see e.g. Leuzinger-Bohleber, 2008, p. 256ff, 2015; Solms, in this volume). Nevertheless, for the further development of psychoanalysis as a scientific discipline, an openness and an attempt for achieving "external coherence" (Strenger, 1991) of psychoanalytical concepts with the knowledge of neighbouring disciplines is inevitable: Psychoanalytical concepts and theories should not be in contradiction with the current knowledge in other scientific disciplines. Surprisingly, many of the central psychoanalytical concepts of Sigmund Freud have proven to be "externally coherent" with the modern neuroscientific understanding of complex psychic processes. Some of them even can be understood more precisely and deeply. On the other hand, we also have to discuss some critical points in our theorising and modify or even re-think some of our psychoanalytical concepts in the light of modern neurosciences (see following introductory paper by Mark Solms).

As will be discussed in this book: challenging epistemological topics are connected to the dialogue between psychoanalysis and the neurosciences. If we don´t take into account epistemological questions of this dialogue carefully, we once more might risk a harmful split in the psychoanalytic community between those who are in favour and those who are against this interdisciplinary exchange. To mention an example: According to our personal experiences in an endeavour of 20 psychoanalysts and neuroscientists studying memory, dreams and cognitive and affective problem-solving in a joint research project 1992–1998 (supported by the Köhler Foundation, Darmstadt, Germany) it seemed essential to critically reflect on its epistemological dimensions (see Leuzinger-Bohleber, Mertens & Koukkou, 1998; Leuzinger-Bohleber, Roth & Buchheim, 2008). Such interdisciplinary exchange, while fascinating and innovative, is challenging and complicated for both sides. We often don't speak the same language, apply different concepts in analogous terms, and often identify with divergent traditions in science and in philosophy of science. Much tolerance and stamina is needed to achieve an intensive exchange of ideas enabling us to reach new intellectual frontiers; to crack up former understandings and concepts and resist idealising tendencies to expect "solutions" for unsolved problems in our own discipline from the other, foreign one, which – like a white screen – attracts projections and projective identifications. To take new findings of the other discipline means to undergo uncertainty and unease; it is painful to leave aside "certainties" and false beliefs developed in your own field. Going through a period of uncertainty and unease is inevitable, a must for a productive and constructive dialogue reaching beyond a rediscovery of already established disciplinary knowledge. The comparison of models developed by both disciplines in order to explain their specific data collected by specific (and very different) research methods is linked to complex and sophisticated problems of philosophy of science and epistemology. The well-known danger of the eliminative reductionism of psychic processes onto neurobiological processes or the consequences of a transfer of concepts, methods and interpretations from one scientific discipline onto another, without reflecting them, need to be prevented.[2]

Therefore, we cannot agree completely with the passionate conviction of Eric Kandel that modern neurosciences really can save the future of psychoanalysis. On the one hand, we share his view that curiosity and openness towards scientific developments, neurosciences included, are a must for innovation and creativity. In order to remain a "Wissenschaft"[3] of the mind, psychoanalysis must refresh and further develop its concepts and theories, showing again and again that psychoanalytic theories are "externally coherent" (Strenger, 1991) with the state of art of other disciplines, e.g. the neurosciences. In this sense, the future of psychoanalysis as a productive "Wissenschaft" depends on openness towards contemporary neurosciences.

But, on the other hand, we must carefully avoid "categorical mistakes" (see e.g. Leuzinger-Bohleber & Pfeifer, 2002; Leuzinger-Bohleber, 2015). The data of the neurosciences are on a completely different level than those of psychoanalysis, aiming to understand and decode meanings of unconscious psychic functioning of human beings. Epistemologically, psychoanalysis is a "specific science" (Wissenschaft) with a specific methodology suited to investigate its specific research object (unconscious conflicts and fantasies) and its specific scientific quality criteria. Psychoanalytic research method has contributed a large body of knowledge and cannot be replaced by any other one, including neuroscientific ones (see e.g. Leuzinger-Bohleber, Dreher & Canestri, 2003; Solms, in this volume).

"External coherence" should not mean losing psychoanalysis' autonomy as a specific "Wissenschaft" nor to reduce it to neurobiology. It can only mean systematically comparing the knowledge base and the models of both disciplines, initiating critical reflection on one's psychoanalytical models' explanatory power again and again, to foster innovative theoretical developments. Neurosciences cannot "solve the unsolved theoretical problems of psychoanalysis". Conceptual problems in psychoanalysis must be "solved" in psychoanalysis' own core field for gaining scientific insights: the genuine psychoanalytical (research) situation (see e.g. Kaplan-Solms & Solms, 2000; Brothers, 2002; Hampe, 2003; Hagner, 2008ab; Kandel, 2005; Leuzinger-Bohleber, 2005, 2006; Mancia, 2006; Leuzinger-Bohleber, 2012ab, 2015; Gullestadt, 2013; Lemma, 2013).

The scientific philosopher and historian Michael Hagner (2008a) investigates thoroughly and in detail how the visualisation of processes which take place in the hidden spaces of our bodies and the brain are influencing our thoughts, fantasies and emotions, as well as our culture in general:

> There is a distinction (in studies on imaging techniques) between disordered thinking from mathematical problem-solving, [. . .] those first memories of childhood experiences, of the last quarrel with one's life

partner or the conflicts with parents, of erotic dreams about the most exciting love relationship. As is well-known, in the twentieth century it was primarily psychoanalysis which was to first single out such phenomena for research. The biographical detail, intimacies and concealed layers this discipline retrieved will doubtless never be matched by screening the brain.

[. . .]

This shift [from psychoanalysis to neuroimaging, L–B] could lead to circumstances in which the multiplicity and relevance of the life of the mind is measured primarily by the methods of visualization. The price for such a development consists in the fact that "the investigation into the deeper connections, the explanation, listing, narration, and evaluation, in short, historical, scientific textual linear thought is displaced by a new, image-based, "superficial way of thinking". The consequence of this shift with respect to the sciences of man is that the analytic depth of former forms of thought, for which psychoanalysis may be considered representative, will be replaced by the superficial insight of neuroimaging. Human understanding is thus relegated to the status of an excrescence of material forms of representation.

(p. 278 ff.)

Conceptualization of the unconscious in contemporary, pluralistic psychoanalysis

As we all know, Freud effectively contributed the third largest insult to mankind by discovering "the dynamic unconscious": Freud shocked mankind with the insight that none of us are "masters of our houses"; we are rather more unwarily driven by unconscious, libidinous and aggressive drive impulses and fantasies. Those parts of our personalities which are prohibited and taboo in our respective culture are exiled to the estranged in us – the unconscious. In 20th-century Vienna, these parts were primarily sexual impulses and fantasies. Nowadays, we are more likely facing unbearable, taboo experiences associated with trauma, impotence, separation, the loss of systems of meaning and value, as well as feelings of insufficiency within a more closely intertwined, globalised, medialised and technically dominated new world. In every one of his works, Freud warned us not to deny these unconscious powers. Only in acknowledging their effectiveness can we guarantee a wise handling of these powers. Turning our backs and negating the unconscious not only leads to psychic illness, it also enhances the danger of uncontrolled outbreaks of drives and threatens human cohabitation and our culture.

Throughout its history of more than a century, psychoanalysis has differentiated itself as a science with 12,000 members of the International Psychoanalytical Association in terms of its central concepts such as "the unconscious" to the point of a "plurality of theories" and the question arises: Does "*the* psychoanalysis" exist at all? Don't we have to speak of "many psychoanalyses"? While modern ego-psychology oriented psychoanalysts such as New York's Fred Pine still refer to the "dynamic unconscious" as the product of fended off impulses and drives which are to be examined by psychoanalysis, others, e.g. Giuseppe Civitarese from Pavia, define a continuum of conscious and unconscious in reference to Bion. The unconscious does not protrude via, for instance, slip of the tongue into the symptoms and stagings of the conscious; rather, every conscious process is accompanied by an unconscious process. Based on neuroscientific findings and experimental psychological research on unconscious forms of information processing, Werner Bohleber also goes by the notion of a *non-repressed unconscious* and differentiates it from the *"dynamic unconscious"* and a *"creative unconscious"*. Jorge Luis Maldonado from Brazil, on the other hand, firmly believes in the concept of the dynamic unconscious and the psychoanalytic structural theory, which distinguishes psychoanalysis from other disciplines examining hidden, non-conscious information processing. Finally, based on Jacques Lacan, Miguel Kolteniuk Krauze from Mexico City advocates two dimensions of the unconscious as a system of primary repression, which is characterised by its inertia and lack of symbolisation capabilities, and a secondary repression, which is characterised by the primary process and its fate – hence André Green's approach concerning the preservation of the drive dimension.

All of these authors were keynote speakers at the IPA in Mexico City themed "Exploring Core Concepts: Sexuality, Dreams, and the Unconscious". This short summary of the diverging views is able to illustrate how the plurality of theories is a characteristic of the prosperity of modern, international psychoanalysis as a discipline, which has always been concerned with highly complex clinical phenomena and has strived to decode conscious, preconscious and unconscious inner workings in joint effort with the patients. When referring to psychoanalysis as a scientific discipline, which just like any other science puts its findings up for a critical discussion in the non-psychoanalytic community, we must always continuously refurbish the lenses of this kaleidoscope in order to recognise commonalities as well as differences to individual conceptualisations of the unconscious and enable fruitful discussions. This is a prerogative for any innovative advancement in psychoanalysis as an internationally acclaimed science (see also following chapter by Mark Solms).

Overview on the chapters of this book

Most of the main papers of this volume have been presented at the *7th Joseph Sandler Research Conference 2014*, which took place at the Goethe University in Frankfurt. It was organised by the International Psychoanalytical Association, the Sigmund-Freud-Institute and the IDeA Center of the Excellency Initiative of the State of Hesse.

Joseph Sandler initiated this conference – together with other leading psychoanalytic clinicians and researchers. His aim was to build bridges between psychoanalysts working mainly in their private offices and those engaged in various forms of extra-clinical research in academic institutions. Joseph Sandler was President of the International Psychoanalytical Association (IPA), Freud Memorial Professor at University College London (UCL) and at the Hebrew University in Jerusalem. He was also senior scientist at the Sigmund-Freud-Institute in Frankfurt between 1986 and 1990.

As already mentioned: In the last hundred years, many other disciplines, among them cognitive science, have studied non-conscious mental functions. Are these conceptualisations relevant for a contemporary understanding of unconscious fantasies and conflicts in psychoanalysis? And are they relevant for clinical psychoanalytical practice?

These sorts of questions are discussed by interdisciplinary researchers and practising psychoanalysts and psychotherapists in this volume. Mark Solms – in his introductory chapter – uses Freud's (1915) essay on "The Unconscious" as starting point. The aim of his paper is to update Freud's classical metapsychology in the light of recent developments in cognitive and affective neuroscience. In doing so, he tries to integrate Freud's concept of repression with contemporary notions of the cognitive- unrepressed- unconscious.

The Project Committee for Conceptual Integration under Werner Bohleber as Chair has been pursuing a similar goal for several years. In their contribution in *PART I*: Conceptual, historical and clinical studies, they will show some of the results of their work as well as the perspectives the discourses concerning the central concept of the unconscious fantasy have taken within psychoanalysis. Ricardo Steiner, a leading expert on psychoanalytic theory development, comments on their work in his chapter and presents his own view on the concept of the unconscious. First, he stresses the cultural context in which Freud started to mention unconscious fantasies and the importance of the German Romantic and European sources used by Freud. Then, he tries to call the attention on the complex issues related to the phylogenetic nature of Freud's Ur-Phantasien, the Primary Fantasies or Phantasies as the Kleinians call them, and shows the importance of Bion's and Segal's work.

Heinz Weiß uses detailed clinical material from the psychoanalysis of a borderline-patient to illustrate the relationship between reparation, the repetition compulsion and the unconscious processing of guilt. He argues that, when mature reparation fails, primitive reparative manoeuvres are brought into play which, instead of acknowledging mourning and guilt, lead to further damage of the patient's internal objects. The technical and clinical implications of this dilemma are discussed in detail.

Part II: Scientific perspectives from psychoanalysis and cognitive neurosciences, explicitly takes up the basic idea of the Sandler Conference by Annemarie and Joe Sandler. In different contributions, the authors contrast the clinical-psychoanalytical papers on the unconscious and neuro-scientific approaches. The renowned neuroscientist and psychiatrist Carlo Semenza from Padua elaborates that some parts of the brain may not know what the other parts do. This fact is reflected in surprising experimental findings and clinical phenomena due to brain damage that show dissociations within the awareness system. Such dissociations provide different insights on the nature and working of consciousness with respect to neuron-based models in neuroscience.

Renowned British neurologist and psychiatrist Karl Friston offers an account of embodied exchange with the world that associates conscious operations which actively inferring the causes of our sensations. The argument has two parts: the first calls on the lawful dynamics of any (weakly mixing ergodic) system that persists in a changing environment – from a single cell organism to a human brain. These lawful dynamics suggest that (internal) states can be interpreted as modeling or predicting the (external) causes of sensory perturbations. In other words, if a system exists, its internal states must encode probabilistic beliefs about external states. Heuristically, this means that if I exist (am) then I must have beliefs (think). The second part of the argument is that the only tenable belief I can entertain about myself is that I exist. This may seem rather facile; however, if we associate existing with ergodicity, then (ergodic) systems that exist by predicting external states can possess only prior beliefs that their environment is predictable. It transpires that this is equivalent to believing that the world – and the way it is sampled – will minimize uncertainty about the causes of sensations. We conclude by illustrating the behavior that emerges under these beliefs using simulations of saccadic searches – and considering them in the light of conscious perception.

The psychoanalysts Marianne Leuzinger-Bohleber and Rolf Pfeifer, experts in the field of so-called Embodied Cognitive Science, illustrate how challenging and fruitful their interdisciplinary dialogue has been for both sides. Centred around the insights from a third psychoanalysis with a patient who suffered from a severe case of childhood polio, they discuss the hypothesis that working through the traumatic experience in the transference with the analyst, as well as the reconstruction of the biographical-historical reality of the trauma suffered, prove to be indispensable for a lasting structural change.

The concept of "embodied memory" proves to be helpful in understanding precisely in what way "early trauma is remembered by the body". Observing in detail the sensory-motor coordination in the analytic relationship enables one to decode the inappropriate intensity of affects and fantasies which match the original traumatic interaction and are revealed as inappropriate reactions in the present, new relationship to the analyst.

In Part III: Clinical Studies, the Israeli psychoanalyst and neuroscientist Yoram Yovell reveals in a pilot study two pattern of amnesia following severe psychological trauma: a fixed, brief memory deficit that appeared to be very common and perhaps unrelated to posttraumatic psychopathology, and an expanding, potentially reversible amnesia that appeared to be related to avoidance and to PTSD. These findings are very interesting for clinicians and are connected to known neurobiological mechanisms for amnesia.

To many psychoanalysts, dreams are a central source of knowledge of the unconscious – the specific research object of psychoanalysis. The dialogue with the neurosciences, devoted to the testing of hypotheses on human behavior and neurophysiology with objective methods, has added to psychoanalytic conceptualisations one motion, memory, sleep and dreams, conflict and trauma. To psychoanalysts as well as neuroscientists, the neurological basis of psychic functioning, particularly concerning trauma, is of special interest. Tamara Fischmann, Michael Russ, Margarete Schoett and Marianne Leuzinger-Bohleber discuss an attempt to bridge the gap between psychoanalytic findings and neuroscientific findings on trauma. They use two independent methods for the investigation of transformation of dreams in psychoanalyses. At first, dreams reported during the cure of chronic depressed analysands were assessed by the treating psychoanalyst. Then, dreams reported in an experimental context were analysed by an independent evaluator using a standardised method to quantify changes in dream content. Single cases are presented, and preliminary results suggest that psychoanalysis-induced transformation can be assessed in an objective way.

The well known US child psychoanalyst and researcher Ted Gaensbauer uses interviews of a four-year-old who suffered a traumatic loss at 22 months. His analyses challenge the traditional view that non-verbal memories of early trauma generally occur outside of conscious awareness. During the interviews, the fluidity with which the child moved back and forth between verbal and non-verbal memory expressions and the contexts in which non-verbal memories were manifested strongly suggested that non-verbal expressions often reflected a conscious communication of his traumatic experience. These findings illustrate that these children were partially able to remember severe traumatisation as "unconscious, embodied memories" and depict them in the interviews, although they had occurred during the first two years of life long before speech development.

Robert Galatzer-Levy, renowned psychoanalyst and researcher from Chicago, summarises in *Part IV*: Conclusions some insights gained at the conference. He takes up some red threads from historical dialogues on the unconscious in psychoanalysis and discusses some of the ideas presented in this volume, basically turning Freudian thinking on its head. For example, Freud's implicit assumption that consciousness is an ordinary accompaniment of mental life is replaced with the idea of consciousness as a likely rare mental process occurring primarily in times of difficulty as a means of slow thinking and careful testing of hypothetical models. Since the most salient part of the world for human beings involves interactions with other human beings Freud's idea that the major computational effort must be devoted to the maintenance of physiological homeostasis comes squarely into question as the maintenance of social connection may be both – a more important and a more challenging computational problem. Finally, he elaborates the relevance of these argumentations for future interdisciplinary dialogues on the unconscious.

Notes

1 The introduction is based on Leuzinger-Bohleber (2015, p. 1–19).
2 A fascinating book by Michael Hagner (2008b) discusses the enormous influence of the neuroimaging techniques onto current science and society. The fantasised possibility of having a "direct look" into the living and working brain involves a huge seduction and fascination (see also Leuzinger-Bohleber & Fischmann, 2006; Hanly, 2008).
3 The German expression"Wissenschaft" means "creating knowledge", a formulation which indicates that "Wissenschaft" should not be equated with (natural) science, as some authors postulate.

References

Brothers, L. (2002). The trouble with neurobiological explanations of mind. *Psychoanalytic Inquiry, 22*, 857–870.

Buchheim, A., Viviani, R., Kessler, H., Kächele, H., Cierpka, M., Roth, G., et al. (2012). Changes in prefrontal-limbic function in major depression after 15 months of long-term psychotherapy. *PLoS ONE, 7*(3), e33745.

Damasio, A. (1999). *The feeling of what happens: Body and emotion in the feeling of consciousness.* London: Heinemann.

Fischmann, T., Russ, M., Baehr, T. & Leuzinger-Bohleber, M. (2012). Changes in dreams of chronic depressed patients: The Frankfurt fMRI/EEG Depression Study (FRED). In P. Fonagy, H. Kächele, M. Leuzinger-Bohleber & D. Taylor (Eds.). *The significance of dreams – Bridging clinical and extraclinical research in psychoanalysis.* London: Karnac, pp. 159–183.

Fischmann, T., Russ, M. O. & Leuzinger-Bohleber, M. (2013). Trauma, dream and psychic change in psychoanalyses: A dialogue between psychoanalysis and the neurosciences. *Frontiers in Human Neuroscience, 7*, 877.

Freud, S. (1895). A Project for a Scientific Psychology. *SE, 1*, 283–397.

Freud, S. (1915). The Unconscious. *SE, 14*, 161–215.

Gullestadt, S. E. (2013). Die Seele im Körper entdecken. Eine Fallstudie. In M. Leuzinger-Bohleber, R. N. Emde, R. Pfeifer (Eds.). *Embodiment – ein innovatives Konzept für Psychoanalyse und Entwicklungsforschung.* Göttingen: Vandenhoeck & Ruprecht, pp. 385–407.

Hagner, M. (2008a). Der Geist bei der Arbeit. Die visuelle Repräsentation zerebraler Prozesse. In: M. Leuzinger-Bohleber, G. Roth, & A. Buchheim (Hrsg.2008). *Psychoanalyse – Neurobiologie – Trauma.* Stuttgart/New York: Schattauer.

Hagner, M. (2008b). *Homo cerebralis: Der Wandel vom Seelenorgan zum Gehirn.* Berlin: Suhrkamp.

Hampe, M. (2003). Pluralism of sciences and the unity of reason. In M. Leuzinger-Bohleber, A. U. Dreher, J. Canestri (Eds.), *Pluralism or unity? Methods of research in psychoanalysis.* London: International Psychoanalytical Association, pp. 45-63.

Hanly, C. (2008). *Logic, meaning and truth in psychoanalytic research.* Paper given at the Joseph Sandler Research Conference: Early development and its disturbances. Frankfurt, 2 March, 2008.

Kandel, E. R. (1998). A new intellectual framework for psychiatry. *American Journal of Psychiatry, 155*(4), 457–469.

Kandel, E. R. (1999). Biology and the future of psychoanalysis: A new intellectual framework for psychiatry revisited. *American Journal of Psychiatry, 156*(4), 505–524.

Kandel, E. R. (2005). *Psychiatrie, Psychoanalyse und die neue Biologie des Geistes.* Frankfurt a.M.: Suhrkamp, 2006.

Kandel, E. R. (2009). The biology of memory: A forty-year perspective. *Journal of Neuroscience, 29*(41), 12748–12756.

Kaplan-Solms, K. & Solms, M. (2000). *Neuro-Psychoanalyse. Eine Einführung mit Fallstudien.* Stuttgart: Klett-Cotta, 2003.

Lemma, A. (2013). *The body one has and the body one is: Understanding the transsexual's need to be seen.* Unpublished paper given at the Joseph Sandler Research Conference in Frankfurt am Main, 2013.

Leuzinger-Bohleber, M. (2005). Chronifizierende depression: eine Indikation für Psychoanalysen und psychoanalytische Langzeitbehandlungen. *Psyche – Zeitschrift für Psychoanalyse und ihre Anwendungen, 59,* 789–815.

Leuzinger-Bohleber, M. (2006). Kriegskindheiten, ihre lebenslangen Folgen – dargestellt an einigen Beispielen aus der DPV Katamnesestudie. In H. Radebold (Ed.). *Kindheiten im Zweiten Weltkrieg. Kriegserfahrungen und deren Folgen aus psychohistorischer Perspektive* (S. 61–82). München: Juventa.

Leuzinger-Bohleber, M. (2008). Biographical truths and their clinical consequences: Understanding 'embodied memories' in a third psychoanalysis with a traumatized patient recovered from serve poliomyelitis. *International Journal of Psychoanalysis, 89,* 1165–1187.

Leuzinger-Bohleber, M. (2012a). Changes in dreams – From a psychoanalysis with a traumatised, chronic depressed patient. In P. Fonagy, H. Kächele, M. Leuzinger-Bohleber & D. Taylor (Eds.). *The significance of dreams: Bridging clinical and extraclinical research in psychoanalysis* (S. 49–85). London: Karnac.

Leuzinger-Bohleber, M. (2012b). The 'Medea fantasy': An unconscious determinant of psychogenic sterility. In P. Mariott (Ed.). *The maternal lineage: Identification, desire, and transgenerational issues* (S. 169–204). London/New York: Routledge.

Leuzinger-Bohleber, M. (2015). Zum Dialog zwischen der Psychoanalyse und den Neurowissenschaften: Trauma, Embodiment und Gedächtnis. Eine Einleitung. In M. Leuzinger-Bohleber, T. Fischmann, T. Böker, G. Northoff & M. Solms (Eds.). *Psychoanalyse und Neurowissenschaften. Chancen – Grenzen – Kontroversen. Reihe Psychoanalyse im 21. Jahrhundert.* Stuttgart: Kohlhammer.

Leuzinger-Bohleber, M., Dreher, A. U. & Canestri, J. (Eds.) (2003). *Pluralism and unity? Methods of research in psychoanalysis.* London: IPA.

Leuzinger-Bohleber, M. & Fischmann, T. in cooperation with the Research Subcommittee for Conceptual Research of the IPA (2006). What is conceptual research in psychoanalysis? *International Journal of Psychoanalysis, 87,* 1355–1386.

Leuzinger-Bohleber, M., Mertens, W. & Koukkou, M. (Eds.) (1998). *Erinnerung von Wirklichkeiten. Psychoanalyse und Neurowissenschaften im Dialog. Bd. 2: Folgerungen für die psychoanalytische Praxis.* Stuttgart: Verlag Internationale Psychoanalyse.

Leuzinger-Bohleber, M. & Pfeifer, R. (2002). Remembering a depressive primary object: Memory in the dialogue between psychoanalysis and cognitive science. *The International Journal of Psychoanalysis, 83,* 3–33.

Leuzinger-Bohleber, M., Röckerath, K. & Strauss, L. V. (Eds.) (2009). *Depression und Neuroplastizität. Psychoanalytische Klinik und Forschung.* Frankfurt a. M.: Brandes & Apsel.

Leuzinger-Bohleber, M., Roth, G. & Buchheim, A. (2008). *Trauma im Fokus von Psychoanalyse und Neurowissenschaften.* Stuttgart: Schattauer.

Mancia, M. (Ed.) (2006). *Psychoanalysis and neuroscience.* Milan [u. a.]: Springer.

Northoff, G. & Böker, H. (2006). Principals of neuronal integration and defence mechanisms: Neuropsychoanalytic hypotheses. *Neuro-Psychoanalysis, 8*(1), 69–84.

Sacks, O. (2007). *Musicophilia: Tales of music and the brain.* New York: Random House.

Solms, M. (1997/2003). Do Unconscious Phantasies Really Exist? In R. Steiner (Ed.). *Unconscious Phantasy.* London: Karnac Books, pp. 89–105.

Strenger, Ç. (1991). *Between hermeneutics and science: An essay on the epistemiology of psychoanalysis.* New York: International Universities Press.

Chapter 2

"The unconscious" in psychoanalysis and neuroscience

An integrated approach to the cognitive unconscious[1]

Mark Solms

CAPE TOWN

Using Freud's (1915a) essay on 'The Unconscious' as my starting point, I will attempt in this chapter to update Freud's classical metapsychology in the light of recent developments in cognitive and affective neuroscience. In doing so, I will try to integrate Freud's concept of repression with contemporary notions of the cognitive – unrepressed – unconscious. I will set out my arguments under eight headings.

Most mental processes are unconscious

Freud wrote:

> Our right to assume the existence of something mental that is unconscious and to employ that assumption for the purposes of our scientific work is disputed in many quarters.
>
> (p. 166)[2]

This statement no longer holds true. In cognitive science today, Freud's insistence that mental processes are not necessarily conscious is widely accepted.

However, the consensus was not won by the arguments that Freud set out in his writings; it derived from a different research tradition. Where Freud cited clinical psychopathological evidence (and the psychopathology of everyday life), modern scientists independently postulated unconscious mental processes on the basis of neuropathological and experimental evidence. Foremost were observations of 'split-brain' cases in which complex psychological responses (e.g. giggling) were elicited in patients by stimuli (e.g. pornographic images) that were exposed only to the isolated right hemisphere, of which the speaking left hemisphere was unaware (Galin 1974). Also influential were reports of 'implicit memory', that is, significant learning effects in amnesic cases, who, following bilateral mesial temporal lobectomy, had lost the ability to encode new *conscious* memories (Milner, Corkin & Teuber 1968). Most striking were reports of 'blindsight': cases of cortical blindness where the patients could localise visual stimuli of which they had no visual consciousness (Weiskrantz 1990). These examples provided evidence of unconscious brain processes that could only be described as *mental*: unconscious embarrassment, unconscious remembering and unconscious seeing. Such examples could easily be multiplied.

Experimental neurophysiological studies, the most celebrated of which was Libet's (1985) demonstration that voluntary motor acts are initiated at the level of supplementary motor area before a subject becomes aware of the decision to move (i.e. unconscious volition), have only strengthened the conviction.

The general view today is just as Freud put it:

> that at any given moment consciousness includes only a small content, so that the greater part of what we call conscious knowledge must in any case be for very considerable periods of time in a state of latency, that is to say, of being psychically unconscious.
>
> (p. 167)

Bargh and Chartrand (1999), for example, estimate that consciousness plays a causal role in less than 5% of cognition. It is likewise now generally agreed that some mental processes are not merely 'in a state of latency'; they are not '*capable* of becoming conscious' (Freud, p. 173). In other words, on the face of it, we all seem to agree that mental activity can be divided into three grades: what Freud called *Cs.*, *Pcs.*, and *Ucs.* (the conscious, not currently conscious, never conscious).

However, at this point, modern notions of the unconscious begin to diverge from Freud's.

Unconscious processes are automatized cognition

It is true that Freud himself gradually came to recognise the inadequacy of his taxonomy, especially when he recognised that many secondary processes, which obey the reality principle, are *never* conscious (Freud 1923). But the existence of unconscious ego processes is not disputed. What is controversial is the very idea of *dynamically* unconscious processes, that is, of all the things that Freud theorised under the headings of 'repression' (and 'resistance' and 'censorship'). For Freud, tendentious *mechanisms for the avoidance of unpleasure* were pivotal to his conception of the unconscious, giving rise as they do to the active *exclusion* of certain mental contents from awareness. With relatively rare exceptions (e.g. Ramachandran 1994, Anderson et al. 2004), the unconscious of contemporary cognitive scientists is theorised without any reference to psychodynamic processes, that is, the unconscious outside of psychoanalysis has no special relationship to *affect*. It is a purely cognitive entity. In contemporary cognitive science, the unconscious is a repository of automatic and automatized information-processing and behavioural capacities (see Kihlstrom 1996 for review). In cognitive neuroscience today there is, in a word, no conception of the 'id'.

Consequently, it makes no sense for modern cognitive scientists to speak of the 'special characteristics of the system unconscious' as Freud did (p.186 ff). Although some neuro*psychoanalysts* draw attention to clinical neurological evidence and experimental psychological findings that confirm Freud's conception (e.g. Shevrin et al. 1996, Kaplan-Solms & Solms 2000), cognitive scientists generally characterise unconscious mental systems in very different terms (e.g. Schacter & Tulving 1994).

Typically they do not even speak of 'conscious' versus 'unconscious' systems; they refer instead to 'explicit' versus 'implicit' and 'declarative' versus 'nondeclarative' systems. This difference, as we shall see, is not entirely accidental.

Consciousness is endogenous

It is important to draw attention to the fact, perhaps not widely recognised among psychoanalysts, that the behavioural neurosciences are just as riven by competing 'schools' as psychoanalysis is. Most pertinent for our purposes is the division between *cognitive* and *affective* neuroscientists. Affective neuroscientists (e.g. Panksepp 1998) bemoan the anthropocentrism of their cognitive colleagues, and their excessive focus on cortical processes. They argue that the cognitive approach overlooks or underplays the fundamental part played in mental life by phylogenetically ancient subcortical structures, and by the instinctual and affective processes associated with them. The affective neuroscience tradition, which relies more on animal than human research, can be traced back to Darwin's *The Expression of Emotions in Man and Animals* (1872), via Paul Maclean (1990) to the work of Jaak Panksepp (1998) – who actually coined the term 'affective neuroscience'.

What I said about cognitive neuroscientists still having no conception of the id does not apply to affective neuroscientists. What Freud called the 'id' is the principal object of study in affective neuroscience (Solms & Panksepp 2012). Panksepp proclaims his research focus to be the 'primary processes' of the mammalian brain, the raw instinctual affects. He argues that these are evolutionarily conserved in humans, where they play a fundamental but largely unrecognised role in behaviour. His findings in this respect are, therefore, of the utmost relevance to psychoanalysts (see Panksepp & Biven 2012).

Unlike his cognitive colleagues, Panksepp would have little difficulty agreeing with this statement of Freud's:

> The content of the *Ucs.* may be compared with an aboriginal population in the mind. If inherited mental formations exist in the human being – something analogous to instinct in animals – these constitute the nucleus of the *Ucs.* Later there is added to them what is discarded during childhood

development as unserviceable; and this need not differ in nature from what is inherited.

(p. 195)

But there is one crucial respect in which Panksepp and colleagues *would* disagree with this statement, and this pulls the carpet right out from under us psychoanalysts. He would not agree that the core content of what Freud first called the system *Ucs.* and subsequently called the id – that is, the deepest stratum of the mind – *is unconscious.* Panksepp, with Damasio (2010) and an increasing number of other scientists (e.g. Merker 2009), would argue that the primitive brain structures that process what Freud called instincts[3] – 'the stimuli originating from within the organism and reaching the mind, as a measure of the demand made upon the mind for work in consequence of its connection with the body' (1915b, p. 122) – are the *very fount of consciousness* (see Solms & Panksepp 2012, Solms 2013). According to these scientists, consciousness derives from the activating core of the upper brainstem, a very ancient arousal mechanism.

We have known this for many years. A mere decade after Freud's death, Moruzzi and Magoun (1949) first demonstrated that the state of being conscious, in the sense measured by EEG activation, is generated in a part of the brainstem thereafter called the 'reticular activating system'. Total destruction of exogenous sensory inputs had no impact on the endogenous consciousness-generating properties of the brainstem (e.g. sleep/waking). Moruzzi and Magoun's conclusions were confirmed by Penfield and Jasper (1954), whose studies led them to the conclusion that *absence* seizures (paroxysmal obliterations of consciousness) could be reliably triggered only at an upper brainstem site. They were also impressed by the fact that removal of large parts of human cortex under local anaesthetic, even total hemispherectomy, had limited effects on consciousness. Cortical removal did not interrupt the presence of the sentient self, of *being* conscious; it merely deprived the patient of 'certain forms of information' (Merker 2009, p. 65). Lesions in the upper brainstem, by contrast, rapidly destroyed all consciousness, just as the induced seizures did. These observations demonstrated a point of fundamental importance: consciousness always depends upon the integrity of upper brainstem structures. This contradicted an assumption of nineteenth-century behavioural neurology, namely that consciousness was derived from perception and attached to higher cortical functions. According to the affective neuroscientists cited above, there appears to be no such thing as intrinsic cortical consciousness; the upper brainstem supplies it all.

Freud never questioned what is now called the 'corticocentric fallacy' (Solms 2013). Despite occasional disclaimers to the effect that 'our psychical topography has *for the present* nothing to do with anatomy' (p. 175), Freud repeatedly asserted that his system *Pcpt.-Cs.* was anatomically localisable and that it was a cortical system. For example:

What consciousness yields consists essentially of perceptions of excitations coming from the external world and of feelings of pleasure and unpleasure which can only arise from within the mental apparatus; it is therefore possible to assign to the system *Pcpt.-Cs.* a position in space. It must lie on the borderline between inside and outside; it must be turned towards the external world and must envelop the other psychical systems. It will be seen that there is nothing daringly new in these assumptions; *we have merely adopted the views on localization held by cerebral anatomy, which locates the 'seat' of consciousness in the cerebral cortex* – the outermost, enveloping layer of the central organ. Cerebral anatomy has no need to consider why, speaking anatomically, consciousness should be lodged on the surface of the brain instead of being safely housed somewhere in its inmost interior.

(Freud 1923, p. 24, emphasis added)

Ironically, as it turns out, consciousness *is* housed in the inmost interior of the brain. The observations of Moruzzi and Magoun (1949) and Penfield and Jasper (1954) have stood the test of time, but greater anatomical precision has been added (see Merker 2009, for review). Significantly, the periaquaductal grey, *an intensely affective structure*, appears to be a nodal point in the brain's 'activating' system. This is the smallest region of brain tissue in which damage leads to complete obliteration of consciousness. This fact underscores a major change in recent conceptions of the brain's activating system: the deep structures that generate consciousness are responsible not only for the *level* (quantity) but also for the core *content* (quality) of consciousness. The conscious states generated in the upper brainstem are inherently *affective*. This realization is now revolutionizing consciousness studies.

The classical conception is turned on its head. Consciousness is not generated in the cortex; it is generated in the brainstem. Moreover, consciousness is not inherently perceptual; it is inherently affective.

Basic (brainstem) consciousness consists in *states* rather than *images* (cf. Mesulam 2000). The upper brainstem structures that generate consciousness do not map our external senses; they map the internal state of the (visceral, autonomic) body. This mapping of the internal milieu generates not perceptual objects but rather the *subject* of perception. It generates the background state of *being* conscious. This is of paramount importance. We may picture this core quality of consciousness as the page upon which external perceptual objects are inscribed. The objects are always perceived *by* an already sentient subject.

Affects are valenced states of the subject. These states are thought to represent the biological meaning of changing internal conditions (e.g. hunger, sexual arousal). When internal conditions favour survival and reproductive success, they feel 'good'; when not, they feel 'bad'. This registers biological *value*, which is evidently what consciousness is *for*. It tells the subject how well it is doing. At this level of the brain, consciousness is closely tied to homeostasis. All of this is entirely consistent with Freud's conception of affect:

The id, cut off from the external world, has a world of perception of its own. It detects with extraordinary acuteness certain changes in its interior, especially oscillations in the tension of its instinctual needs, and these changes become conscious as feelings in the pleasure-unpleasure series. It is hard to say, to be sure, by what means and with the help of what sensory terminal organs these perceptions come about. But it is an established fact that self-perceptions – coenaesthetic feelings and feelings of pleasure-unpleasure – govern the passage of events in the id with despotic force. The id obeys the inexorable pleasure principle.

(Freud 1940, p. 198)

Affect may accordingly be described as an interoceptive sensory modality, but that is not all it is. Affect is an intrinsic property of the brain. And this property is also *expressed* in emotions; emotions are, above all, peremptory forms of motor discharge. This reflects the fact that the changing internal conditions mentioned above are closely tied to changing external conditions. This is because, firstly, vital needs (represented as deviations from homeostatic setpoints) can be satisfied only through interactions with the external world. Secondly, certain changes in external conditions have predictable implications for survival and reproductive success. Therefore, affects, although inherently subjective, are typically directed towards objects: "I feel like this *about* that" (cf. the philosophical concept of 'aboutness' – or intentionality). Damasio (1999) defines the object relation "I feel like this about that" as the basic unit of consciousness.

On this view, consciousness derives from the deepest strata of the mind, it is inherently affective, and it is only secondarily 'extended' (to use Damasio's term) upwards to the higher perceptual and cognitive mechanisms that Freud described as the systems *Pcpt.-Cs.* and *Pcs.* In other words, it is the *higher* systems that are unconscious in themselves. They borrow consciousness via associative links from the lower system, not the other way round.

Despite this apparently fundamental contradiction of Freud's model, a moment's reflection reveals that it could not be otherwise. If the reality principle inhibits the pleasure principle, as it obviously must do, then where do the inexorable feelings of pleasure (and unpleasure) come from? Surely not from above. 'The id obeys the inexorable pleasure principle' (Freud, op cit.) The pleasure principle is not a top-down control mechanism; quite the opposite. And how can one speak of *feelings* of pleasure and unpleasure without speaking of consciousness? The consciousness must come from below.

But this is not how Freud saw it:

The process of something becoming conscious is above all linked with the perceptions which our sense organs receive from the external world. From the topographical point of view, therefore, it is a phenomenon which takes place in the outermost cortex of the ego. It is true that we also receive information from the inside of the body – the feelings, which actually exercise a more peremptory influence on our mental life than external perceptions; moreover, in certain circumstances the sense organs themselves transmit feelings, sensations of pain, in addition to the perceptions specific to them. Since, however, these sensations (as we call them in contrast to conscious perceptions) also emanate from the terminal organs *and since we regard all these as prolongations or offshoots of the cortical layer*, we are still able to maintain the assertion made above. The only distinction would be that, as regards the terminal organs of sensation and feeling, the body itself would take the place of the external world.

(Freud 1940, pp. 161–2; emphasis added)[4]

There is a clear contradiction here. The pleasure principle cannot simultaneously be a bottom-up force *and* a top-down sensory 'offshoot of the cortical layer'.

Affect is always conscious

On the other hand, Freud had no difficulty in recognising that affectivity is 'more primordial, more elementary, than perceptions arising externally' (p. 22), in other words, that it is a more ancient form of consciousness than perception (see Freud 1911, p. 220). He also readily admitted that affects are consciously felt from the start: that *there is no such thing as unconscious affect*, nothing analogous to unconscious ideas:

It is surely of the essence of an emotion that we should be aware of it, i.e. that it should become known to consciousness. Thus the possibility of the attribute of unconsciousness would be completely excluded as far as emotions, feelings and affects are concerned.

(p. 177)

Freud explained:

The whole difference arises from the fact that ideas are cathexes – basically of memory-traces – whilst affects and emotions correspond to processes of discharge, the final manifestation of which are perceived as feelings. In the present state of our knowledge of affects and emotions we cannot express this difference more clearly.

(ibid.)

In other words, affects are not stable *structures* that persist in the mind whether activated or not; they discharge *the activation* itself. Freud put this more clearly in his earliest metapsychological writings (1894), when he still theorised activation as 'quotas of affect . . . spread over the memory-traces of ideas somewhat as an electric charge is spread over the surface of a body' (p. 60). Later, however, he conceived of the activating process as unconscious drive energy, only the terminal discharge of which was perceived as affect.

Strachey added a footnote to the last sentence of the quotation above (where Freud says that 'in the present state of our knowledge of affects and emotions we cannot express this difference more clearly') referring the reader to the following passage in *The Ego and the Id*. This passage is of such basic importance that I must quote it in full, despite its length:

> Whereas the relation of *external* perceptions to the ego is quite perspicuous, that of *internal* perceptions to the ego requires special investigation. It gives rise once more to a doubt whether we are really right in referring the whole of consciousness to the single superficial system *Pcpt.-Cs.* Internal perceptions yield sensations of processes arising in the most diverse and certainly also the deepest strata of the mental apparatus. Very little is known about these sensations and feelings; those belonging to the pleasure-unpleasure series may still be regarded as the best examples of them. They are more primordial, more elementary, than perceptions arising externally and they can come about even when consciousness is clouded. I have elsewhere expressed my views about their greater economic significance and the metapsychological reasons for this. These sensations are multilocular, like external perceptions; they may come from different places simultaneously and may thus have different and even opposite qualities. Sensations of a pleasurable nature have not anything inherently impelling about them, whereas unpleasurable ones have in the highest degree. The latter impel towards change, towards discharge, and that is why we interpret unpleasure as implying a heightening and pleasure a lowering of energic cathexis. Let us call what becomes pleasure and unpleasure a quantitative and qualitative 'something' in the course of mental events; the question then is whether this 'something' can become conscious in the place where it is, or whether it must first be transmitted to the system *Pcpt.* Clinical experience decides for the latter. It shows us that this 'something' behaves like a repressed impulse. It can exert driving force without the ego noticing the compulsion. Not until there is resistance to the compulsion, a hold-up in the discharge reaction, does the 'something' at once become conscious as unpleasure. [. . .] It remains true, therefore, that sensations and feelings, too, only become conscious through reaching the system *Pcpt.*; if the way forward is barred, they do not come into being as sensations, although the 'something' that corresponds to them in the course of the excitation is the same as if they did. We then come to speak, in a condensed and not entirely correct manner, of 'unconscious feelings', keeping up an analogy with unconscious ideas which is not altogether justifiable. Actually the difference is that, whereas with *Ucs. ideas* connecting links must be created before they can be brought into *Cs.*, with *feelings*, which are themselves transmitted directly, this does not occur. In other words: the distinction between *Cs.* and *Pcs.* has no meaning where feelings are concerned; the *Pcs.* here drops out – and feelings are either conscious or unconscious. Even when they are attached to

word-presentations, their becoming conscious is not due to that circumstance, but they become so directly.

(1923, pp. 21–3)

Two points must be noted here. The first is that research in affective neuroscience strongly suggests that Freud's 'something' *can and does* become conscious 'in
the place where it is' (in the upper brainstem and associated subcortical structures). There are multiple lines of evidence for this (see Merker 2009, Damasio
2010 for reviews), but perhaps the most striking is the fact that children who are
born without cortex (without any system *Pcpt.-Cs.*) display abundant evidence
of affective consciousness.

These children are blind and deaf, etc.,[5] but they are not unconscious. They
display normal sleep–waking cycles, and they suffer *absence* seizures in which
their parents have no trouble recognising the lapses of consciousness and when
the child is 'back' again. Detailed clinical reports (Shewmon et al. 1999) give
further proof that the children not only qualify as 'conscious' by the behavioural criteria of the Glasgow Coma Scale, they also show vivid emotional
reactions:

> They express pleasure by smiling and laughter, and aversion by "fuss-
> ing," arching of the back and crying (in many gradations), their faces
> being animated by these emotional states. A familiar adult can employ
> this responsiveness to build up play sequences predictably progressing
> from smiling, through giggling, to laughter and great excitement on the
> part of the child.
>
> (Merker 2009, p. 79)

They also show associative emotional learning. They:

> take behavioral initiatives within the severe limitations of their motor dis-
> abilities, in the form of instrumental behaviors such as making noise by
> kicking trinkets hanging in a special frame constructed for the purpose
> ("little room"), or activating favorite toys by switches, presumably based
> upon associative learning of the connection between actions and their
> effects. Such behaviors are accompanied by situationally appropriate signs
> of pleasure and excitement on the part of the child.
>
> (ibid.)

Although there is in these children significant degradation of the types of consciousness that are normally associated with adult cognition, there can be no doubt
that they are conscious, both quantitatively and qualitatively. They are not only
awake and alert, but also experience and express a full range of instinctual emotions.
In short, subjective 'being' is fully present. The fact that the cortex is absent in these

cases proves that core consciousness is both generated *and felt* subcortically – that instinctual energy can become conscious 'in the place where it is', without being transmitted to the system *Pcpt.-Cs.* This contradicts the theoretical assumptions of Freud, quoted above, to the effect that 'feelings, too, only become conscious through reaching the system *Pcpt.*' It appears that affects truly are *conscious in themselves*.

The only possible reason to doubt this is the fact that children without cortex cannot *tell* us what they feel (they cannot 'declare' their feelings). The same applies to animals. They also cannot declare their feelings to themselves; that is, they can feel their feelings but they cannot *think about* them. This leads to a second point that needs to be made in relation to my lengthy quotation from *The Ego and the Id*, concerning the inherently conscious nature of affect.

Not all consciousness is declarative

In the closing sentences of the long quotation above Freud says:

> Actually the difference is that, whereas with *Ucs. ideas* connecting links must be created before they can be brought into *Cs.*, with *feelings*, which are themselves transmitted directly, this does not occur. In other words: the distinction between *Cs.* and *Pcs.* has no meaning where feelings are concerned; the *Pcs.* here drops out – and feelings are either conscious or unconscious. Even when they are attached to word-presentations, their becoming conscious is not due to that circumstance, but they become so directly.
>
> (op cit)

In 'The Unconscious' Freud adds:

> The system *Ucs.* is at every moment overlaid by the *Pcs.* which has taken over access to motility. Discharge from the system *Ucs.* passes into somatic innervations that leads to the development of affect; but even this path of discharge is, as we have seen, contested by the *Pcs.* By itself, the system *Ucs.* would not in normal conditions be able to bring about any expedient muscular acts, with the exception of those already organized as reflexes.
>
> (pp. 187–8)

What is introduced here is a *developmental* point of view. Initially, the *Ucs.* has direct access to affectivity and motility, which are normally controlled by the *Cs.* (see p. 179), but this control is gradually 'contested' and eventually 'taken over' (p. 187) by the *Pcs.*

Freud concludes:

> We are describing the state of affairs as it appears in the adult human being, in whom the system *Ucs.* operates, strictly speaking, only as a preliminary

stage of the higher [*Pcs.*] organization. The question of what the content and connections of that system are during the development of the individual, and of what significance it possesses in animals – these are points on which no conclusion can be deduced from our descriptions: they must be investigated independently.

(p. 189)

This greatly clarifies the point at hand. The primordial plan of the mental apparatus (which pertains to many animals and young children) probably did not include the *Pcs.* organisation to which Freud attributes control of motility and consciousness (including, to a limited extent, affect).

The *Pcs.* organisation is bound up, more than anything else, with 'word-presentations'. Thus we learn that, for Freud, consciousness in adult human beings is largely dependent upon *language*.

Let us make Freud's position absolutely clear:

> We now seem to know all at once what the difference is between a conscious and an unconscious presentation. [. . .] The conscious presentation comprises the presentation of the thing plus the presentation of the word belonging to it, while the unconscious is the presentation of the thing alone. The system *Ucs.* contains the thing-cathexes of the objects, the first and true object-cathexes; the system *Pcs.* comes about by this thing-presentation being hypercathected through being linked with the word-presentations corresponding to it. It is these hypercathexes, we may suppose, that bring about a higher psychical organization and make it possible for the primary process to be succeeded by the secondary process which is dominant in the *Pcs.* [. . .] A presentation which is not put into words, or a psychical act which is not hypercathected, remains thereafter in the *Ucs.* in a state of repression. [. . .] Moreover, by being linked with words, cathexes can be provided with quality even when they represent only the *relations* between presentations of objects and are thus unable to derive any quality from perceptions.

(pp. 210–212)

What this conception precludes is the distinction between what is nowadays called 'primary' versus 'secondary' consciousness (Edelman 1993). *Freud's usage of the word 'consciousness' typically refers to* **secondary** *consciousness, that is to awareness of consciousness as opposed to consciousness itself.* Secondary consciousness is given various names by different theorists, such as 'declarative' consciousness, 'reflective' consciousness, 'access' consciousness, 'autonoetic' consciousness, 'extended' consciousness, 'higher-order' thought, etc. Primary consciousness, by contrast, refers to the direct, concrete, phenomenal *stuff* of sentience. As we have seen, Freud was dimly aware of this distinction, but he did not think through the implications.

In light of contemporary knowledge, we can clarify: alongside the secondary (declarative, reflective) form of consciousness that Freud typically emphasised, two other (primary) forms of consciousness exist, namely *affective* consciousness and pre-reflexive perceptual consciousness. These latter forms are not dependent on language. *Primary affective consciousness is the 'something' that Freud referred to in the long quotation above.* It is *not* unconscious. It can be felt, but it cannot be thought about.[6]

As we have seen already, despite his topographic uncertainties, Freud recognised the primary nature of affective consciousness. He seems also to have indirectly recognised that even pre-reflexive perceptual consciousness is activated endogenously. Consider the following passage (which has several equivalents elsewhere in his writings):

> Cathectic innervations are sent out and withdrawn in rapid periodic impulses from within into the completely pervious system *Pcpt.-Cs.* So long as that system is cathected in this manner it receives perceptions (which are accompanied by consciousness) and passes the excitation onwards to the unconscious mnemic systems; but as soon as the [endogenous] cathexis is withdrawn, consciousness is extinguished and the functioning of the system comes to a standstill. It is as though the unconscious stretches out feelers, through the medium of the system *Pcpt.-Cs.*, towards the external world and hastily withdraws them as soon as they have sampled the excitations coming from it.
> (Freud 1925, p. 231)

Please note that – for Freud – it is 'the unconscious'[7] that stretches out the feelers of perception 'from within'. However, the cathexes in question remain unconscious until they reach the cortical system *Pcpt.-Cs.* This reveals that even simple perceptual consciousness, in Freud's model, is ultimately endogenous. If we now add that he was *mistaken* in thinking that the cathectic 'feelers' cannot generate consciousness until they reach cortex (as we must do; see above) then we arrive at a different formulation – one that is more consistent with the findings of modern neuroscience: consciousness is *affective* until it reaches the cortex, at which point it becomes conscious *perception* ('. . . *about that*'). This gives rise to primary consciousness of objects, which may or may not then be *re-represented* in words (in 'declarative' secondary consciousness: 'this feeling belongs to me and I am feeling it about that').

The systems CS. and PCS. are unconscious in themselves

This formulation has substantial implications for Freudian metapsychology, some of which are addressed elsewhere (see Solms 2013 for a start, as well as footnote 6 above). In this section, I would like to address only the most basic implication of the insight that the cognitive systems *Pcpt.-Cs.* and *Pcs.* are unconscious in themselves. In the next section, I will consider the implications for the system *Ucs.*

I will begin by returning to an observation I have cited twice already, namely that vision can occur unconsciously ('blindsight'). This implies that perception itself is an unconscious process, and begs the question: what does consciousness *add* to perception?

The answer is that consciousness adds *feeling* (Damasio 1999, 2010), ultimately derived from the pleasure–unpleasure series. That is, consciousness adds *valence* to perception; it enables us to know: 'how do I feel about this; is this good or bad for me?' In terms of the scale of biological values which gave rise to consciousness in the first place, it enables us to decide: 'does this situation enhance or reduce my chances of survival and reproductive success?' This is what consciousness adds to perception. It tells us what a particular situation *means*, and thereby tells us what to *do* about it – in the simplest terms: whether to approach or withdraw. Some such decisions are 'unconditioned'; that is, they are made automatically. This is what instinctual responses are; they provide generic predictive models which spare us the dangers inherent in learning for ourselves.[8]

Such automatic responses are accounted for by the primitive mode of mental functioning that Freud called the 'pleasure principle'. However, a vast number of situations occur in life that cannot be predicted by stereotyped instincts. This is the purpose of *learning* from experience, and therefore the whole mode of functioning that Freud called the 'reality principle'. The reality principle utilises secondary process inhibition (the mode of cognition that dominates in the *Pcs.*) to constrain the pleasure principle, and replaces instinct with the flexible solutions that only *thinking* can provide. The purpose of the reality principle, therefore, is to construct an *individualised* predictive model of the world.

Freud refers to thinking as 'experimental action' (i.e. virtual or imaginary action). In contemporary neuropsychology, this is called 'working memory'. Working memory is conscious by definition. (Not all cognition is conscious; but here we are concerned only with conscious cognition.) The function of working memory is to 'feel your way through' a problem until you find a solution. The feeling tells you how you are doing within the biological scale of values described above, which determines when you have hit upon a good solution (cf. Freud's concept of 'signal anxiety').

Thinking is necessary only when problems arise. This (the problem) generates the conscious 'presence' of affect and, thereby, *attention* to the objects of perception and cognition. However, the whole purpose of the reality principle (of learning from experience) is to improve one's predictive model: that is, to minimise the chances of surprise – to solve problems – and thereby to *minimise the need for consciousness*. The classical model, therefore, is again turned on its head.

Freud's secondary process rests on the binding of 'free' drive energies. Such binding (i.e. inhibition) creates a reserve of tonic activation that can be utilised for the function of thinking, just described, which Freud attributed to the *Pcs.* ego. In fact Freud's earliest conception of the ego defined it as a network of 'constantly cathected' neurons which exert collateral inhibitory effects on each other (Freud 1895). This prompted Carhart-Harris and Friston (2010) to equate Freud's ego 'reservoir' with the 'default mode network' of contemporary neuroscience. Be that as it may, Karl Friston's work is grounded in the same Helmholtzian energy concepts as Freud's (see Friston 2010). His model (in terms of which prediction-error or 'surprise' – equated with free energy – is minimised through the encoding of more accurate models of the world, resulting in better predictions) is entirely consistent with Freud's. His model reconceptualises Freud's reality principle in computational terms, with all of the advantages this entails for quantification and experimental modelling. On this view, *free energy is untransformed affect* – energy released from the bound state, or blocked from the bound state, due to prediction errors (see Solms & Friston 2014).

It is of the utmost interest to note that in Friston's model, prediction error (mediated by surprise), which increases 'incentive salience' (and therefore conscious attention) in perception and cognition, *is a bad thing* biologically speaking. The more veridical the brain's predictive model of the world, the less surprise, the less salience, the less attention, the more automaticity, the better. One is reminded of Freud's 'Nirvana principle'.

The very purpose of the reality principle, which first gave rise to secondary process cognition, is to find solutions via learning from experience. Once a solution is found, it is automatised in the form of an unconscious predictive model: "When this happens, I just do that; I don't even think about it." Thinking is no longer necessary once a problem is solved. The goal of the thinking, therefore, is non-thinking, *automaticity*, which obviates the need for the subject to 'feel its way through' unpredictable situations. In other words, *the ideal purpose of cognition is to forego conscious processing, and replace it with automatised processing* – to shift from representational 'episodic' to associative 'procedural' modes of functioning (and thereby from cortical to subcortical circuits). It appears that consciousness in cognition is intended only to be a temporary measure: a compromise. (Cf. Freud's 'constancy principle'.)

With reality being what it is – always uncertain and unpredictable, always full of surprises – there is little risk that we shall in our lifetimes actually reach the zombie-like state of Nirvana that we now learn is what cognition aspires to. Affect is not so easily overcome.

Repression is premature automatisation

I will now reformulate the metapsychology of repression, and link it with the role that consciousness plays in thinking. I have described this role already but now I want to point out that the aim of thinking (of problem solving) is the updating of memory traces: a process nowadays called 'reconsolidation' (see Nader & Einarsson 2010).

Reconsolidation is the neural process by which previously consolidated memories are made labile again through *reactivation of the consolidated memory traces*.

My principle claim is that repressed memories are *prematurely consolidated solutions* – that is, non-solutions – predictions that constantly give rise to prediction errors. Hence the ever-present threat of a 'return of the repressed', which gives rise to neurotic symptom formation.

Why do we automatise inadequate solutions? The answer is that *cognitive consciousness is an extremely limited resource*. The typical human brain is capable of holding only seven bits of information in working memory at any one moment. Comparing this paltry figure with the amount of information that is permanently stored gives some indication of the extent of our need to automatise. My proposal is this: when confronted with an insoluble problem, *it is better to automatise an inadequate solution than to devote the precious resources of working memory to a lost cause.*

Needless to say, insoluble problems are more ubiquitous in childhood than in adulthood. How does the child ever solve problems like: "I want to be big like him, I want a job like him, I want a wife like his, I want *his* wife, I want to make babies with her," etc.? It is also clear why mental *conflicts* are particularly apt to become repressed. 'Conflict' in this context is just another word for 'insoluble problem'. ('I want this *and* I want that although I can't have both.')[9]

The tragedy of repression (of premature automatisation) is that it renders childish solutions immune to updating. Hence *the central task in psychoanalytic therapy is to de-automatise*, to render conscious once more, to permit reconsolidation to take place, and then to automatise better solutions.

The purpose of learning is not to maintain veridical records of the past so much as to guide future behaviour on the basis of past experience. The purpose of learning is, in a word, to shape predictions, predictive models of reality, predictive models of how we can meet our needs in the world.

That is why memory functions implicitly for the most part; it serves no useful purpose to be consciously aware of the past basis of your present actions, so long as the actions in question bring about the predicted (desired) outcomes. In fact, *conscious reflection upon an automatised motor programme undermines the intended behaviour because it destabilises the underlying programme.* It becomes necessary to bring past experience to consciousness only when predicted outcomes fail to materialise, when prediction error ('surprise') occurs. Prediction error renders the basis of present actions salient again – and deserving of attention (of consciousness) once more – precisely because the prediction that was generated by the past learning episode is now in need of revision. Reconsolidation, then, simply improves prediction.

Biologically successful memories are reliable predictive algorithms – what Helmholtz (1866) called 'unconscious inferences'. There is no need for them to be conscious. In fact, as soon as they become conscious, they no longer deserve to be called memories, because at that point they become labile again. *This seems to be what Freud had in mind when he famously declared that 'consciousness arises instead of a memory-trace'* (1920, p. 25). The two states – consciousness and automatised algorithm – are mutually incompatible. They cannot arise from the same neural assemblage at the same time.

In short: the 'cognitive' unconscious does not consist only in viable predictive algorithms. While it is true that the ultimate aim of learning is the genera- tion of perfect predictive models – a state of affairs in which there is no need for consciousness (Nirvana) – the complexity of life is such that this ideal is unattainable. Real life teems with uncertainty and surprise, and therefore with consciousness. That is to say, it teems with unsolved problems. As a result, we frequently have to automatise less-than-perfect predictive algorithms so that we can get on with the job of living, considering the limited capacity of con- sciousness. Many behavioural programmes therefore have to be automatised – rendered unconscious – before they adequately predict how to meet a need in the world. This applies especially to predictions generated in childhood, when it is impossible for us to achieve the things we want – when there is so much about reality that we cannot master.

The consequently rampant necessity for premature automatisation is, I believe, the basis of repression. I hope this makes clear why repressed memories are always threatening to return to consciousness. They do not square with reality. (For example, in the transference.) I hope this also clarifies why the repressed part of the unconscious is the part of the mind that most urgently demands reconsolidation, and therefore most richly rewards psychotherapeutic attention.

Most importantly, I also hope it is clear that the above formulation *does away with the distinction between the cognitive and the dynamic unconscious.* The dynamic unconscious is formed in just the same way as the cognitive unconscious; the only difference is the legitimacy of the basis upon which the automatised pre- dictions are formed.

Conclusions

This review of Freud's metapsychology of 'The Unconscious' in relation to some findings of contemporary cognitive and affective neuroscience suggests that his model is in need of major revision:

(1) The core processes of the system *Ucs.* (the processes that Freud later called 'id') are not unconscious. *The id is the fount of consciousness,* and conscious- ness is primarily affective. I therefore propose that *the Ucs. and the id are different mental systems, and that they should be located separately.*

(2) The primary consciousness generated in the id is of a different kind to that gen- erated in Freud's system *Cs.* Freud's systems *Pcpt.-Cs.* And *Pcs.* are concerned primarily with what is now called secondary or 'declarative' consciousness.

(3) The systems *Pcpt.-Cs.* and *Pcs.* (the systems that Freud later called 'ego') are *unconscious in themselves,* and by inhibiting the id *they aspire to remain so.* They inhibit the id in order to supplement stereotyped instincts with learning from

experience. Unsuccessful instinctual predictions generate affective consciousness (prediction error; free energy), which can be tamed only through thinking (problem solving).

(4) The ego systems borrow consciousness as a compromise measure; they *tolerate* consciousness in order to solve problems and resolve uncertainties (to bind affect). Once a realistic solution is found for an id demand, however, the *raison d'être* of consciousness disappears. *Then a memory-trace arises instead of consciousness.* This is 'Nirvana'.

(5) The system *Ucs.* includes all such automatised predictions. This system is not the id; the *Ucs.* is hived off from the ego. The 'dynamic' part of the *Ucs.* is simply the part of it that malfunctions, that causes prediction errors (causes affect; re-awakens the id). The dynamic ('repressed') part of the *Ucs.* therefore *tends to re-attract consciousness.* This is the threat of the 'return of the repressed.'

(6) The task of psychoanalytic therapy is to connect the affect (the 'free energy' of the id) generated by prediction errors (by 'surprises' in reality) with the illegitimately automatised predictions that gave rise to it (the 'repressed' in the *Ucs.*). This enables the individual (the conscious ego) to *think* its way through an unsolved problem once more, and then to *reconsolidate* (to re-automatise in the unconscious ego) the memory traces in question. Conscious thinking is thus a temporary state, located half way between affect (problems), on the one hand, and automatized behaviour (solutions), on the other.

Notes

1 This is a revised version of a paper first published as Solms (2013) 'The Unconscious' in Psychoanalysis and Neuropsychology. In S. Akhtar & M. O'Neil (eds.) *On Freud's 'The Unconscious'.* London: Karnac, pp. 101–118.

2 Unless otherwise indicated, all Freud citations in this chapter are from 'The Unconscious' (1915a).

3 Actually, Freud's term was 'drives', *Triebe* in German.

4 Freud's localisation of the system *Cs.* underwent many vicissitudes. Initially, he made no distinction between perceptual and affective consciousness (Freud 1894). Rather, he distinguished between *memory traces of perception* ('ideas') and the *energy that activates them*. This distinction coincided with the conventional assumptions of British empiricist philosophy, but Freud interestingly described the activating energy as 'quotas of affect' which are 'spread over the memory-traces of ideas somewhat as an electric charge is spread over the surface of a body' (Freud 1894, p. 60). Strachey (1962, p. 63) rightly described this as the 'most fundamental of all [Freud's] hypotheses' but there is every reason to believe that Freud envisaged such activated memory traces of 'ideas' as *cortical* processes. In his more elaborated (1895) 'Project' model, he explicitly attributed consciousness to a special system of cortical neurons (ω), which he located at the *motor* end of the forebrain. This location enabled consciousness to register discharge (or lack thereof) of the energy that accumulates inside the system of memory traces (then called the ψ system) from both endogenous and sensory sources. Please note: from (1895) onward Freud described mental energy as being *unconscious* in itself; it was no longer described as a 'quota of affect'. Consciousness, which Freud now divided into two forms, arose from *the manner in which the energy excited the ω neurons*. It gave rise to *affective* consciousness when differences in the quantitative level of energy in the ψ system (caused by degrees of motor

discharge) was registered in ω as pleasure-unpleasure; and it gave rise to *perceptual* consciousness when differences in qualitative aspects of exogenous energies (e.g. wavelength or frequency) derived from the different sense organs were transmitted, via perceptual (φ) neurons, through the memory traces of ideas (ψ), onto ω. In an (1896) revision of this 'Project' model, Freud moved the ω neurons to a position between φ and ψ, and simultaneously acknowledged that all energy in the mental apparatus was endogenously generated; energy did not literally enter the apparatus through the perceptual system. (Freud seemed to forget this later; e.g. 1920). In *The Interpretation of Dreams* (1900), however, Freud reverted to the 'Project' arrangement, and again located the perceptual and consciousness systems at opposite (sensory and motor) ends of the mental apparatus. His indecision in this respect seems mainly to have derived from the fact that his perceptual (sensory) and consciousness (motor) systems formed an integrated functional unit, since motor discharge necessarily produced kinaesthetic (sensory) information. Freud accordingly settled (in 1917) on a hybrid localization of the perceptual and consciousness systems. In this final arrangement, φ (renamed '*Pcpt*' in 1900) and ω (renamed '*Cs*') were combined into a single functional unit, the system '*Pcpt-Cs*'. At this point, Freud clarified that the *Pcpt-Cs* system is really a single system which is *excitable from two directions*: exogenous stimuli generate perceptual consciousness, endogenous stimuli generate affective consciousness. However, he again emphasised that this combined system is *cortical* (Freud 1923, p. 24). Freud also retreated at this point from the notion that affective consciousness registers the quantitative 'level' of excitation within the ψ system, and suggested instead that it – like perceptual consciousness – registers something qualitative, like wavelength (i.e. fluctuations in the level of energy within the *Pcs* system over a unit of time; see Freud 1920). The main thing to notice in this brief history of Freud's localisation of consciousness is that it was from first to last conceptualised as a cortical process. (Although Freud did seem to have fleeting doubts about this at times; e.g. 1923, p. 21.) See Solms (1997) for a first intimation that something was wrong with Freud's superficial localisation of the internal (affective) surface of the system *Pcpt-Cs*. See also Solms (2013).

5 They lack perceptual *consciousness*. This does not mean they cannot process perceptual *information* via subcortical pathways. Consciousness is not a prerequisite for perception (cf. 'blindsight').

6 This has massive clinical implications. For one thing, it implies that both patient and analyst register the relevant affects directly; they just don't know what they *mean*. This, then, becomes the principal analytic task: to attach (or re-attach) missing ideas to troublesome affects. I also think these affects are the principal source of the countertransference. I think they are the medium by which patient and analyst communicate 'unconsciously'. I am inclined to paraphrase Freud's famous assertion about hysterics suffering mainly from reminiscences and say: our patients suffer mainly from *feelings*.

7 This despite the fact that he was writing in (1925). He should have said 'the id'. And as we have seen above, the id is conscious. (See my concluding Section 8 below.)

8 Please note: I am using the word 'instinctual' in the modern sense here, not in the misleading way that Strachey used it to translate Freud's term *Trieb* ['drive']. See footnote 3 above.

9 Hence the 'tolerance of mutual contradiction' in the system *Ucs*. In the following sentence we discover the basis for its 'timelessness' (cf. Freud 1915a).

References

Anderson, M., Ochsner, K., Kuhl, B., Cooper, J., Robertson, E., Gabrieli, S., Glover, G. & Gabrieli, J. (2004) Neural systems underlying the suppression of unwanted memories. *Science*, 303: 232–235.

Bargh, J. & Chartrand, T. (1999) The unbearable automaticity of being. *The Am. Psychol.*, 54: 462–479.

Carhart-Harris, R. & Friston, K. (2010) The default mode, ego functions and free energy: a neurobiological account of Freudian ideas. *Brain*, 133: 1265–1283.

Damasio, A. (1999) *The Feeling of What Happens*. New York: Harvest.

Damasio, A. (2010) *Self Comes to Mind*. New York: Pantheon.

Darwin, C. (1872) *The Expression of Emotions in Man and Animals*. London: John Murray.

Edelman, G. (1993) *Bright Air, Brilliant Fire*. New York: Basic.

Freud, S. (1894) The neuro-psychoses of defence. *SE*, 3: 45–61.

Freud, S. (1895) Project for a scientific psychology. *SE*, 1: 281–397.

Freud, S. (1896) Letter of January 1, 1896 [extract]. *SE*, 1: 388–391.

Freud, S. (1900) The interpretation of dreams. *SE*, 4–5.

Freud, S. (1911) Formulations on the two principles of mental functioning. *SE*, 12: 215–226.

Freud, S. (1915a) The unconscious. *SE*, 14: 166–204.

Freud, S. (1915b) Instincts and their vicissitudes. *SE*, 14: 117–140.

Freud, S. (1917) Metapsychological supplement to the theory of dreams. *SE*, 14: 222–235.

Freud, S. (1920) Beyond the pleasure principle. *SE*, 18: 7–64.

Freud, S. (1923) The ego and the id. *SE*, 19: 12–59.

Freud, S. (1925) A note upon "the mystic writing-pad". *SE*, 16: 227–232.

Freud, S. (1940) An outline of psychoanalysis. *SE*, 23: 144–207.

Friston, K. (2010) The free-energy principle: a unified brain theory? *Nat. Rev. Neurosci.*, 11: 127–138.

Galin, D. (1974) Implications for psychiatry of left and right cerebral specialization. *Am. J. Psychiatr.*, 31: 572–583.

Helmholtz, H. (1866) Concerning the perceptions in general. In *Treatise on Physiological Optics*, 3rd ed. New York: Dover. [Southall, J. trans.]

Kaplan-Solms, K. & Solms, M. (2000) *Clinical Studies in Neuropsychoanalysis*. London: Karnac.

Kihlstrom, J. (1996) Perception without awareness of what is perceived, learning without awareness of what is learned. In M. Velmans (ed) *The Science of Consciousness: Psychological, Neuropsychological and Clinical Reviews*. London: Routledge, pp. 23–46.

Libet, B. (1985) Unconscious cerebral initiative and the role of conscious will in voluntary action. *Behav. Brain Sci.*, 8: 529–539.

Maclean, P. (1990) *The Triune Brain in Evolution*. New York: Plenum.

Merker, B. (2009) Consciousness without a cerebral cortex: a challenge for neuroscience and medicine. *Behav. Brain Sci.*, 30: 63–134.

Mesulam, M.M. (2000) Behavioral neuroanatomy: large-scale networks, association cortex, frontal syndromes, the limbic system and hemispheric lateralization. In *Principles of Behavioral and Cognitive Neurology*, 2nd ed. New York: Oxford University Press, pp. 1–120.

Milner, B., Corkin, S. & Teuber, H.-L. (1968) Further analysis of the hippocampal amnesic syndrome: 14 year follow-up study of HM. *Neuropsychologia*, 6: 215–234.

Moruzzi, G. & Magoun, H. (1949) Brain stem reticular formation and activation of the EEG. *Electroencephalog. Clin. Neurol.*, 1: 455–473.

Nader, K. & Einarsson, E. (2010) Memory reconsolidation: an update. *Ann. NY Acad. Sci.*, 1191: 27–41.

Panksepp, J. (1998) *Affective Neuroscience*. New York: Oxford University Press.

Panksepp, J. & Biven, L. (2012) *Archaeology of Mind*. New York: Norton.

Penfield, W. & Jasper, H. (1954) *Epilepsy and the Functional Anatomy of the Human Brain*. Oxford: Little & Brown.

Ramachandran, V. (1994) Phantom limbs, neglect syndromes, repressed memories, and Freudian psychology. *Int. Rev. Neurobiol.*, 37: 291–333.

Schacter, D. & Tulving, E. (1994) *Memory Systems.* Cambridge, MA: MIT.

Shevrin, H., Bond, J., Brakel, L., Hertel, R. & Williams, W. (1996) *Conscious and Unonscious Processes: Psychodynamic, Cognitive and Neurophysiological Convergences.* New York: Guildford.

Shewmon, D., Holmse, D. & Byrne, P. (1999) Consciousness in congenitally decorticate children: developmental vegetative state as a self-fulfilling prophecy. *Dev. Med. Child Neurol.,* 41: 364–374.

Solms, M. (1997) What is consciousness? *J. Am. Psychoanal. Assn.,* 45: 681–778.

Solms, M. (2013) The conscious id. *Neuropsychoanalysis,* 15 (1): 5–19.

Solms, M. & Friston, K. (2014) Consciousness by surprise: oral presentation (Solms) and discussion (Friston) at the International Psychoanalytical Association Research Conference, Sigmund Freud Institute, Frankfurt. (https://www.youtube.com/watch?v=xP8Y2f1I0jE)

Solms, M. & Panksepp, J. (2012) The id knows more than the ego admits. *Brain Sci.,* 2: 147–175.

Strachey, J. (1962) The emergence of Freud's fundamental hypotheses. *SE,* 3: 62–68.

Weiskrantz, L. (1990) *Blindsight.* New York: Oxford University Press.

Part I

Conceptual, historical and clinical studies

Chapter 3

Unconscious fantasy

An attempt at conceptual integration

Werner Bohleber

FRANKFURT

Juan Pablo Jiménez

SANTIAGO DE CHILE

Dominique Scarfone

MONTREAL

Sverre Varin

OSLO

Samuel Zysman

BUENOS AIRES

Introduction

Acknowledging the plurality of theories in psychoanalysis constituted a liberating advance within the analytic community, but it also concealed a potential inhibitive factor in attempts to integrate concepts. In fact, to date, there is no consensus on how to decide in favor of one or the other competing, at times mutually contradictory theory, and how to integrate divergent concepts and theories. In response to an initiative by IPA President, Charles Hanly, from 2009 to 2013, an IPA Committee on Conceptual Integration[1] studied the possibility of integrating concepts which, originating in different psychoanalytic traditions, differ entirely with respect to their fundamental assumptions and philosophies. In view of the theoretical and clinical diversity of psychoanalytic concepts, we realized the necessity of developing a method for comparing the different conceptualizations and their underlying theories and, further, placing them in a frame of reference that would allow for a more objective assessment of similarities and differences. Using this method, we began by studying the concept of enactment, the results of which were then published in a paper.[2] This was followed by a study of unconscious phantasy.

Unconscious phantasy[3] is one of the central concepts in psychoanalytic theory and practice. Due to its clinical and theoretical importance, all psychoanalytic schools have developed their own concept of unconscious phantasy. In view of the pluralistic status of theory, it is hardly surprising to discover a large number of definitions, ranging from the classic wishful activity and psychic representative of instincts to a definition of a "not-me experience" as enacted in the analytic relationship.

In order to limit the spectrum of investigation, we were obliged to make a selection of the main papers. We have established a canon of important contributions from different psychoanalytic traditions: from *Kleinian* psychoanalysis Isaacs (1948), Segal (1991; 1994), and Britton (1995; 1998); from the *Contemporary Freudians* Sandler and Sandler (1994); from the modern American *Ego Psychology* Arlow (1969a; 1969b) and Abend (2008); from *Self Psychology* Ornstein and Ornstein (2008); from *Relational Psychoanalysis* Bromberg (2008); from *French psychoanalysis* Laplanche and Pontalis (1968), and Aulagnier (1975).

A model for comparing concepts applied to unconscious phantasy

In group discussions, we reflected repeatedly on the "philosophy" of integration on which our model is based. Recognizing the plurality of concepts is imperative. There are several perspectives and horizons under which phenomena are studied and conceptualized. Consequently, integration is an ideal to which we must adhere without thereby falling prey to the illusion that it can ever actually be attained. We are convinced, however, that steps towards better integration are possible, although we may expect to achieve only a partial integration. With this in view, there can be no justification for partisan or geopolitical reductionism. As we have observed, the terrain is shot through with many difficulties and potential misunderstandings between discussants. As Grossman (1995) and Hamilton (1996) have indicated, there is a danger that theories can come to represent the inner identity of a group to which the analyst wishes to be a part. Furthermore, he or she enters into an attachment relationship to specific theories, which, in turn, convey to him or her a sense of security. Theories are also "internal objects" (Zysman, 2012). This function of theory has become a particularly relevant factor in controversial discussions, as is often the case where the concept, such as unconscious phantasy, happens to be one of the most central concepts of psychoanalysis. Our own experience in group discussions has been that the various members became personally involved to a far greater degree than was the case in discussions on "enactment". It took time to identify tensions, to focus on them in discussion and to open-mindedly follow one of the member's detailed explanations of his theoretical convictions.

We have developed a model comprising five steps:

Step 1: The history of the concept
Step 2: Phenomenology of the concept
Step 3: The rules of discourse when discussing concepts
Step 4: Dimensional analysis of the concept
Step 5: Integration as an objective

Before moving on to a more detailed discussion of the steps, we would like to emphasize that our task is not to provide a detailed discussion of unconscious phantasy as such, but to elaborate a conceptual map or a schema for classifying the various conceptualizations.

Step 1: History of the concept "unconscious phantasy"

The history of the concept "unconscious phantasy" dates back to the Studies on Hysteria (Breuer & Freud, 1893–95), the Fliess papers (particularly May 25, 1897, p. 252), and the Project for a Scientific Psychology (1895). Earlier terms used for the same concept (such as "unconscious ideas", Breuer & Freud, 1893–95, e.g. p. 222) were later subsumed under "phantasy". According to Freud's "central usage" – a term introduced by Bott Spillius (2001) – phantasies are wish fulfillments arising from instinctual frustrations due to repression. The theoretical background originates in Freud's topographical model. While phantasies may be conscious, they may pass over to the preconscious, from where they are retrieved once again. This standpoint remained unchanged following the introduction of the structural model. Freud differentiates between two forms of unconscious phantasies: "Unconscious phantasies have either been unconscious all along and have been formed in the unconscious; or – as is more often the case – they were once conscious phantasies, day-dreams, and have since been purposely forgotten and have become unconscious through 'repression'" (1908, p. 161). This expression "unconscious all along" puts us in contact with what Freud referred to as primal phantasies (Urphantasien). *Freud* claimed that they are transmitted phylogenetically, as memories from mankind's prehistory. They are not a product of repression: they are mankind's current phantasies of primal scene, seduction, and castration.

The Kleinian approach introduced by Susan Isaacs (1948) in the Controversial Discussions at the British Society, introduces radical changes to the concept. Unconscious phantasies are not limited to the repressed phantasies, but are the mind's content underlying – and accompanying (at least) from birth onwards – the entire structure of mental functioning. This entails accepting the existence of an early psychic activity, which, however rudimentary, establishes the infant's connection to an external world. The introduction of the concept of projective identification (Klein, 1946) pursued this direction yet further in stressing the idea that the introjection of objects is preceded by projective identifications on them. Existing "real" objects are not the "real" contents of our mind; our internal objects are unconscious phantasies about given "real" objects. According to Klein and her disciples, unconscious phantasies exist prior to the acquisition of verbal language, and the non-verbalized ones are primarily expressed through feelings, sensations, and corporal states and movements. They may be equated with what Bion referred to as preconceptions in his theory on the development of thinking. From the clinical perspective, unconscious phantasies are also the stuff of which transference is made. In the Kleinian clinical approach, the analysis of the transferential phantasies represents the via regia to the problems of the patient and to the interpretation thereof. A first ever approach to unconscious phantasies as a co-construction by the patient and the analyst was made by Baranger and Baranger (1969 [2008]). They started from Isaacs's classical definition and, based on the dialogical nature of psychoanalytical therapy, and with references to Merleau-Ponty and to the concept of "field" in the Gestalt psychology, they postulated the existence of a shared "psychoanalytic field" where a "field phantasy" can be identified and analyzed. Many problems coming to the fore in this perspective, as e.g. communicational consequences of mutual projective identification, were dealt with by David Liberman (1974). The Kleinian expansion of the concept also highlights the intimate connection of unconscious phantasies with human creativity. Accordingly, Hanna Segal explores the relationship between unconscious phantasies and symbolization, and children's play (equated to free associations) with art and sublimation. She asserts that art and play differ from dream and daydream "because unlike those they are also an attempt at translating phantasy into reality" (1991, p. 101).

In modern North American ego psychology, Jacob Arlow's conception of unconscious fantasy remains the most influential (1969a; 1969b). In contrast to the Kleinians, for Arlow, the difficulty of the concept arises from the fact that unconscious fantasies are composed of elements with fixed verbal content, and that they have an inner consistency, namely, that they are highly organized. Arlow used the term fantasy in the sense of daydream, and finds it of greater relevance to speak of unconscious fantasy functioning as a constant feature of mental life. He grouped fantasies around basic childhood wishes. Arlow adopts a visual model to illustrate the interaction between fantasy thinking and the perception of reality. Two centers of perceptual input supply data from both the inner and outer eye. Whereas unconscious fantasy activity supplies the "mental set" in which perceptual input is perceived and integrated, external events, by contrast, stimulate and organize the reemergence of unconscious fantasies. However, the function of a third agency of the ego is to integrate, correlate, judge, and discard the competing data of perceptual experience. The result is a composite mixture of the two inputs. Not only the id, but also the ego and the superego play a part in the formation of unconscious fantasies. They are compromise formations.

As contemporary Freudians, *Sandler and Sandler (1994)* criticize the Kleinian extension of the concept of unconscious phantasy as covering practically every variety of unconscious mental content and thereby overloading it. The Sandlers sought to solve the conceptual problem by distinguishing between two sorts of unconscious phantasies: past unconscious and present unconscious phantasies. Phantasies of the past unconscious occur in the first 4–5 years of life. They are accessible only by reconstructions based on the patient's material and our interpretations of the past as are rooted in psychoanalytic theory. Phantasies in the present unconscious may be considered partial derivatives of the past unconscious. When the adult individual experiences pressure of any sort his immediate unconscious response issues from his past unconscious as a move towards action or phantasy. However, these derivatives that undergo changes over the course of development, are linked more closely to representations of present-day persons, and are subject to a higher level of unconscious secondary process functioning. In so far as they arouse conflict they disturb the equilibrium of the present unconscious. Here, the entire range of defense mechanisms together with compensatory mechanisms comes into play. Phantasies in the present unconscious function in an adaptational manner by way of involving constant defensive modifications of self- and object representations, and in so doing repeatedly restore the individual's equilibrium. They have a stabilizing function that maintains safety and well-being in the face of disruptive urges of various kinds, such as humiliating experiences.

In the self-psychological conceptualization of Ornstein and Ornstein (2008) the drive wishes are no longer motivating factors of the unconscious fantasy and its content. This place is now occupied by environmental responses. Unconscious fantasies have a variety of contents directly dependent on environmental influences and specific, individual childhood experiences. If the environment is good enough, fantasies become the source of many of our passions and ambitions. If caretakers are unavailable, or humiliate and treat the child sadistically, unconscious fantasies may become the foundation for symptomatic behavior and for retaliative fantasies. The Ornsteins describe two classes of unconscious fantasies that depend on the dual function of self-object transferences. Not only are they repetitions organized by traumatic experiences, they also represent the search for an experience capable of inducing a desired change. These hopes for change are then organized into a so-called "curative fantasy". This may be organized at various levels of consciousness and assumes the form of a deep inner conviction that some very specific experiences must first be undergone for recovery to begin.

Philip Bromberg (2008) is a representative of the relational perspective. For the latter, unconscious fantasy has lost its universal character as representative of the drives, and has become a function of dissociated self-states that aids symbolization. In the first stage, the fantasy is a "not-me" experience, dissociated from self-narratives and from narrative memory. It is largely unsymbolized by language and, in the transference-countertransference relationship, assumes the function of an enactment. If areas of dissociation are no longer foreclosed and the capacity for internal conflict has already begun to develop, this would provide an opportunity for symbolizing the enactment. The enactment creates a new perceptual context and allows its symbolization as an unconscious fantasy. In this process, the unconscious fantasy has a hermeneutic function along the way from an action to the conscious understanding of the analytic relationship.

Contemporary findings in *developmental research* have introduced some new ideas on unconscious fantasy. Freud's concept of primary process thinking, such as early cognitive functioning in infants and young children, which also manifests itself in the production of unconscious fantasies, was not supported. Research has shown that the child acquires an implicit knowledge of interaction with the caretaker at an early stage and forms expectations and interactional representations thereof. These representations are considered the basic building blocks that constitute unconscious fantasies. They assume the form of unconscious belief statements about the self and the other, and the patterns of their relationship. Here, unconscious is understood as being that which is only implicitly available to the child. Developmental research confronts psychoanalysis with findings emphasizing the significance of exogenous events and their mental representations. While this ongoing debate is interesting, the question remains as to how, if at all, this kind of research can be integrated into the various psychoanalytic concepts of unconscious fantasy (see, for example, Erreich, 2003; Lyon, 2003; Litowitz, 2005; Eagle, 2011; Schimek, 2011).

The reader now has, perhaps, an impression of just how divergent are the conceptualizations of the different psychoanalytic schools. What they all take for granted is that this concept describes a phenomenon that emerges in the analyst's mind at some point of the psychoanalytic process. Our second step now involves taking a closer look at this clinical phenomenon.

Step 2: Unconscious fantasy as clinical phenomenon

The description of the process whereby the analyst's mind embraces the idea that an emerging phenomenon in the relationship with the patient can be defined as unconscious fantasy is important. Monitoring countertransference has become a key tool in this process. The analyst is oriented to going beyond the explicit words of the patient in an endeavor to unveil what we may call unconscious experience. He seeks to obtain a picture of the patient beyond his immediate and concrete presentation. Hence, the focus shifts to the inconsistencies within the patient's verbal narrative and the relation of the former to non-verbal behavior. Sooner or later, both analyst and patient will face a discontinuous, somewhat fragmented and inconsistent reality. Very slowly, a creative process evolves in the analyst's mind by way of selecting certain relations within the network of possible relations as these are established in the patient's presentation. No matter what these relations are, they will inevitably lead us to an unfamiliar world. We select those facts that appear closest to our own world, thus allowing us to participate in the patient's world. A shared world begins to take shape, a kind of joint "illusion" that overlaps in the otherwise respective worlds of the patient and the analyst; this shared world "appears" in the analyst's mind as a fantasy, that is, as a complex visual image – a short figurative narrative – which simultaneously describes multiple dimensions in the patient (and in the analyst), within the 'here and now' of the analytic relationship. The unconscious fantasies we "find" during the process of "discovering" the patient's inner world constitute a way of describing the experience of the unconscious as it emerges at the interface of the analyst's and patient's interpersonal/intersubjective contact.

Implicit in the phenomenology as described in the above, is a close theoretical relation between the concept of enactment and that of unconscious fantasy. It would be erroneous to think that enactment acts out a fantasy existing prior to the act itself. What the analyst calls unconscious fantasy is rather the verbal articulation of an unsymbolized affective experience. Consequently, the illusion that the fantasy exists prior to the affective shared experience, or prior to the act itself, would belong to the phenomenology of unconscious fantasy. The concept of unconscious fantasy can thus be understood as a metaphor that assists in understanding the patient's psychic material and behavior.

However, it is at this point that a controversy arises with respect to the idea of a genetic continuity of unconscious phantasies. For Kleinians, above all, phantasy exists prior to the affective shared experience in the analytic session. Based on metapsychology, this argument is something that phenomenology is incapable of solving alone, since it refers to a broader and more complex epistemological problem, namely, how we come to know others' minds. Here, the point is that, as psychoanalysts, we attempt to draw meticulous distinctions between the patient's phantasy world and our own, without thereby excluding the possibility that the one resonates or interacts with, and may actually exercise a mutual impact upon the other.

Step 3: The "rules of discourse" regarding the concept of unconscious phantasy

In our previous work (Bohleber et al., 2013), we identified seven criteria for assessing the extent to which a concept is unique. Here, we carry out the same assessment with unconscious phantasy.

In terms of *relevance*, there is no problem whatsoever. Unconscious phantasy is inextricably embedded in psychoanalytic theory.

As for *refutability*, the idea is to search for the possibility in which a clinical state points to the lack of unconscious phantasy. At any rate, at the phenomenological level it is possible to imagine situations in which no unconscious phantasy can be accessed.

The *operational definition* refers to the procedure by which it is possible to invoke the workings of an unconscious phantasy. In this connection, the sources vary, ranging from the first-person, second-person, and third-person perspectives. We rely, above all, on the heuristic value of the concept in making sense of otherwise absurd symptoms and other clinical manifestations.

In sum, these first three criteria seem to have been more or less well met.

Internal consistency is made more problematic by the fact that there is no general agreement as to whether a true difference can be established between conscious, preconscious, and unconscious phantasy. While, for some, there is a radical difference both in the nature and in the function of these levels, for others (beginning with Freud), the three levels form a continuum and are without major ontological differences. However, one may assert justifiably that with respect to unconscious phantasy proper all usually refer to the same general idea, with any differences emanating chiefly from the broader theoretical context.

Speaking of context, *contextual or intra-theoretical consistency* is probably the one criterion posing the greatest challenge to any smooth integration of the concept. Let us begin by making clear that what we mean to reach by this criterion is not an agreement between different theories, but to ensure that any given concept belongs to – and is not contradictory with – psychoanalytic theory at large. If it is not intra-theoretically consistent, then the concept must be reformulated or rejected, or else the theory must be revised in order to accommodate the recalcitrant concept. As for unconscious phantasy, it may be said to belong to a considerably large cluster of psychoanalytic concepts and is thus naturally consistent with the theory as a whole; the problem here is that these concepts overlap significantly. Consider, for instance, such concepts as complex, infantile theory, personal myth, family romance, unconscious wish, psychic reality, internal object, reminiscence etc. The problem, as one can see, does not lie in the concept of unconscious phantasy itself so much as in the theory as a whole. Some seem to be at the same level, while others may appear as subordinate concepts.

For the same reason, the criterion of *parsimony* is poorly met since these related concepts all refer to unconscious phantasy.

Finally, due to its exclusively psychoanalytic origin, unconscious phantasy can receive little in terms of *extra-analytic convergence*, in the sense that no biological or other non-analytic means can really support or deny its existence and the function psychoanalysts attribute to it.

Step 4: The dimensional analysis of the different concepts of unconscious phantasy

The dimensional analysis of the different concepts represents the core step in our approach. Here we attempt a detailed analysis of the concept's "meaning-space". As we have shown in the above, concepts do not possess a single unambiguous, determinable meaning, but rather a spectrum of meanings. Our method aims to secure a comprehensive meaning-space that enables us to place the different versions of the concept within it. It is a multidimensional, not merely a three-dimensional space – in our case a five-dimensional one. The positions the various conceptualizations of unconscious phantasy may assume in dimensions of this space will show us whether they belong to the same conceptual "family", or if divergences in the meaning context and in the construction of psychic reality make all integration impossible. We have identified five dichotomized dimensions, which we now move on to discuss in greater detail.

Dimensional analysis of the concepts of unconscious phantasy

Dimension I (reality factor): Phantasy endogenously generated/total imagination vs. accurate representation of actual events

The relation between fantasy and reality has always preoccupied psychoanalytic theory. The German word "Phantasie" is rather used to denote the imagination and less the capacity of imagining. "Phantasie" invariably contains an illusory element. We go further in claiming that if there is no element of reality, then fantasy as a whole would be a complete illusion, or delusion. Hence, the polarity of pure imagination and external reality is part of the structural definition of fantasy. As *Laplanche & Pontalis* have shown, Freud consistently sought firm ground for fantasies in reality: First in real seduction, in spontaneous sexuality and finally in a hypothetical past as the actual grounds of primal fantasy. Freud found the solution to this problem in the creation of an intermediate field: psychic reality. However, as Laplanche and Pontalis emphasized, "the difficulty and ambiguity lie[s] in the very nature of its relationship to the real and to the imaginary, as is shown in the central domain of fantasy" (1968, p. 3). Let us now consider the ways in which the different conceptions of unconscious fantasy attempt to solve this conceptual difficulty. We employ the idea of a continuum extending from "pure intrinsic factors" to "fantasy as an accurate representation of reality" so as to bring order to the different conceptions.

We situate *Kleinian* conceptions close to one pole of the continuum. For Kleinians, the entire content of the unconscious mind consists of unconscious phantasies. They operate within the world of imagination, whereby thought in reality and rational action cannot operate without concurrent and supporting unconscious phantasies. For *Isaacs* phantasy is the psychic representative of instinct. Phantasy lends mental existence and form to instinct. The infant experiences desire as a specific phantasy without words, such as: "I want to suck the nipple". The reality factor here is the sensations and affects that give phantasy a concrete bodily quality, a 'me-ness'. Isaacs emphasized that the earliest phantasies are an internal and subjective reality, but are from the outset concomitantly "bound up with an actual, however limited and narrow, experience of objective reality" (1948, p. 86). *Segal* describes how, in normal infants, phantasy is tested to see whether satisfaction may be obtained from the object. It implies the infant's capacity to perceive a reality different to phantasy. Segal speaks of an "in-built attitude to the world" in phantasies, which allows for repeated reality-testing (1994, p. 400). This attitude is based on a depressive-position organization.

Britton (1995; 1998) adopts a different position. Phantasies are generated and persist unconsciously from infancy onwards. They have no consequences unless belief is attached to a phantasy. For Britton, belief is the function that confers the status of reality to phantasies. Reality testing helps beliefs become knowledge. In this sense, beliefs occupy an intermediate position between pure fantasy and external reality.

For Arlow (1969a), understanding the unconscious fantasy has been substantially hindered by drawing too sharp a line between unconscious and conscious, as Kleinians do. For Arlow, fantasies are grouped around certain basic instinctual wishes. He uses the concept of unconscious fantasy in the sense of unconscious fantasy thinking. The ego's perceptual apparatus operates simultaneously in two different directions. It looks outward towards the sensory stimuli of the external world of objects, while focusing inward, reacting to a constant stream of inner stimulation. The organized mental representation of this stream of inner stimulation is fantasy thinking. It includes memory schemata related to the significant conflicts and traumatic events of the individual's life. Fantasy and perception constantly intermingle. While unconscious fantasies occasionally have subtle forms, they can also have an intrusive and powerful influence in organizing perceptual data into illusions, misconceptions, and parapraxes. However, in principle, fantasy and objective reality can be separated once again. The analyst ought to search for unconscious fantasy in order to help patients distinguish between their unconscious fantasy and reality.

For Sandler and Sandler (1994), unconscious phantasies, as part of the past unconscious, involve age-appropriate secondary processes as well as primary process functioning. Constant pressure is exerted to anchor phantasies that form part of present unconscious in reality. Wishful past unconscious phantasies arising in the preconscious have to be modified, disguised, or repressed by mechanisms of defense before entering consciousness. The actualization of our unconscious wishful phantasies has to be achieved in a way that is plausible to us. For the Sandlers, reality and the affects experienced in reality have an important organizing function for unconscious phantasies.

For Ornstein and Ornstein (2008), environmental responses to the child's developmental needs are crucial for the formation and variety of unconscious fantasy content. Depending on the child's environment, fantasies can become beneficial for the development of passions and ambitions, or they can act as pathogenic agents. Under these latter circumstances, unconscious fantasies are organized by traumatic experiences. In treating such patients, unconscious fantasies of hope and expectations for reparative experiences have a curative function. Unconscious fantasies have a variety of contents that depend directly on environmental influence and specific individual childhood experiences.

For Bromberg (2008), the concept of unconscious fantasy possesses only a heuristic power of giving meaning to an action or an enactment with the status of an unformulated experience. An unconscious fantasy is a not-me experience dissociated from self-narrative and from narrative memory. Should a sphere of dissociation no longer be encapsulated but dissolves as happens in the analytic relationship, then the generative elasticity of fantasy makes room for the multiple realities and multiple self-states of both patient and analyst. Some enactments are capable of creating a new perceptual context allowing it to be symbolized as an unconscious fantasy.

If we situate the different concepts on a continuum of the "reality factor" dimension in which phantasy, as total imagination, is situated at one pole, and phantasy, as an accurate representation of actual events, at the other, we may then classify them in the following way:

Total imagination   Accurate representations
                                                         of actual events

X_____X

Isaacs   Segal   Britton   Arlow   Sandler & Sandler   Ornsteins   Bromberg

When comparing them one observes that only partial integration of some concepts seems possible. The Kleinian concepts of Isaacs, Segal, Britton, the ego psychological concept of Arlow, and the Sandlers' concept all outline a constant reciprocal interplay between reality and unconscious phantasy, which forms a mix of fact and phantasy. The differences and divergences result from the accentuation or weight placed on fact or phantasy, whereby Kleinians lean more towards phantasy, and Arlow and the Sandlers more towards reality. For the Ornsteins, the agent for forming unconscious fantasy is the experience of reality, particularly the caregiver's responses to the developmental needs of the child. The background for this position is the results of developmental and attachment research on the naïve cognition of the child and the possibility of veridical perception.

In structural terms, Bromberg adopts a position similar to that of the Ornsteins: fantasy as a result and expression of real, previously unformulated experience.

Dimension 2: Essentialism versus nominalism: Unconscious fantasy as underlying structure of mental life, or as an interpretive category

In the following, we attempt to classify the various texts of our canon according to two questions: Firstly, is unconscious fantasy an organizing structure of mental life, existing independently of the analyst's interpretive activity? And secondly, as relating to the first question: is unconscious fantasy observed directly, or else only inferred from observable behavioral evidence?

1   We begin by considering the Kleinian texts (Isaacs, 1948; Segal, 1994; Britton, 1995), which, located at one end of the spectrum, fall into what we can call *essentialism*, namely, that the concept of unconscious fantasy is defined by its underlying nature, whereby analytic work primarily consists in the "apprehension" of the unconscious phantasy; the very act of interpreting does not modify the inferred phantasy. In a successful treatment, unconscious phantasy, of course, changes, though as a result of the process as a whole. Segal and Britton essentially agree with Isaacs, who according to Klein, holds that unconscious phantasies are the primary content of unconscious mental processes. Segal (1994) and Britton (1995) start out from the idea of the structuring function of unconscious phantasy for mental life. Kleinians believe in a very early active ego involved from the outset in object relations consisting in unconsciously phantasized actions of love and hate as are associated with the good or bad maternal breast, the mother's body, and the parents' sexual life. The earliest phantasies remain directly connected with somatic experience and are non-visual. In later development, they may be expressed visually through verbal terms. And yet, as Isaacs clearly states, "unconscious phantasies are always inferred, not observed as such" (Isaacs, 1948, p. 73).

2   We can place Bromberg's text (2008) at the other end of the spectrum
    in this dimension. For the latter, the phenomenon denoted by the con-
    cept of unconscious fantasy is acknowledged as a dissociated, affect-driven
    experience rather than a form of repressed symbolized thought. What is
    assumed as evidence of a buried unconscious is an illusion created by the
    interpersonal/relational nature of the analytic process during the ongoing
    symbolization of unprocessed affect. As cognitive and linguistic symbol-
    ization gradually replaces dissociation, increased self-reflection fosters the
    illusion of something emerging that, though always known, has been previ-
    ously warded off. Ergo, unconscious fantasies are co-constructed or, more
    emphatically, though they do not pre-exist in the unconscious mind of the
    child or of the patient, they do come to life during the very process of relat-
    ing with significant others throughout the course of personal development
    or in analysis, by interpreting enactments. Bromberg's position can be clas-
    sified as *radical nominalism*, in short, that the existence of unconscious fan-
    tasies is understood as a given by virtue of the analyst's interpretive activity;
    the concept possesses only heuristic value. In this context, the question as
    to whether unconscious fantasies are inferred is superfluous.

    > The other authors in our canon can be situated along different points of
    > a continuum extending from Isaacs at one end, through to Bromberg at
    > the other. They may be classified as *moderate nominalists* who contend,
    > namely, that while something real exists as "unconscious fantasy", it is
    > possible to modify/construct this psychic reality by way of interaction
    > with 'external reality', either by way of significant others or by the ana-
    > lyst through interpretation.

3   For Aulagnier (1975), all psychic processes are representational activities
    accompanying the development of subjectivity. There are, however, differ-
    ent kinds of representations. The first step in this development is the *pri-
    mal (originaire) process*, during which the infant mind recognizes the pleasant
    or unpleasant quality of emerging stimuli that provide initial orientation in
    relating to world. This process is governed by the postulate of "self-procre-
    ation", namely, that representation as such is the activity that creates the state
    of pleasure and that prefigures the complementary object (the breast). The
    act of representation is the *pictogram* that may be of "conjunction", when
    the experience is pleasurable, or o of "rejection", when the experience is
    predominantly of displeasure. The second step in subjectivization is the pro-
    cess of *primary and scenic* representation, which is a *fantasy* understood as the
    imaginary fulfillment of desires to avoid suffering caused by the absence of
    the initial link with the mother. The third moment is the *process* of second-
    ary and ideational representation with the apparition of ideation as repre-
    sentation, language, and thinking, the seat of the ego. Unlike the Kleinian
    conception, in the primary process, the proper place of unconscious fan-
    tasy, recognition of external reality and of a mother who frustrates is already

implicit; unconscious fantasy is the way the child appropriates an otherwise foreign reality. However, the mother may modify the fantasy life of the child: Through what Aulagnier refers to as *primary violence*, the mother, both by way of interpretation and in being motivated by her desire, imposes in the child's psyche options, thoughts, ways of circulation and the discharge of pleasure, etc. In this sense, fantasy life is open to interaction; her conception thus departs from the Kleinian view that conceives psychic reality as being more autarkic.

4   Sandler and Sandler (1994) may be grouped typically as *moderate nominalists*; namely, while agreeing that there is some structure in the psyche that might be called unconscious phantasy they also argue that there are different ways of construing it, each with different consequences for analytic treatment. The phantasies assumed as existing in the past unconscious are our own reconstructions based upon the patient's analytic material, on our *interpretation* of the past. This interpretation, moreover, is rooted in our psychoanalytic theory of mental functioning and our theory of child development. However, contrary to this, phantasies in the present unconscious exist in the "here-and-now", are accessible to analytic work, are more closely linked with representation of present-day persons, and are subject to a higher level of unconscious secondary-process functioning. Thus, unconscious transference phantasies exist in the present unconscious, not in the past unconscious.

5   Arlow's (1969a; 1969b) and Abend's (2008) texts may be placed in the same category, for they both contend that there is no sharp distinction between daydreaming and unconscious fantasy and that conscious and unconscious fantasy activity is a constant feature of mental life. Hence, they prefer to speak of *unconscious fantasy function*. Unconscious fantasies tend to be clustered around certain basic instinctual wishes, affording a means of wishful gratification; different versions of related fantasies may appear at different developmental stages and yet include defensive components as well as superego components, along with the important wishes they contain. To this extent, they seem to be essentialists, and are in this sense closer to Kleinian ideas. "We tend to regard [unconscious fantasies] as *concrete entities in patient's minds* whose presence we first infer, then detect, and finally reconstruct. . . . We think we can detect underlying formations [. . .] that we call unconscious fantasies, and which are giving shape to the surface material" (Abend, 2008, p. 124; our italics). We tend to think of them, however, as *moderate nominalists*, especially Abend when asserting that "evaluation of the data of experience and outcome is a process that is itself *not entirely free of the influence of the evaluator's unconscious fantasy function*, as Arlow's formulation makes clear" (2008, p. 126; our italics). They assume, moreover, that fantasies, like all clinical material, may also be affected by actual experiences.

6   Finally, the Kohutian Ornstein and Ornstein (2008) may likewise be grouped among moderate nominalists, albeit closer to Bromberg inasmuch as they both recognize the crucial importance of the analyst's participation

in the patient's mental processes. For these authors, so-called self-object transferences contain unconscious fantasies that organize early traumatic experiences and reparative unconscious fantasies of hopes and expectations.

In sum, the possibilities of integration between the authors of the canon along the dimension considered depend on the role the authors assign to the other and to the analyst during an analytical session, in the constitution of the phenomenon "unconscious fantasy". In this sense, there are more possibilities for integration between moderate nominalists when disregarding either pole, namely, Kleinian essentialists and radical nominalists like Bromberg.

Dimension 3: The problem of the organizational dimension of unconscious phantasies

Although, for the most part, the question is addressed only indirectly in the canonical texts, differences may be discerned among the various schools of thought with respect to organization. In his text "The Unconscious" (1915), Freud thought of phantasy as an intermediate yet highly organized formation between the systems Ucs. and Pcs. In Klein, unconscious phantasies are essentially that which constitutes the unconscious, in other words relations between unconscious objects. In such a conception, firstly, the primitiveness of phantasies does not rule out a high degree of organization, and, secondly, organization does not necessarily reflect symbolic value. At the other end of the spectrum, relational/intersubjective psychoanalysts such as Bromberg feel that they would rather do without unconscious phantasy. Hence, Bromberg deems the question of organization as most likely irrelevant. He does, however, concede the possibility of a posthumous narrative that constructs what other schools have considered as being an ontologically existent unconscious phantasy. For their part, ego psychologists and contemporary Freudians would probably acknowledge a variable degree of organization in accordance with their view of a continuum that spans from daydreaming to unconscious phantasy and depending on the degree to which phantasy is subject to primary process. It may well be said of the "French school", in spite of its many variants, that it not only views organization as a feature of phantasy but, for instance, gives phantasy itself an organizational role in the creation of symptoms. This is conspicuous in Lacan when positing a central phantasy that organizes the existential stance of the subject.

That said, we believe that the question must be addressed differently. Above all, a sound epistemological procedure should, in our view, enquire into legitimate inferences, as in terms of unconscious phantasies that might be extracted from clinical practice – especially in view of the fact that such phantasies can, indeed, be articulated only in the après-coup of the analysis of clinical phenomena. Phantasies are, by definition, described retrospectively, either directly by the person entertaining them (conscious phantasies, daydreams) or indirectly through the work of reconstruction by the analysand and the analyst. This après-coup character poses a formidable challenge when seeking to determine the degree of organization in unconscious phantasies, and where the same would hold, at least to some extent, for conscious and preconscious phantasies. For the implication is that these are never accessible to naturalistic description: they resist analysis as positive entities the constituents of which could be dismantled so as to determine their architecture.

Hence, there is no way of distinguishing between a phantasy supposedly present "in" the unconscious layers of the psyche and its eventual construction or reconstruction by the analytic dyad. Consequently, it is impossible to establish whether a phantasy formulated at some point in the session was more or less organized in its supposedly "initial" state, or if its degree of organization merely reflects the preconscious/conscious capacity for elaboration as the subject becomes increasingly capable of formulating, in situ, the phantasy in question. For instance, instead of imagining that a well-formed phantasy is already "there" and waiting to be uncovered, one might just as well posit an unconscious kernel of mnemonic traces forming a very "primal" presentation in the mind (e.g. Aulagnier's pictogram; Freud's "Ding" in contrast to "predicate" in the Project). This quite "raw" or non-elaborated form may serve as the starting point of a process whereby a truly psychic script becomes more elaborate the closer it approaches the state in which it can be articulated in words. In such a case, one may be tempted to believe that it was highly organized from the start. One might also imagine that the nucleus remains in its "raw" state, as reflected only in non-verbal manifestations (e.g. acting out, somatization, hallucinatory experience). The bottom line is that unconscious phantasy need not be deemed an entity but rather a living process; not a state of affairs to be uncovered, but a way of elaborating the dialectical relationship between external and psychic realities. In any case, all we can really establish is whether or not the subject (or the analytic dyad) was capable of formulating a more or less elaborate phantasy, regardless of the nature of the unobservable unconscious contents or processes. In other words, we can ascertain only the capacity for "phantasizing" (i.e. arriving at a formulated, hence conscious phantasy as the end-product) and not the existence of such phantasy "in" the unconscious, as is true of any other assertion about unconscious 'content'.

Dimension 4: Unconscious phantasies "global" or "particularized"

In our work, we endeavor to infer the patient's phantasies since our interpretations would otherwise be subject to error. This is why the concept is a constant presence in theoretical and clinical writings; when not explicit, it can be perceived as an underlying presence. Some papers in the literature on the subject define unconscious phantasies predominantly as findings related to particular life situations, with precise and specific content (referred to as "particularized"). Others, with a different perspective, tend to describe them rather as unconscious permanent companions, encompassing a broader range, or even the complete extent of a human life, including mental products (referred to as "global"). Inevitably, each author's theoretical position about the nature of unconscious phantasies as such becomes evident in their descriptions. At the same time, pathogenic or curative capabilities are also attributed to them. When expanding on this dimension focus will be placed both on the terms "global" and "particularized", together with their theoretical assumptions, also in an attempt to establish their impact on the definition of the concept.

A more detailed revision of all existing views held on this matter would go beyond the scope of this paragraph, but a few examples may help to grasp the key issues involved. The first concerns the difficulty in drawing a clear boundary between "global" and "particularized" phantasies. Arlow (1969a), for example, sees phantasies as compromising formations between ideals, standards, and considerations of reality. In this perspective, phantasies may be considered as defensive maneuvers linked to "disturbances of conscious experience" facilitating expression to all the components. Up to this point, it might seem acceptable to speak of particularized phantasies; but Arlow also speaks of a "streaming" of fantasies, memories, experiences and reality testing, which apparently justifies entertaining both categories, global and particularized, as present. Kris is evidently more disposed to present phantasies as "global", relating them to family romances and personal myths: "The autobiographical self image has taken the place of a repressed fantasy" (1956a, p. 674). Interestingly enough, he refers to one of Anna Freud's (1951) statements, which is worthwhile citing in this connection: "What the analytic patient reports as an event which had taken place once appears in the life of the growing child as a more or less typical experience, which may have been repeated many times. Her suggestion, then, is that analysts tend to be misled by the "telescopic character of memory" (Kris, 1956b, p. 73).

A second, important issue to consider is the temporal perspective: the unconscious is timeless, but its productions are spotted consciously in the measurable times in which we live. In turn, the psychoanalytic process that develops (consciously) in measurable time can be seen from two different perspectives: synchronic and diachronic. Characterizing phantasies as either global or particularized is difficult outside these temporal references (see A. Freud's quotation above). An unconscious phantasy can be inferred at any given moment during a session, which may mislead us into believing that their existence is due, and extends only to, those moments in which we infer them. To avoid this error, we must recall that there are different reasons why we frequently fail to identify an existing phantasy. Clearly, when we succeed in identifying an active phantasy at a given moment during a session, we dispose over better possibilities for correct interpretation; we might say that in such circumstance we were "synchronized" with the patient.

Sometimes, it is not possible to obtain this idyllic picture, and only in the long run (the diachronic perspective) is it possible to infer active phantasies in a previous stage of the treatment along with the present ones. One may consequently infer lost opportunities of interpretation, and if there was not such loss, the accuracy of past interpretations may become accessible to assessment. In any case, what we cannot rule out is the presence of the same phantasy, its transformations, or else different phantasies throughout the course of a psychoanalytic process, as these depend on the patient's psychopathology and development. "Global" and "particularized" phantasies, therefore, (in so far as these terms are used to refer to their intrinsic nature) can coexist in given clinical situations. The same terms, when used chiefly as adjectives, supposedly aid the identification of unconscious phantasies expected as having distinctive traits. This entails some difficulty when it comes to defining clear limits in the use of each separate term; hence, it is not easy to sustain them as a basis for inclusive classification. However, they may well instead be used in more limited contexts for qualifying given unconscious phantasies, such as at specific moments in a session or at some stage over the course of analysis. From this point of view, we may assume some interrelation with the analyst's interventions, as these may be valid only in specific circumstances, or may be assumed over the course of treatment.

A caveat connection relating to the title of this dimension might consist in the following questions: a) does the existence of phantasies depend of our inferences, or is the converse the case? And b) the nature of unconscious phantasies may largely be inferred from their contents, but do these suffice for "ontological definition of them"? To speak of a "particularized" phantasy is to refer to a precise phantasy in a given person, though one may also assume that it forms part of a wider repertoire of phantasies common to mankind ("global"). A provisional conclusion would be that the categories "global" and "particularized" can best be employed in cases in which we are able to explicitly delineate the limits within which we apply them. Epistemologically, it is impossible to discard the coexistence of both categories in clinical material of the same patient; all we may claim is that either we did or did not find them in a given material.

Freud not only reformulated his theories; in some cases, he retained opposing opinions throughout his life, though specifically retained one of them. With respect to unconscious phantasies, he never relinquished his pivotal idea: phantasies are wish fulfillments induced by instinctual frustration and repression (we ought not to forget that repressions constituted the building blocks of the unconscious). He also maintained, however, that some may have been unconscious "all along" and formed in the unconscious. Following the latter line of thought, primal phantasies as well as primary repressions were the "attractors" of the repressed element and constituted an aid to the formation of the unconscious. In light of the dimension currently under discussion, adhering to one or the other of these assertions may be important. One may claim that the category "particularized" appears more compatible with the classical definition as linked to repression and wish fulfillment. Conversely, the existence of phantasies unconscious "all along" seems more compatible with the category "global". Naturally, there is no lack of instinctual conflict in them, though it may better be expressed in broader terms, such as "ways to be in the world" and "longings for psychic stability", which may be active over extended periods of time. In this sense, compatibility with the category "global" and the Kleinian hypothesis of unconscious phantasies as the permanent correlates of every psychic activity seems more feasible.

We conclude with a brief comment on "curative" (Ornstein & Ornstein, 2008) or "pathogenic" qualities attributed to unconscious phantasies. These are terms used for findings relating to individual persons and later "generalized". The risk here is that such generalizations contain personal and ideological elements, since the semantic content of the terms we use are always subject to cultural changes simultaneously affecting both patient and analyst. Hence, the logical conclusion would be that this is a matter to be considered separately in each case. One must also consider, therefore, alternative ways to understand such supposed attributes in unconscious phantasies. One may claim with reservation that, in themselves, phantasies are neither curative nor pathogenic, but that their structure and formal traits are such that we are able to grasp the existence of those pathogenic or curative characteristics of the person with the phantasy. By extension, this would also appear compatible with "global" phantasies: while different persons may have similar phantasies, the fact of their being curative or pathogenic differs in each case.

The question as to whether we may assume the existence of some degree of theoretical integration where we used the word "compatible" is now open. By way of a very tentative, positive answer, a reformulation of basic theoretical hypotheses – even partial – might to some extent be possible, and would necessarily entail concurrence on commonly employed terms. Naturally, this would necessitate further, in-depth discussion.

Dimension 5: The age at which phantasy formation is possible: Available from birth on vs. available only in the first or second year of life

This dimension concerns the conception of early infant mental life, its characteristics, its origins, and development. Does early mental life have the character of phantasy and, if so, at what stage does phantasizing commence? Furthermore, as previously discussed, in what form do infantile phantasies influence adult mental life?

Freud held that no unconscious and conscious life exists in the infant during the first six or seven months of life. In an attempt to solve the problem of emerging phantasies as part of mental life, Freud postulated the notion of primal phantasies or "Urphantasien". These are inherited (phylogenetic) memory traces of prehistoric events elaborated as individual phantasies. For Freud, phantasy is connected with the origin of the drive. He further held that phantasy constitutes the object of the sexual drive when drive-related wishes are not met, and when autoerotism creates a phantasy scene that may provide some satisfaction. Phantasy thus creates sexuality. Phantasies have an organizing function in mental life; they constitute attempts at wish-fulfillment, primitive defense (turning against oneself, projection, negation, and so forth), and conflict mastery. Phantasies interact with life experiences, and thus form phantasy life. The ambiguity inherent in Freud's position laid the grounds for divergent positions in psychoanalysis regarding the way in which and at what stage phantasy life is initiated, what kind of developmental line was conceptualized, and the status phantasy might occupy in mental life.

For Kleinians, unconscious phantasies are present "as mental expression of instincts" (Isaacs, 1948, p. 80) from birth on and, further, the aim and direction of the impulses "is inherent in the character and direction of the impulse itself, and in its related affects", (Isaacs, 1948, pp. 85–86). While Freud maintained that primal phantasies help in organizing drive-related wishes and impulses, here they become "inherent", as if the impulses themselves contained the organizing factor.

Laplanche and Pontalis (1968) suggest that the pre-historical origin of primal fantasies might be understood as a "prestructure actualized and transmitted by the parental fantasies" (p. 16).

This line of thought was developed further by Aulagnier (1975). She postulated mental activity from early infancy as primal processes necessitating the word of the Other for the development of fantasies capable of preparing the infant for symbolic and narrative functions. Unconscious fantasies are based on the infant's largely self-created pictograms that represent the experience of being loved or rejected. Unconscious fantasies are created in the infant's bodily relation to the Other's/mother's body and formulated according to this Others' discourse. The child would achieve separateness and triangulation only if the mother is capable of representing a third position, which implies *not* being its sole object. Fantasies are thus more organized and are developmentally later than primal processes and pictograms.

For Ornstein and Ornstein (2008), fantasies commence very early in infant-caregiver interaction. They are related to self-object relations, internal and external. For the Ornsteins, unconscious fantasies emerging in analysis with adults derive from mental representations of gratifying experiences (giving rise to development and creativity) or from frustrating experiences (giving rise, for example, to curative fantasies as mentioned earlier).

Sandler and Sandler (1994) distinguish present and past unconscious phantasies. Phantasies are constituted early in mental life. The phantasies of the past unconscious issuing in early childhood are different from the phantasies of present unconscious. They "date from before the construction of the repression barrier and the resulting infantile amnesia" (1994, p. 390).

Without specifying when it "starts", for Arlow (1969a) and Abend (2008), fantasies relate to childhood. They are grouped together around certain basic childhood wishes and experiences. One version of the fantasy wish may represent a later version or defensive distortion of an earlier fantasy.

One fundamental tenet of *empirical developmental research* is that mental activity exists at least from birth onwards and that these processes relate both to innate dispositions and infant and child interaction with caregivers and others. Erreich (2003) proposes that the infant develops relational knowledge at an early stage, and that this is based on mental capacities described as wishful thinking, veridical perception, and naive cognition. She poses the question as to whether this relational knowledge can be conceptualized as fantasy. She maintains that there is a need for a mental construct capable of encompassing these three mental capacities and goes on to argue that the concept of unconscious fantasy may be a suitable construct facilitating the integration of knowledge on early development as elaborated in developmental research in psychoanalytic theory. Erreich, consequently, retains the term unconscious fantasy and defines it as unconscious belief statement resulting from the intersection of all three mental capacities and the inborn temperament of the child.

Freud's position that infant mental life is characterized by primary process thinking was not confirmed by developmental research. Litowitz (2005) argues, however, that even though recent research on children's mental processes cannot sustain primary process as a model for their mental processes, the unique contribution of psychoanalysis in this field demonstrates how children use mental processes for motivational purpose and how, in this context, they construct unconscious fantasies.

Bromberg (2008), on the other hand, doubts whether the concept of unconscious fantasy can be retained as a characterizing developmental process. However, that the dissociated parts have a developmental history represented in procedural memory, albeit not as unconscious fantasies with motivational characteristics, would seem inherent in his position.

A developmental line of unconscious phantasy could then briefly be summarized thus:

Table 3.1 A developmental line of unconscious phantasy

	pre-birth	*0–1yrs.*	*1.5 yrs.*	*1.5+yrs.*
Freudian	phylogenetic memory	self-part-object relations	self-whole object representation	towards object-constancy/ permanence
Post-Freudian Pluralism	pre-conceptions	development of models of relations to others/caregivers = unconscious fantasy	several models to different caretakers	consolidation of relational knowledge: unconscious fantasies
Attachment theory Cognitive developmental research	temperament	Mentation: wish, veridical perception, naive cognition	Attachment: secure, avoidant, enmeshed RIGS	Unconscious/ conscious relational knowledge
Interpersonal position		Dissociated: procedural and implicit knowledge	Dissociated: procedural and implicit knowledge	Dissociated: procedural and implicit knowledge

Is integration possible with respect to this dimension?

There seems to be a consensus that infants and children are involved with the world from the outset, and that active/motivated mental processes are set in motion for the purpose of mastery, adaptation and defense. Theorists such as Aulagnier seem to be in accord with developmental research when demonstrating how the development of the child's ability to form phantasies and its propensity for symbolic thinking depends on the interaction with the mother and her capacity to be in a third position. The concept of innate or primal phantasies proposed by Freud and retained to a large degree by Kleinians is apparently incompatible with this view.

However, the concept of unconscious phantasy does not depend on the idea that the infant's/child's mentation is characterized by primary process thinking. Moreover – according to Erreich and Litowitz – findings in developmental research are compatible with the concept of unconscious phantasy and its early development. This view is also implicit in Ornstein's and Ornstein's perspective. For the Kleinians, unconscious phantasy is the expression of the instincts as influenced by interaction, thus illustrating a significant divergence to Bromberg's merely heuristic and tentative use of the concept in connection with procedural unsymbolized memory.

Conclusion: Is integration of the different concepts of unconscious phantasy possible?

Today, the concept of unconscious phantasy is incorporated in different theories and their respective perspectives. Pragmatically considered, unconscious phantasy has become a rather flexible concept. Sandler and Sandler, though understanding it as being a consequence of the elastic nature of psychoanalytic concepts, would caution that concepts "can only be stretched to a certain point before they snap" (1994, p. 388). This could result in the concept assuming an amorphous character concealing within it the danger of abandoning the idea of comparing the different versions for points of convergence or divergence.

With our model, we have chosen five dimensions for analyzing the meaning-space of concepts. A number of dimensions thus distinguish the different versions of the concept "unconscious phantasy" very well, demonstrating that while some versions share similarities, others are so divergent that they resist integration with at least a few of the other versions. Above all, these key divergences turn on the fundamental assumptions of the various school traditions as these combine with different metapsychological frames of references and with unresolved epistemological problems.

We would like to give a brief illustration of these problems by way of two topics:

1. Unconscious phantasy is one of the central concepts of psychoanalysis. However, with regard to the question as to the centrality of this concept,

differences remain between the school traditions. For Kleinians, it is *the* central concept. Unconscious phantasy is the primary mental activity present from birth onwards. The unconscious is quasi identical with unconscious phantasies, and reality thinking cannot operate without unconscious phantasies. For Kleinians, psychoanalysis stands and falls with the concept of unconscious phantasy. The other conceptions of unconscious phantasies tend to be more specific and limited in form. The content of the unconscious is not identical with unconscious phantasies and the conception of reality thinking is different. For Arlow, the ego psychologists, the Sandlers, and contemporary Freudians, the significance of the concept of unconscious phantasy represents greater value than the Ornsteins ascribe to it, who do not differentiate conscious from unconscious phantasies, as is the case for Bromberg, who opts for retaining it because of its heuristic value.

The differences are created by the position reality occupies as an independent factor related to unconscious phantasy. For Kleinians, unconscious phantasy is the basic mental activity underlying all later thought that gives specific form to the reality we encounter. For Arlow, there is a constant interplay between reality (perception) and unconscious phantasy, though, in principle, they can be separated again. For Kleinians and for Arlow, drives constitute the instigator of unconscious phantasies; for the Sandlers, the stabilizing function of unconscious phantasy so as to eliminate painful affects and maintain safety is added to the drives as instigator. Other conceptions, however, abandon the drives as instigator and substitute it by reality. Phantasy is constructed from experiences in reality. Results of developmental research support the argument that unconscious phantasy is an unconscious belief statement formed from the child's wishful thinking, veridical perception, and naïve cognition. The Ornsteins and Bromberg emphasize that disturbing, traumatic, and dissociated "unformulated" experiences are the instigator of conscious or unconscious phantasies. Here, one might ask whether we can start with "real experiences" without looking for the relationship of this reality with unconscious phantasies. However, such a dialogue about reality and unconscious phantasy would be conducted with different basic assumptions and background metapsychologies. This we consider to be one of the essential problems regarding the question of the integration of concepts and theories.

Ludwik Fleck (1935) – whose philosophy and sociology of knowledge has become increasingly influential in recent decades – has coined the term "thought collective", which has a special "thought style". Thought collectives construct so-called "systems of opinion" and possess "solidarity of thinking". Fleck emphasized that our perception of a clinical fact is formed by the thought collective of which we are part, as well as its style. For one colleague, a particular fact is clearly conceptualized or has a specific "Gestalt", whereas, for another it either remains unclear or he/she has a different understanding thereof. Only if the "constraint of thought" is loosened and an "intercollective" exchange of ideas initiated would a change of meaning with respect to concretizations of theoretical statements then be possible. We hold that Fleck's description of thought collectives is transferable to psychoanalysis and its various schools. The work of our committee is just such an example of "intercollective" exchange. Each of us has studied one particular step of the model together with one particular dimension and its different conceptions. Inevitably, each of us set his own theoretical priorities in the description of dimensional problems. This was followed by a group discussion where the objective was to integrate the divergent points of view in a final description of a particular step and dimension in the model. The reader will gain an impression of our different approaches and priorities in the analysis of each of respective dimension. We should again emphasize, however, that one of our working principles was to hold our own psychoanalytic theoretical preferences in the balance in an attempt to do justice to each conceptualization. It was a precondition for using our model as a frame of reference for comparing the concepts of unconscious phantasy as it was for highlighting the degree to which they diverge and converge.

2. As our dimensional analysis has shown, there are epistemological differences between the conceptions. Is unconscious phantasy an analyst and patient construct as it emerges in the analytic process, or does the patient have the unconscious phantasy "in himself"? In other words, is it ontologically existent as a concrete entity in the mind? For Freud, unconscious phantasies can be only partially known. They are to be inferred from the derivatives of the unconscious itself. Kleinians agree that, while unconscious phantasies must be inferred from the patient's clinical material, their existence is independent of the inference. Arlow thinks similarly on this matter. He speaks of an unconscious fantasy function. The stream of inner stimulation is organized by fantasy thinking. The Sandlers adopt a middle position: past unconscious phantasies are our reconstruction as based on clinical material. Relational psychoanalysts are situated at the other end of the spectrum, as we see especially in the case of Bromberg. For them, unconscious fantasy is the patient/analyst co-construction of an experience that had hitherto remained unformulated. These divergences must be subject to rigorous epistemological discussion. One such epistemological position might be that unconscious phantasies must, by definition, be described retrospectively. They are understood as patient/analyst constructs. Another position would be that unconscious phantasies exist independently of a retrospective definition by analyst and patient. They are accessible to naturalistic description.

With respect to the various viewpoints regarding the world of phantasies, it would be undoubtedly advantageous to adopt a position capable of tackling several epistemological problems. To this end we propose the following procedure:

1   We acknowledge that whatever we believe about unconscious phantasy (pre-existing structure yet to be uncovered or "end-product" of a process) ultimately rests on the manifest articulation thereof (i.e. on the "end-product").

2   By acknowledging that we can describe only the overt articulation of a phantasy, we are spared the problem of how to distinguish between unconscious, preconscious, and conscious phantasies. Indeed, at any level of consciousness, phantasy life shares the following characteristics:

a)   Phantasy is a private creation of the mind and belongs to a different kind of reality than the shared one (i.e. it constitutes what we call psychic reality);

b)   Phantasy, at any level, is presented to mind as an accomplished wish, or fear, and therefore represents the manner in which the psyche has been capable of dealing with the challenges posed either by external reality or internal demands. Hence, we are not required to choose, for example, between positing phantasy as the expression of the drives (Klein) or as a response to the enigma of the other (Laplanche). In all cases, either by way of its content or by the mere fact of its being created, a phantasy amounts to a form of compromise between the satisfaction of the internal pull – whether referred to as drive or some other designation – and taking into account the existence of the other (of outer reality). This approach to phantasy life has brought us closer to an approach that facilitates a description of phenomena independently of theoretical preferences.

We propose, therefore, focusing on the description of the elaborative capacity of the subject (aided or unaided by the analyst). We have thus shifted the spotlight away from a content that could not be described directly to a readily observable capacity or process, and achieve this by reference to a shared clinical material. Indeed, whether we believe we express the phantasy as it "was" in the unconscious, or else entertain the idea that we have "constructed" the content from an unfathomable primal source, in either case, we demonstrate precisely the capacity of formulating a phantasy as phantasy. In so doing, we also spare ourselves the question as to whether or not we believe that unconscious phantasies exist at all, since we are required neither to assert nor deny such a prior existence in order to describe the process of elaboration which, in the end, does formulate phantasy as phantasy.

This epistemological starting point helps us hold our own theoretical preferences in the balance. While this is not the place for a discussion of the far-reaching epistemological problems implicit in the divergent concepts of unconscious phantasy, it does not imply that we deny the complex relationship between something inferred and the question as to its independent existence. The articulation of our inference of an unconscious phantasy does not merely "attach words" to what is inferred. Assuming that the articulation is not too far off the mark, it will tap into "something" at work unconsciously. But should we go further and attempt to state what this "something" really "is", we would be obliged to discuss the subject of controversial epistemological starting points. Some theories operate on the basis that unconscious phantasy exists and "is", while others resist going beyond claiming that the formulation of a phantasy is precisely what is meant by the word formulation: it lends that "something" form.

With our model, we have studied the differing and diverging conceptualizations of unconscious phantasy. We have deconstructed them in our various steps. And with our dimensions we have sought to identify their differences and similarities for the purposes of discussing the problem of the possibility of integration. Judging their veracity is beyond the scope of our working principle. Clearly, considerable ground has yet to be covered with respect to the comparison and possible integration of divergent psychoanalytic concepts: a veritable work in progress.

Notes

1 The members were Werner Bohleber (chair), Juan Pablo Jiménez, Dominique Scarfone, Sverre Varvin, Samuel Zysman. Until August 2010, other members also included Dale Boesky, and until November 2012, Peter Fonagy.
2 Bohleber et al. (2013).
3 The spelling of the word "phantasy" is heterogeneous in psychoanalytic literature. The Kleinians use "phantasy" in order to differentiate unconscious phantasies from conscious ones. Other psychoanalysts have adopted this spelling. North American analysts prefer mostly "fantasy". In our text we follow the orthographic usage of the authors we discuss. For the most part, we use "phantasy" in our arguments.

References

Abend, S. (2008). Unconscious fantasy and modern conflict theory. *Psychoanal Inquiry* 28: 117–130.

Arlow, J.A. (1969a). Unconscious fantasy and disturbances of conscious experience. *Psychoanal Quarterly* 38: 1–27.

Arlow, J.A. (1969b). Fantasy, memory, and reality testing. *Psychoanal Quarterly* 38: 28–51.

Aulagnier, P. (1975). *The violence of interpretation: From pictogram to statement*. London: Brunner-Routledge, 2001.

Baranger, M. & Baranger, W. (1969 [2008]). The analytic situation as a dynamic field. *Int J Psychoanal* 89: 795–826.

Bohleber, W., Fonagy, P., Jiménez, J.P., Scarfone, D., Varvin, S. & Zysman, S. (2013). Towards a better use of psychoanalytic concepts: A model illustrated using the concept of enactment. *Int J Psychoanal* 94: 501–530.

Breuer, J. & Freud, S. (1893–95). Studies on hysteria. *SE* 2.

Britton, R. (1995). Psychic reality and unconscious belief. *Int J Psychoanal* 76: 19–23.

Britton, R. (1998). *Belief and imagination: Explorations in psychoanalysis*. London: Karnac.

Bromberg, Ph.M. (2008). "Grown-up" words: An interpersonal/relational perspective on unconscious fantasy. *Psychoanal Inquiry* 28: 131–150.

Eagle, M. (2011). *From classical to contemporary psychoanalysis. A critique and integration*. New York and London: Routledge.

Erreich, A. (2003). A modest proposal: (Re) defining unconscious fantasy. *Psychoanal Quarterly* 72: 541–574.

Fleck, L. (1935). *Genesis and development of a scientific fact*. Chicago: The University of Chicago Press, 1979.

Freud, A. (1951). Observations on child development. *Psychoanal Study Child* 6: 18–30.

Freud, S. (1908). Hysterical phantasies and their relationship to bisexuality. *SE* 9: 155–166.

Freud, S. (1915). The unconscious. *SE* 14: 159–215.

Grossman, W. (1995). Psychological vicissitudes of theory in clinical work. *Int J Psychoanal* 76: 885–899.

Hamilton, V. (1996). *The analyst's preconscious*. Hillsdale, NJ: The Analytic Press.

Isaacs, S. (1948). The nature and function of phantasy. *Int J Psychoanal* 29: 73–97. Also in: Steiner R (Ed.). *Unconscious phantasy*, pp. 145–198. London: Karnac, 2003.

Klein, M. (1946). Notes on some schizoid mechanisms. In: *The writings of Melanie Klein*, III, pp. 1–24. London: Hogarth Press, 1975.

Kris, E. (1956a). The personal myth – A problem in psychoanalytic technique. *J Am Psychoanal Assoc* 4: 653–681.

Kris, E. (1956b). The recovery of childhood memories in psychoanalysis. *Psychoanal Study Child* 11: 54–88.

Laplanche, J. & Pontalis, J.B. (1968). Fantasy and the origins of sexuality. *Int J Psychoanal* 49: 1–18.

Liberman, D. (1974). Verbalization and unconscious phantasy. *Contemp Psychoanal* 10: 41–55.

Litowitz, B.E. (2005). Unconscious fantasy: A once and future concept. *J Am Psychoanal Assoc* 55: 199–228.

Lyon, K. (2003). Unconscious fantasy: Its scientific status and clinical utility. *J Am Psychoanal Assoc* 51: 957–967.

Ornstein, A. & Ornstein, P. (2008). The structure and function of unconscious fantasy in the psychoanalytic treatment process. *Psychoanal Inquiry* 28: 206–230.

Sandler, J. & Sandler, A.M. (1994). Phantasy and its transfomations. *Int J Psychoanal* 75: 387–394.

Schimek, J.G. (2011). *Memory, myth, and seduction: Unconscious fantasy and the interpretive process*. New York and London: Routledge.

Segal, H. (1991). *Dream, phantasy, art*. London: Routledge.

Segal, H. (1994). Phantasy and reality. *Int J Psychoanal* 75: 395–401.

Spillius, E.B. (2001). Freud and Klein on the concept of phantasy. *Int J Psychoanal* 82: 361–373.

Zysman, S. (2012). Theories as objects: A psychoanalytic inquiry into minds and theories. In: Canestri J, editor. *Putting theory to work: How are theories actually used in practice?* pp. 135–156. London: Karnac.

Chapter 4

Reply to W. Bohleber and colleagues' paper on unconscious phantasy

Riccardo Steiner

LONDON

Italo Calvino (1988), a great writer of the cultural tradition to which I belong, wrote that simplifications are extremely dangerous and should be avoided. I would agree with this statement. Indeed, I have been given very little space to comment on this complex and dense text by Werner Bohleber and his colleagues. Furthermore, I have been given too little time to study and write some plausible notes. Therefore, the task to answer such a rich and inevitably complicated paper has been quite difficult. I am compelled to simplify enormously what I want to say, and I am not even sure I have understood all that Werner and his colleagues have written. Instead of being able to expand on their statements, sometimes I will have to ask Werner to answer, if he can, some of my own questions. I must apologize for any inevitable misunderstandings.

First of all, I would like to touch on two general issues. I think they have to be mentioned in order to better understand what we are trying to speak about.

I quite accept that the first issue I want to raise and remind you of could be considered to be, if not my 'pathology,' then at the very least an *idée fixe* of mine. I am interested in the history of psychoanalysis and its concepts, and the history of psychoanalysis is not always a very popular approach to our discipline. Yet, I hope my approach can lead to something that is worth considering.

Die Phantasie and *Traumphantasie* are concepts which belong to the prehistory of psychoanalysis. These terms do not belong so much to the natural sciences, but rather to German romantic philosophy and literature. This means that they belong to a tradition that had filtered into the German culture of the 18th and 19th centuries through texts and commentaries from the European Renaissance and from the period of the Baroque. Always linked to strong feelings and emotions or desires, the cultural roots of these terms in Western culture can be traced as far back as Ancient Greece. Just think of Plato, not to mention the later neo-platonic, Plotinus.[1]

As far as our discipline is concerned, we find these terms, for instance, in the *Brautbriefe* (Fichtner, Grubrich Simitis & Hirschmueller, 2011) – the love letters exchanged between Freud and Martha Bernays during the long period of their engagement. Already in 1882, in the first letters they exchanged, they both tried to make sense of their dreams – their internal passionate emotional life – using expressions like *die Phantasie* and *die Traumphantasie*, not to mention *das Unbewusst*. These expressions came from their cultural, philosophical and poetical background and from readings very much related to the German and European Romanticism just mentioned, without forgetting – particularly in the case of Freud – Shakespeare and Milton. (Grubrich-Simitis, 2011; Steiner, 2013a).

To understand what these terms started to mean in our discipline, we would need to explore the Freud/Fliess correspondence of 1882–1904 (Masson, 1985) and examine the revolutionary role that *die Phantasie* played in the discovery of the unconscious, as Freud understood it. We should also consider the Oedipal fantasies linked, again in an attempt to find a sort of universal evidence for their existence, not to experimental research but to literary works, such as Sophocles's *Oedipus Rex*, Shakespeare's *Hamlet* and even Grillparzer's description of incest between siblings in *Die Ahnfrau*. I am referring to the famous letters to Fliess, from September to November 1897 (*Ibid.*, pp. 264–285), in which Freud told his friend that he had come to the conclusion that he must, if not totally abandon, then certainly to side-line traumatic infantile events as the main cause of neuroses in his adult patients: hysteria, obsessional neurosis and other mental disturbances. Indeed, he had become more and more convinced of the important causal role played by unconscious sexual phantasies, both individual and universal (Steiner, 1998, 2003). Without forgetting its links to the cultural tradition I have just mentioned, in these letters and in Freud's early work, the term '*die Phantasie*' gradually became charged with more or less unconscious meanings and emotional implications linked to infantile sexuality (and also aggression). Later on, as I and others have tried to show, Freud further developed these hypotheses and observations (Steiner, 2003).

But alongside all that I have just reminded you of, there is something more specific that I would like to briefly mention – something else related to the cultural background of Freud that I have alluded to. When we refer in our field to *die Phantasie* and to *phantasieren* in the dream – terms which have been translated by Strachey into English as 'imagination' and 'imagining' – it is amazing (to my mind) how still today we are, to use the language of the semioticians and scholars interested in intertextuality, 'spoken' by a text – that of Scherner's: *Das Leben des Traumes* (1861), together with Volkelt's *Die Traumphantasie* (1875). Please note the title of the book! The latter is largely an attempt to explain Scherner's very mystical and complicated thinking. Freud too, used Volkelt's work to clarify Scherner (Freud, 1900, pp. 83–84). These authors, and others I should mention, are the sources Freud used in his *Traumdeutung*. The way Freud used them was unique.

Freud (1900, pp. 83–86, pp. 224–227) took Scherner very seriously. He was a rather odd, mad, mystical theologian-philosopher (Goldmann, 2003, p.25) and he was a follower of Schelling, the great German idealist philosopher who, despite this, had an extremely interesting view concerning the origin of the self in the body. If somebody in our field today were to take a contemporary equivalent of Scherner's *Das Leben des Traumes* so seriously he would be looked upon with great suspicion. But had I the time, I could show that Freud's genius succeeded in making sense of Scherner's theory about the role played by '*die unbewusste active Tätigkeit der Phantasie*' – the unconscious activity of the imagination – dream imagination linked to symbolization. Psychoanalysis perhaps owes even more to Scherner than Freud himself acknowledged in *The Intepretation of Dreams*. Indeed, Scherner tried to make sense of some of the symbols we interpret in dreams – including some that have a sexual meaning. Freud accepted most of his views. Of course, he also elaborated them and did not accept the mechanical link between parts of the body as a stimulus for the dream and the symbols which appear in it. Freud stressed above all the role played by '*das unbewusste Wunsch*' (the unconscious wish).

I do not have space here to mention what Scherner (1861), Volkelt (1875) and Radestock (1879) and others described as dream work or as the logical process which dominates the dream (Steiner, 1988) but at times one has the impression of reading something akin to Matte Blanco's *The Unconscious as Infinite Sets* (1985) and his notion of the logic of the primary process. However, it is to the notion of a creative, active role played by *das phantasieren* in dreams that I would most like to call your attention. In the discussion of our subject, one of the main difficulties is to maintain both the differentiation and the link between the activity of unconscious phantasizing (or imagining), the unconscious wish and the content of some sexual and aggressive phantasies expressed through their symbolization, not to mention the problem touched upon by Werner and his colleagues of the difference between imagining and thinking. For instance, for the Kleinians (for example, Bion's and Segal's work, to which I will return) thinking cannot be invoked without the cooperation of unconscious phantasizing or imagining, linked to what they mean by unconscious phantasies and the way they are expressed symbolically. In particular, where Bion is concerned, there is also the role played by dreaming, as he understood it, and its constant connection with conscious thinking.

Therefore, the differentiation between the activity of *die Traumphantasie* and the sexual content of some symbols created by the dream already existed in outline, particularly in Scherner's work but also in that of Volkelt. In stressing the importance of '*das unbewusste Wunsch*' – not only in what he meant by dreams and the links between *die Unbewusste Phantasie* and *Unbewusste Symbolik* – Freud made these issues immensely more complicated. But here again, we can see the importance of Freud's German Romantic tradition, because he expresses these ideas using the sources I have mentioned and thus in a language which is not that of the natural sciences (with its emphasis on precision), but rather in a vague, metaphoric language, similar to that used by certain philosophers and poets. This language belongs to a particular culture, but simultaneously finds an echo in other cultures. This can be observed in the way Freud has been translated.[2]

Restricting myself to English, which after all remains the official language of the IPA, Strachey and other translators were quite aware of the cultural resonances present in Freud's language. They tried to use a terminology which would respect these cultural implications, and very often they used terms which could be traced back to the English romantic poet Coleridge, amongst others. Even Bion, Britton, Milner, Segal and Winnicott, to mention only a few, were or are, in their own personal way, influenced by what Coleridge meant by 'the imagination', 'imagining' and so on. Coleridge himself had been greatly influenced by German Romantic philosophy and poetry![3]

To give just one more example of how rich and complicated this issue is, and of the necessity to consider its complex intercultural roots, in Italian, for instance, one can find links going back[4] at least to the Renaissance and to theoreticians and artists of the Baroque, whose work influenced the very important notion of 'Fantasia' and 'universali fantastici' ('imaginative universals') of an Italian philosopher and polymath of the late seventeenth century, G. B. Vico. His book *Principi di Scienza Nuova* (1744) had a very significant impact (Berlin, 1975) on the German Romantic polymath Herder, and on Goethe and Nietzsche, amongst others, all of whom were extremely well known to the young Freud (not to mention, later on, Dilthey, Joyce and others). The sources I have quoted remind us that we need to take into account the cultural traditions of the language Freud used, and the languages into which we translate and interpret Freud and his followers. This is not a purely antiquarian 'curiosity'; it is one of the problems that, even today, we have to face when we deal with the notions of 'unconscious fantasy' and 'phantasy' within our discipline.

I think it is important to consider all this, particularly at this moment in time when there is such stress on empirical research and on empirical psychoanalysis, which seems to totally ignore these issues. Indeed, Freud's specific cultural background raises the question of what we gain and lose if we forget this or if we sever these links and start to give a different meaning to these terms. Would it still be Freud's psychoanalysis, and the psychoanalysis of those he influenced so much, such as Melanie Klein and her followers, who tried to develop it further? Please do not misunderstand me; I am not defending the principle of the *ipse dixit* – the blind principle of authority – I am simply trying to do my job and I am quite aware that Freud's background cannot be reduced to his romantic literary and philosophical sources alone (Sulloway, 1979; Steiner, 1988, 2000). To quote and paraphrase an old Jewish proverb: to remember at least partially where we and our concepts come from helps us to better know where we are going, or what we are referring to, and to understand what we give up or reject if we apply a different meaning to those old concepts today.

The second general problem I would like to touch upon is one that particularly concerns the nature (the ontological and epistemological status) of the so-called *Urphantasien* (the 'primal phantasies', translated with a 'ph' by Strachey). In many ways – if I have correctly understood Werner's, Jimenez's, Scarfone's, Zysman's and even Vervin's contributions[5] – this is a problem that lingers behind many of their statements. Probably, it lies at the heart of some of the difficulties in attempting to integrate, that is, to find real common ground, between the ways contemporary schools of psychoanalysis both understand the meaning of and clinically use (or not) the notion of *Urphantasien*. This relates to the primal scene and the seduction and castration phantasies 'and no doubt a few others', to quote Freud in his XXIII lecture on 'The Paths to Symptom-Formation' in his *Introductory Lectures on Psychoanalysis* (1916–1917, pp. 370–371).

From Werner's and, for instance, Vervin's graphics, it is obvious that the Kleinians are considered to be the ones who insist more on the innate character of unconscious phantasies, because in some ways they stick with, or have extended and developed in their own way (as I will try to show in a moment), some of Freud's most questionable hypotheses: the phylogenetic nature of these unconscious phantasies. Of course, in the case of the Kleinians, there is also the issue relating to the chronology of these unconscious phantasies. Indeed, they claim that the unconscious phantasies are present and active from the beginning of life (Isaacs, 1943/2003; Klein, 1944). At times, the newborn baby has a very primitive, rudimentary and partial sense of the other (the smell and tactile perception of the breast and body of the mother, etc.) as separate from him. In other words, the infant has a sort of rudimentary ego from the start (Isaacs, 1943/2003; Klein, 1944, 1946, 1952). These problematic and daring hypotheses, as you all know, attracted many serious criticisms, but thinking also about the fact that Werner comes from Frankfurt, one is tempted to quote Adorno's aphorism in *Minima Moralia*: 'In psychoanalysis nothing is true except the exaggerations' (1951[1974], p. 49).

I noticed in Werner's and colleagues' paper that there has been a slight difficulty in clarifying why the Kleinians refer to unconscious phantasies using a 'ph' and not an 'f', as the Freudian and the neo-Freudians do (although the Sandlers sometimes oscillate in using 'ph' and 'f', and the Americans and Werner and his colleagues sometimes do, too). Isaacs (1943/2003) clearly states that the way Klein and her followers understood the notion of unconscious phantasies, starting with that of the breast (see particularly Klein, 1944) made them choose the 'ph' only when referring to unconscious phantasies. But it is Klein, obviously inspired by Freud, who insists on the phylogenetic origin of that kind of phantasy (Klein, 1944, in King & Steiner, 1992, p.757).[6] There is no doubt, therefore, that even graphically following one of the ways Strachey chose to translate *unbewusste Phantasie*, the Kleinians tried to stress what they meant by the pervasive presence of unconscious phantasies in the mind of the human being from the beginning of his life.

I hope what I have just pointed to can better clarify our issues and the difficulties in making sense between so many different approaches. I am not saying that the Kleinians are right in their choice, which of course implies a particular way of looking at Freud's notion of day dreaming and fantasies (translated with an 'f' by Strachey) and a particular way of interpreting the interaction between what is conscious, preconscious and unconscious. Nevertheless, the *Urphantasien* or primal phantasies, as you all know, do indeed present us with a big problem. To be fair, we should add to this the problem of the so-called universal

or phylogenetic symbolism strictly related to them, because Freud started hint-
ing at this problem in Lecture X of the *Introductory Lectures on Psychoanalysis*
(1915–1916, pp. 164–166). He explicitly mentioned the phylogenetic origins
of symbolism in Lecture XIII (*Ibid.*, p. 199) and at the same time, he started dealing with the phylogenetic origins of *Urphantasien*.[7] He came back to these issues
later on, for instance in *Analysis Terminable and Interminable* (1937, pp. 240–241)
and in *Moses and Monotheism* (1939, pp. 132–133), where he again mentioned
the universal and phylogenetic character of symbolism.

The key problem related to primal phantasies and their phylogenetic origins
is Lamarck, whose views have been heavily criticized and have become unac-
ceptable today (Medawar, 1985; Gould, 2002). Do we still accept the Lamarckian hypotheses of Freud? We all know that to the end of his life, Freud held
to his own convictions on this score, implicitly rejecting any new biological
views that dismissed Lamarck (see Freud's *Outline of Psychoanalysis*, 1940, pp.
188–189; Steiner, 2003). Freud started mentioning *Die Urphantasien* and their
phylogenetic origins in Lecture XXIII of his *Introductory Lectures on Psychoanalysis* (1916–1917, pp. 370–371) but, together with Laplanche & Pontalis (1967;
Steiner, 2003), I have tried to show that in some ways we could even go back to
the *Urzenes* ('primal scenes') – and their limited number – mentioned by Freud
in the Fliess correspondence of 1892–1904 (Masson, 1985; see Freud to Fliess, 2
May 1897, pp. 240–242) due to Freud's constant need to find universal evidence
with which to support his discoveries.[8]

The Lamarckian phylogenetic hypotheses used by Freud to explain his
Urphantasien can be understood only if one also takes into account what he
wrote in the case history of the *Wolf Man* in 1914 (although published in 1918),
to which I would like to return below. Furthermore, we should consider the fan-
tascientific but fascinating *Übersicht der Übertragungsneurosen* (written in 1915),
discussed with Ferenczi but never published. This text was discovered and carefully introduced with very important and still unsurpassed statements about
Freud's Lamarckism by Grubrich-Simitis[9] (1987), stressing what lies behind 'A
Phylogenetic Fantasy.'

Remember again what Freud wrote in *Moses and Monotheism* (1939, pp. 78–79)
concerning the archaic inheritances, the primal scene and the killing of the primal father, but also what he wrote in *An Outline of Psychoanalysis* (1940,
pp. 188–189) where the primal phantasy of seduction and its phylogenetic origin is described in detail, starting with mother's breast as the primal seducing
object for the baby, followed a bit later by the body of mother itself. Of course, in
this text there is the *vexata quaestio* of the awareness of the breast by the baby during the first months of life, which Freud denies here. But here, incidentally, Freud
is not so far away from Klein's (1944) views as far as the phantasy of the breast
and the body of the mother, their phylogenetic origin and the role they play in
the baby's development are concerned (King & Steiner, 1992, pp. 753–757).[10]

In those last papers and books, as Strachey has clearly demonstrated in his
editorial note to *Moses and Monotheism* (1939, p. 102, fn. 1), Freud even oscillates

between the terms '*Trieb*' ('drive') and '*Instinkt*' ('instinct'), reminding us how the archaic, primeval inheritance transmitted phylogenetically poses the problem of our biological links with the animal species we descend from. After all, according to contemporary research, only 6 million years have passed since we differentiated ourselves from the chimpanzees with which we share – according to the great biologist-palaeontologist and anthropologist Cavalli Sforza (Cavalli Sforza and Padoan, 2013, pp. 20–53) – 98 percent of our DNA. Leaving aside the complex vicissitudes which lead from the hominids to homo sapiens, it was only 100,000 years ago that we started to spread from Africa, 500,000–200,000 years ago that the predecessors of homo sapiens started to use language and, what really matters: only between 12,000 and 8,000 years ago did homo sapiens become a relatively stable farmer, having previously been a hunter-gatherer (like other primates) in constant motion. This is something that involved an extraordinarily important change in the structure of both the family and of groups.

Of course, Freud was not aware of this contemporary research, but he knew that his attempt to universalize through Lamarck – and his questionable theories – was limited by chronological data, and we have to bear this in mind, too. Indeed, how far back can those *Urphantasien* be traced today, with all the prehistoric data at our disposal? Are they universal and transcultural; how were they transmitted and how are they being transmitted? When did the prohibition of incest and primal repression begin? Or is it nonsense to think in these terms and ask these questions today, here in Europe?

Indeed, even if we can no longer accept Freud's Lamarckian hypotheses, the problems relating to the origins, existence and extent of the presence in the Unconscious of *die Urphantasien* in different peoples and cultures cannot be ignored, not to mention that of unconscious symbolism. This is true at least for most of the contemporary schools of psychoanalysis studied and compared by Werner and his colleagues. Thus, it is not only a theoretical problem; it is something we have to face every day in our clinical practice, working in different geographical, cultural and socio-political settings all over the world.

Laplanche & Pontalis (1967, pp. 331–332) already stressed the importance of this problem, which lingers in many of Werner's and his colleagues' statements. Consider Zysman's contribution, with his notion of 'global phantasies'. I very much liked Scarfone's elegant and sophisticated attempt to bypass the problem, but I am not totally persuaded by his way of tackling it. Maybe this is because I belong to a different generation of psychoanalysts. If I understood him correctly, he seems to go beyond the already sophisticated structuralist reinterpretation of the phylogenetic origins of the *Urphantasien* of his master Laplanche, which I have to confess I still prefer, although I do not completely agree with him either.

I am not an expert in the field, but I wonder if one could find some help in understanding these issues using contemporary epigenetics. Jorge Canestri, whom I consulted (personal communication, 2015), told me that epigenetics – which he understands far more than myself – could help us make sense, in contemporary terms, of Freud's Lamarckism. Perhaps Mark Solms, to whom we

owe a very important but often ignored neuropsychoanalytic paper on unconscious phantasies (Solms, 1997/2003) could also help us. But of course, it is
another question that I am asking Werner and his colleagues to answer.

I also wonder what Werner and his colleagues think of the attempts made by
Money-Kyrle and Bion in England in the sixties and seventies of the last century (and here we see the importance of local cultural influences and traditions)
to bypass the problem of Lamarck. This is something that even Bowlby (1969),
who nevertheless always referred to Darwin and neo-Darwinism, tried to do a
bit later from the point of view of attachment.

Money-Kyrle, in his *Man's Picture of His World* (1960, pp. 42–59), and Bion,
in *Learning from Experience* (1962b, p.91), tried to make sense of the chrono-
logically most archaic primal phantasy: the unconscious phantasy of the breast,
stressed so much by Klein. Money-Kyrle (1960, p.46) also insisted on the presence of primal intercourse. Money-Kyrle and Bion introduced the hypothesis
of pre-programmed, inborn phantasies of expectation of the breast and the
primary scene in the mind of the baby, rooted in biology. They considered their
hypotheses more empirically viable than Freud's and never mentioned Lamarck.
Bion called them 'preconceptions', a notion similar to what Kant meant by
'empty thoughts'. This refers to a sort of unconscious expectation, a very confused sort of knowledge in phantasy, which needs to be 'saturated' by the actual
experience of the mother and father. Initially, such phantasies are extremely
partial, confused, distorted and exaggerated. Money-Kyrle rightly called them
'misconceptions', which need to be gradually transformed and then repressed.
Only with the depressive position do these partial preconceptions start to lose
their distorted and often hallucinatory character. With the constant interaction
between the baby and the mother (and I would add also, the father) they start
to be felt to be outside and are gradually internalized as (external and internal)
whole objects, in a more realistic way. See Bion's notion of 'commensal' in
Learning from Experience (1962b).[11]

I know this is only a superficial analogy, because Laplanche and Pontalis were
completely against any attempt to link primal phantasies to their instinctual
biological roots, but curiously enough Money-Kyrle and Bion can remind one
of their notion of prestructured primal phantasies (1968 [2003], pp. 121–129).
The latter authors were enormously influenced by Lacan, but also by Levi
Strauss and by the structuralism and linguistics of Roman Jakobson.[12] Although
Jakobson (personal communication, 1979) told me that he did not follow Lacan
and was also interested in the biological roots of language, as is Chomsky. I will
come back to Chomsky, briefly, later on.

Yet Money-Kyrle, who studied philosophy in Austria with Schlick and was
deeply influenced by neokantianism and by Bion's hypotheses (whatever one
may think of the way Bion reads Kant), seems also to resemble what Freud said
in the *Wolf Man*. I am always surprised that his statements have been so readily
forgotten. I am thinking particularly about his claim that primal phantasies could
be considered 'as phylogentically inherited schemata which like the categories

of philosophy[13] are concerned with the business of "placing" the impressions derived from sexual experiences' (Freud, 1918, pp. 119–120). Freud claims a few lines before, when he defines phantasies as 'some sort of hardly definable knowledge . . . something as it were preparatory to understanding . . . something analogous to the far reaching instinctive knowledge of animals', that they constitute 'the nucleus of the unconscious, a primitive kind of mental activity' (Freud, 1918, pp. 118–120).

Of course, cultural echoes and analogies should always be carefully scrutinized and not taken out of context so as to avoid simplifications and misreadings. But if one considers some of these statements by Freud, one can perhaps understand why Klein and Isaacs were stimulated to come to some of their conclusions. Even Bion, with his theory of preconceptions, protomental systems and thinking, or Segal (1994 [2003], pp. 200–203; following Bion, 1962a, pp. 110–119 and 1962b, pp. 90–92), insists on the fact that phantasies and phantasizing are necessary preliminary forms of knowledge that need to be constantly tested and shaped by reality. Reality for the baby is strictly related to the experience of containment by the mother and father. It depends on the type of interaction between the baby and the parental couple, whether these primitive phantasies can lose their distorting characteristics. Under the influence, I think, of her son, who studied with Chomsky, Segal, in her last work (1990 [2007], pp. 115–116) compared unconscious phantasies with the inborn generative grammar of Chomsky, something which also interested Andre Green (personal communication, 2006). I had come to a similar conclusion (Steiner, 1975). I do not know what Werner and his colleagues think of what I have just tried to recall. It nevertheless shows that Kleinian thinking has also tried to develop.

In reading the contributions of Werner and his colleagues, particularly those of Jimenez and Vervin, it is obvious that they rightly, in some way, tend to isolate the Kleinian way of understanding unconscious phantasies from the rest of contemporary psychoanalytic thinking. The Kleinians are presented – to use the philosophical jargon – as the essentialists, the idealists, although *a la* Schelling, I would say, given the importance they attribute to the early body. Indeed, if one reads Isaacs (1943/2003, p.185) correctly, the first primordial unconscious phantasies are not visual. They are based on confused coenaesthetic bodily sensations, linked to raw emotions of good or bad, togetherness or not-togetherness, and inside or outside. This is something that Bion would develop further in his numerous papers and books on protothinking or paleothinking, beta or alpha elements, and so on.

The Kleinians have also been called the totalitarian fundamentalists of the unconscious (equated with unconscious phantasies) because their conception becomes synonymous, or linked with, other mental mechanisms, even the mechanisms of defence. But I do not totally agree with Werner when he claims that, for the Kleinians, the unconscious is synonymous with unconscious phantasy. Segal, for instance, told me and others: do not forget that the *unbewusste Wunsch* is the father of unconscious phantasies and, therefore, for her, recalling

Freud, the unconscious wish is at the core of the deep unconscious. As you all know, if we start to take the road of the unconscious *unbewusste Wunsch*, we end up at a sort of navel of the unknown, at that 'mycelium', to use Freud's famous metaphor in *The Interpretation of Dreams* (1900, p.525) concerning the ultimate interpretability of the dream.

What I mean is that we still do not know how far back the unconscious wish can lead us, and what sort of proto-paleo-primal phantasies (if one can call them that) remain to be discovered. Just think of the work of Levine, Reed, Scarfone and others (2013) on the 'unrepresented states' of the mind, at least partially inspired by Bion (1975 [1977], pp. 43–57; 1997, pp. 50–51) and based on what he claimed – using a statement of Freud's – about the fragile caesura between pre and post-natal life and the inaccessible unconscious. In this case, one is tempted to again recall Adorno's aphorism from *Minima Moralia*.

Without ending up in one of those fascinating but rather labyrinthine and daring alleys, I would simply like to point out the following: in one way or another, Werner and his colleagues all stress the difficulty of finding links between the Kleinian way of understanding unconscious phantasies and that of the other schools, not to mention the difficulties that also exist in the other schools as far as our issue is concerned. The Sandlers – with whom I had many friendly intellectual exchanges discussing the problem – tried in England to reduce the gap between themselves and the Kleinians, but in developing their model of the past and present unconscious (1984, 1994) they practically isolated what they understood as unconscious primal phantasies in a nearly inaccessible past. I do not have space to comment on other analysts' contributions, mentioned by Werner and his colleagues, but just think of some of Aulagnier's (1975 [2001], pp. 20–37) statements concerning the pictograms, reminiscent of Bion's ideographs (1957 [1967], pp. 49–50). I still remember a panel in Rome during the IPA Congress in 1989, where Aulagnier was presenting, during which I reminded her of Bion's work on proto or paleo thinking during the paranoid-schizoid position and his views on ideographs. Even Andre Green agreed with me. All I have said here shows *a fortiori* that the Kleinians, in spite of their so-called essentialism and fundamentalism, have, as I already said, tried to further develop their views concerning unconscious phantasies.

I am insisting on this because what has struck me in all the papers by Werner and his colleagues is the fact that Bion is never properly taken into account. It is true that it is difficult to understand what Bion means by a 'contact barrier' between the conscious and unconscious and his way of describing the formation of the unconscious, without referring to what Klein and Isaacs (who incidentally seems to anticipate Bion's preconceptions) were stressing in the thirties, forties and fifties about the relationship between conscious and unconscious and primitive unconscious phantasies, using the theory of 'genetic continuity'. It is true that the Kleinians, particularly at that time, did not refer to the notion of *Nachträglichkeit*, which of course plays its role, even as widely different schools deal with the *Urphantasien*. Nevertheless, it is curious that even Laplanche and

Pontalis said at one point: 'In our view the idea of primal phantasy serves in a way as a counterweight to the notion of deferred action' (1967, p.332).

Of course, I do not want to claim that what they had in mind was the theory of genetic continuity, but there is no doubt that Klein and Isaacs, basing themselves on the analysis of very small children and using the play technique, employed the notion of genetic continuity, which was used in academic psychology. Nevertheless, genetic continuity, which we sometimes find even in Freud, does not exclude *Nachträglichkeit*. Indeed, neither Klein nor Isaacs, nor even Bion or Segal or any contemporary Kleinian, really think that they can have direct access to unconscious phantasies. I agree with the warning contained in Mark Solms's paper concerning how we deal with unconscious phantasies, even regarding the Kleinians (Steiner, 2003, pp. 104–105). Yet Klein and Isaacs, and then of course Bion, nevertheless arrived at a notion of greater permeability between unconscious phantasies and primal repression – and that is something which characterizes the Kleinians, for better or worse.[14] Bion, as we know, tried in several of his works to give all this a more sophisticated theoretical status.

I do not claim that everybody should accept what I have just said, and I am the first to agree that some aspects of the thinking of Bion and his colleagues can be problematic. Yet, at the risk of sounding repetitive, what I really find missing in Werner's and his colleagues' paper in particular is a more articulated evaluation of Bion's notions of container, the mother's reverie and alpha function. I would have liked a more articulated evaluation of the way in which Bion (1957 [1962a], pp. 118–20), Rosenfeld (1986, pp. 157–207) and Segal (1994 [2003], pp. 202–203) have described, in various ways, the communicative and the pathological aspects of projective identification – but also of introjective identification, based on communicative or pathological introjective identification, linked to the intensity or violence of the emotions of libidinal and destructive drives and wishes, acting together with the unconscious phantasies of the baby. All of what I have just mentioned is also linked to the responses of the mother (and also of the father), of what I call the reverie of the parental couple (Steiner, 2006, 2013a) – its presence or its absence in responding to the needs, projections and reintrojection of the unconscious phantasies of the baby.

As Werner rightly says, unconscious phantasies are a sort of theoretical-conceptual extrapolation from our clinical practice. Yet, in analysis, one has just to feel and try to understand the confused, primitive, rough quality of, for instance, the primal scene to understand the value of Bion's notion of container, reverie and alpha function. It can sometimes appear split off in dreams which the adult patient cannot tolerate and accept as his own, in which he watches his father and brother raping his mother, or in which he swallows an anaconda as the first incorporation of father's penis, due to the pathological and at times traumatic interaction between himself and his parents in the past. In the 'normal process' of projective and introjective identification, when the container and the parental reverie and alpha functions are good enough, unconscious primal phantasies act as a preliminary, necessary way of testing reality and coming to a better understanding of it in time and through development; but they are also shaped and molded by good enough experiences coming from the outside world.

I do not know if Werner and his colleagues are familiar with the last work of Segal on these issues (1992 [2007], pp. 104–107) in which, alongside a discussion with Wolheim,[15] she utilizes Bion, Rosenfeld and her own clinical material to deal clearly with these problems which I have had to condense and simplify here. Projective identification implies that, with the projected phantasy, the baby also projects its embryonic perceptual and thinking apparatus. If the baby finds a container that can fulfill, understand and metabolize the projection of his phantasies, then the baby gradually re-introjects a capacity to tolerate frustration, which also enables him to gradually use his own alpha function. In other words, the baby gradually becomes able to think and to perceive his own external (but also internal) reality in a fluid, non-delusional, non-rigid and less-paranoid-schizoid way and repression can gradually take place. A satisfying, containing breast, a containing primal scene, helps the baby to gradually build up a more realistic perception of internal and external reality. Otherwise, one ends up with Segal's symbolic equations, or with Bion's unmetabolized beta elements: the creation of a pathological and disturbed internal and external world in the baby, where his perceptual and thinking apparatus is mutilated or fragmented and cannot develop properly. Then the primal phantasies remain unchanged, with all their misperceptions, as I said, which leads to psychotic or borderline disturbances.

All that I have just stated leads to a contemporary view of unconscious phantasy that is much less secluded, less concentrated exclusively on the internal world of the baby or of the adult, than that which Werner and his colleagues are claiming, as far as the Kleinian approach to this issue is concerned. It is true, nevertheless, that Kleinians acknowledge problems related to the constitution of the baby. But Freud had done the same. I wonder if Werner and his colleagues have an answer to the so-called constitutional factors in us and the role they play both in our disturbances and in our mental health? All these aspects of Kleinian thinking, if taken more fully into account, would perhaps have allowed further integration with the views of the other schools. Finally, I would like to add that the way in which all the Kleinian scholars and clinicians I have quoted understand unconscious phantasies, and in this context I would like to add also the work of Betty Joseph (1989), leads to a very specific way of conceiving thinking, non-verbal but also verbal language. They constantly interact with the dynamic nature of the unconscious phantasies via projective and introjective identification and can never be conceived without them even in their most mature and abstract form. In 1992, also using some of Schafer's views, I advanced the hypothesis (Steiner, 1992, p.7) that the Kleinian notion of enactment in the transference, and I would also add, *mutatis mutandi*, Joseph Sandler's views on this subject (1987), could perhaps be usefully compared with Austin's theory (1962) of some aspects of what he called 'speech acts', particularly the interlocutory ones.

But I have to stop here. I quite agree with many of Werner's conclusions on the difficulties of finding a real integration regarding this issue. I do not know whether he is familiar with the book *Understanding Dissidences and Controversies in Psychoanalysis* (Bergman, 2004), which is a collection of papers given in New York by Bergman, Green, Kernberg, Blum and others, in which, incidentally, the Controversial Discussions between Anna Freud and Klein focusing on unconscious phantasies were deeply studied and used. In the end, many of those who took part in the meetings came to the conclusion that *pace* the great and understandable efforts of Bob Wallerstein, it is not possible to reach a real common ground and integration in contemporary psychoanalysis. As Andre Green said (*Ibid.*, p.126–127) there is no dissidence today because there is such a widespread dissent and we have to face it together.

Joseph Sandler, who, as we all know, had such an interest in integrating new ideas in his way of reading and following Freud, once jokingly told me – after I had mentioned to him that in his way of understanding the here and now he sometimes sounded like Betty Joseph – 'Riccardo, *vive la différence*'. Freud had already said something similar about Adler, but particularly about Jung and what Jung meant by the analysis of the here and now. Sometimes we have to accept that we take different routes: 'This may be a school of wisdom; but it is no longer psychoanalysis' (Freud, 1933, p.143).

I will end with a biblical quotation, which curiously enough seems to be very suitable when considering some aspects of primal unconscious phantasies. It comes from Isaiah, chapter 11: 'The wolf also shall dwell with the lamb and the leopard shall lie down with the kid and the calf and the young lion will lie together . . . and the lion will eat straw like the ox and the earth shall be full of knowledge of the Lord'. This quotation is a marvellous utopian phantasy but it does not belong to psychoanalysis, even as far as the integration of various way of understanding *die Urphantasien* today is concerned. We must go on trying – reading and studying the work of each other in depth and without prejudices, meeting, discussing, confronting our views, following the rule of hermeneutic dialogue. In this way we can all learn from each other.

Notes

1 It is interesting that Freud was aware of this. In the (1914) edition of *The Interpretation of Dreams* he wanted to remind the reader that the links between *Die Phantasie* (translated in this instance as 'imagination' by Strachey) and what he called *Wunsch* (translated as 'desire') are very old. He quotes Plotinus: 'When our desires are aroused, imagination comes along and, as it were, presents us with the objects of those desires (Ennead, IV, 4, 17)' (Freud, 1900, p.134). Plotinus had obviously been influenced by Plato. Freud took the quotation from the work of Carl du Prel, a German scholar whom he admired very much. Freud called Du Prel "that brilliant mystic" (Freud, 1900, p.63).

2 Unfortunately, I do not have space here to discuss how these terms have been translated in other languages, but this would be a very interesting way of looking at our issues, due to the theoretical and linguistic problems that translations of Freud evoke.

3 To give an example, in the British Library in London there is a text written by von Schubert, *Die Symbolik des Traumes* (1814), an extremely fascinating small book belonging to the most characteristic period of German Romanticism. Freud knew von Schubert quite well (Steiner, 1982, 1988) and the copy of the text in the possession of the British Library is annotated in the margins by Coleridge.

4 Leaving aside Dante.
5 Not to mention what one could find in the rich and exhaustive bibliography that Werner and his colleagues refer to.
6 'First the whole interest and love focus is on the nipple and on the breast. . . . I have on several occasions expressed the view that the relation of the infant to his mother is based on phylogenetic inheritance and is ontogenetically the most fundamental of all human patterns. . . . Freud described unconscious sexual theories of children as a phylogenetic inheritance. The analysis of young children has not only confirmed this discovery, but revealed in many details the significance of these infantile theories in the intellectual and emotional life of the children' (Klein, 1944, in King & Steiner, 1992, p.757).
7 See Strachey's very exhaustive editorial note in Freud's *Moses and Monotheism* (1939, p.102, fn.1) where he is able to inform us about the whole issue of the so-called archaic or phylogenetic heritage of dream symbols and primal phantasies in Freud's work, from a chronological point of view. He claims that the "the possibility of the inheritance of actual ancestral experiences", which lies at the core of phylogenesis, had appeared relatively late in Freud's writings: around 1912–1913 with *Totem and Taboo*.
8 One can consider the way Freud tried to address his need to find universal evidence of the Oedipal phantasies (discovered just a few years before he wrote *The Interpretation of Dreams*) through his research on the universality of the Oedipal myth of a polymath named Constant (Steiner, 1998; See also Steiner, 2013a).
9 Translated into English rather questionably.
10 Klein (1944) did not insist so much on the seductive quality of the mother. Later, particularly in *Envy and Gratitude*, Klein (1957) mentioned the confusion created by an overly erotized relationship to the breast, where the mother, too, plays a part.
11 'By commensal, I mean that contained and container are dependent on each other for mutual benefit and without harm to either. In terms of a model, the mother derives benefit and achieves mental growth from the experience: the infant likewise abstracts benefits and achieves growth' (Bion, 1962b, p.91).
12 I personally agree with Laplanche and Pontalis's view (1968 [2003]), stimulated by Lacan, of the presence of what they mean by primal phantasies, when they stress the structural presence of the father together with that of the mother from the beginning of the life of the baby. I have never been totally persuaded by the chronology suggested by Klein and Isaacs that first there is only a relationship with the mother and then later on, after 2–3 months, the father also starts to become important. Bion (1962b, p.36) also stresses the importance of the father and the mother's love for him as an essential part of her feeding reverie. Although historically one has to acknowledge what Klein claimed during the Freud-Klein Controversies of 1941–1945 (King & Steiner, 1992, pp. 936–937) that she was going beyond Freud in stressing both the role of the father and the mother during the first months of life.
13 It is here that he had Kant in mind, if not even Plato.
14 See, for instance, the discussion between Segal and the Sandlers (1994 [2003], p.208).
15 One of the leading English speaking philosophers interested in psychoanalysis (see Steiner, 2003, pp. 199–208)

References

Adorno, T.W. (1951[1974]). *Minima Moralia*. London: NBL.
Aulagnier, P. (1975[2001]). *The Violence of the Interpretation*. London: Routledge.
Austin, J.L. (1962). *How to Do Things with Words*. Oxford: Oxford University Press.
Bergmann, M. (Ed.) (2004). *Understanding Dissidences and Controversies in Psychoanalysis*. New York: The Other Press.
Berlin, I. (1975). *Vico and Herder: Two Essays in the History of Ideas*. London: Chatto and Windus.

Bion, W.R. (1957[1967]). The Differentiation of the Psychotic from the Non-Psychotic Part of the Personality. In *Second Thoughts*. London: Heinemann Books, pp. 43–64.

Bion, W.R. (1962a[1967]). A Theory of Thinking. In *Second Thoughts*. London: Heinemann Books, pp. 110–119.

Bion, W.R. (1962b). *Learning from Experience*. London: Heinemann Books.

Bion, W.R. (1967). *Second Thoughts*. London: Heinemann Books.

Bion, W.R. (1975[1977]). *Coesura*. Rio de Janeiro: Imago.

Bion, W.R. (1977[1997]). Untitled 29 May 1977. In *Taming Wild Thoughts*. Bion, F. (Ed.). London: Karnac Books, pp. 39–54.

Bowlby, J. (1969). *Attachment and loss*. London: Hogarth.

Calvino, I. (1988). *Six Memoirs for the Next Millennium*. Cambridge, MA: Harvard University Press.

Cavalli Sforza, L.L. & Padoan, D. (2013). *Razzismo e Noismo*. Turin: Einaudi.

Fichtner, G., Grubrich Simitis, I. & Hirschmueller, A. (Eds.) (2011). *Sigmund Freud und Martha Bernays: Die Brautbriefe Vol. 1 (1882–83)*. Frankfurt am Main: Fischer Verlag.

Freud, S. (1900). The Interpretation of Dreams. *S.E.*, 4–5.

Freud, S. (1914[1918]). From the History of and Infantile Neurosis. *S.E.*, 17, p.3.

Freud, S. (1915). *A Phylogenetic Fantasy*. Grubrich Simitis, I. (Ed.). Cambridge, MA: Harvard University Press, 1987.

Freud, S. (1915–1916). Introductory Lectures on Psychoanalysis. *S.E.*, 15, Parts 1–2.

Freud, S. (1916–1917). Introductory Lectures on Psychoanalysis. *S.E.*, 16, Part 3.

Freud, S. (1933). New Introductory Lectures on Psychoanalysis. *S.E.*, 22, p.7.

Freud, S. (1937). Analysis Terminable and Interminable. *S.E.*, 23, p.211.

Freud, S. (1939). Moses and Monotheism. *S.E.*, 23, p.17.

Freud, S. (1940). An Outline of Psychoanalysis. *S.E.*, 23, p.141.Goldmann, S. (2003). *Via Regia zum Unbewussten*. Giessen: Psychosozial Verlag.

Gould, S. J. (2002). *The Structure of Evolutionary Theory*. Cambridge, MA: Harvard University Press.

Grubrich Simitis, I. (1987). Introduction. In *Sigmund Freud a Phylogenetic Fantasy (1915)*. Grubrich Simitis, I. (Ed.). Cambridge, MA: Harvard University Press.

Grubrich Simitis, I. (2011). Einleitung. In *Sigmund Freud und Martha Bernays: Die Brautbriefe (1882–83), Vol. 1*. Frankfurt am Main: Fischer Verlag.

Isaacs, S. (1943/2003). The Nature and Function of Phantasy. In *Unconscious Phantasy*. Steiner, R. (Ed.). London: Karnac Books, pp. 145–198.

Joseph, B. (1989). *Psychic Equilibrium and Psychic Change: Selected Papers*. Feldmann, M. & Spillius, E. (Eds.). London: Routledge.

King, P. & Steiner, R. (Eds.) (1992). *The Freud–Klein Controversies 1941–1945*. London: Routledge.

Klein, M. (1944). The Emotional Life and the Ego Development of the Infant with Special Reference to the Depressive Position. In *The Freud–Klein Controversies 1941–1945*. King, P. & Steiner, R. (Eds.). London: Routledge, 1992, pp. 452–797.

Klein, M. (1946[1975]). Notes on some Schizoid Mechanisms. In *The Writings of Melanie Klein: Envy and Gratitude and Other Works, Vol. 3*. Money Kyrle, R. (Ed.). London: The Hogarth Press, pp. 1–24.

Klein, M. (1952[1975]). On Observing the Behaviour of Young Infants. In *The Writings of Melanie Klein: Envy and Gratitude and Other Works, Vol. 3*. Money Kyrle, R. (Ed.). London: The Hogarth Press, pp. 94–121.

Klein, M. (1957[1975]). Envy and Gratitude. In *The Writings of Melanie Klein: Envy and Gratitude and Other Works, Vol. 3*. Money Kyrle, R. (Ed.). London: The Hogarth Press, pp. 146–235.

Laplanche, J. & Pontalis, J.-B. (1967). *The Language of Psychoanalysis*. London: Karnac Books.
Laplanche, J. & Pontalis, J.-B. (1968[2003]). Fantasy and the Origins of Sexuality. In *Unconscious Phantasy*. Steiner, R. (Ed.). London: Karnac Books, pp. 107–143.
Levine, H.B., Reed, G.S., Scarfone, D. et al. (Eds.) (2013). *Unrepresented States and the Construction of Meaning*. London: Karnac Books.
Masson, M.J. (Ed.) (1985). *The Complete Letters of Sigmund Freud to Wilhelm Fliess (1887–1904)*. Cambridge, MA: Harvard University Press.
Matte Blanco, I. (1985). *The Unconscious as Infinite Sets*. London: Duckworth.
Medawar, J.S. (1985). *Aristotle to Zoos: A Philosophical Dictionary of Biology*. Cambridge, MA: Harvard University Press.
Money Kyrle, R. (1960). *Man's Picture of His World*. London: Duckworth.
Radestock, P. (1879). *Schlaf und Traum: eine physiologisch-psychologische Untersuchung*. Wiesbaden: Breitkopf und Härtel.
Rosenfeld, H.A. (1986). *Impasse and Interpretation*. London: Tavistock Books.
Sandler, J. (1987). *From Safety to Superego*. London: Karnac Books.
Sandler, J. & Sandler, A.M. (1984). The Past Unconscious, The Present Unconscious and the Interpretation of the Transference. *Psychoanalytic Inquiry*, 4, pp. 376–379.
Sandler, J. & Sandler, A.M. (1994). Phantasy and Its Transformations: A Contemporary Freudian View. *International Journal of Psychoanalysis*, 75, pp. 387–394.
Scherner, C.A. (1861). *Das Leben des Traumes*. Berlin: Schindler.
Segal, H. (1992[2007]). Acting on Phantasy, Acting on Desire. In *Yesterday, Today, Tomorrow*. Abel Hirsch, N. (Ed.). London/New York: Routledge, pp. 96–110.
Segal, H. (1994[2003]). Phantasy and Reality. In *Unconscious Phantasy*. Steiner, R. (Ed.). London: Karnac Books, pp. 199–209.
Solms, M. (1997[2003]). Do Unconscious Phantasies Really Exist? In *Unconscious Phantasy*. Steiner, R. (Ed.). London: Karnac Books, pp. 89–105.
Steiner, R. (1975). *Il Processo di Simbolizzazione nell'Opera di Melanie Klein*. Turin: Boringhieri.
Steiner, R. (1982). Es Ludens? In *La Comunicazione Spritosa*. Fornari, F. (Ed.). Florence: Sansoni, pp. 103–164.
Steiner, R. (1988). Paths to Xanadu. *International Review of Psychoanalysis*, 15, Part 4, pp. 415–454.
Steiner, R. (1992). Some Historical and Critical Notes on Hermeneutics and Psychoanalysis. *Bulletin of the British Psychoanalytic Society*, 28(10), pp. 7–43.
Steiner, R. (1998). In Vienna Veritas? *International Journal of Psychoanalysis*, 74, Part 4, pp. 511–583.
Steiner, R. (2000). *Einleitung zur Sigmund Freud Zur Psychopatologie des Alltags Leben*. Frankfurt am Main: Fischer Tachenbuch Verlag, pp. 7–60.
Steiner, R. (Ed.) (2003). *Unconscious Phantasy*. London: Karnac Books.
Steiner, R. (2006). Does the Pierce' Semiotic Model Based on Index, Icon, Symbol Have Anything to do with Psychoanalysis? In *Language, Symbolization and Psychosis*. Ambrosio, G. & Canestri, J. (Eds.). London: Karnac Books, pp. 219–272.
Steiner, R. (2013a). Die Brautbriefe: The Sigmund Freud and Martha Bernays Correspondence. *International Journal of Psychoanalysis*, 94, pp. 863–935.
Steiner, R. (2013b). Paper Given in Prague, August 2nd 2013 at the 48th Congress of the IPA. See Cohen, J. (2013) Panel Report: Transformations of Emotional Experience. *International Journal of Psychoanalysis*, 94, pp. 1167–1168.
Sulloway, F.J. (1979). *Freud: Biologist of the Mind*. New York: Basic Books.
Vico, G.B. (1744). *Principi di Scienza Nuova*. Naples: Muziana.
Volkelt, J. (1875). *Die Traum Phantasie*. Stuttgart: Meyer & Zeller's.
Von Schubert, G.H. (1814). *Die Symbolik des Traumes*. Bamberg: Kunz.

Chapter 5

Reflections on primitive reparation, the repetition compulsion and the unconscious processing of guilt

Heinz Weiss

STUTTGART/FRANKFURT

Introduction

In my clinical presentation, I would like to show that reparation is largely bound to the unconscious processing of guilt. I will further argue that, if mature reparation fails, primitive reparative attempts are brought into play, which remain unsuccessful because of their concreteness, the denial of separateness and the omnipotent control of anxiety and guilt (Rey 1986; Segal 1964; 1978; 1991). The tragedy of these primitive forms of reparation lies in the fact, that, instead of allowing a sense of forgiveness, they often lead to further damage of the patient's internal objects. This may be one of the mechanisms fueling the repetition compulsion *which in its own right can be understood as a failing and desperate reparative attempt.* In a way, these patients resemble the tragic heroes of Greek mythology (Sisyphus, Prometheus, Tantalos), whose rebellion against the gods – the primitive super-ego – leads to endless torment and punishment.

It is this primitive super-ego that makes reparation so difficult. But, on the other hand, reparation is also required to transform the archaic super-ego into a containing structure that enables the ego to deal with feelings of mourning and guilt (Klein 1958; O'Shaughnessy 1999).[1]

In my clinical contribution, I'd like to show how this development can be impeded, especially when a pathological organization of the personality is brought into play and feelings of *grievance* and *wrath* come to dominate healthier parts of the personality (Steiner 1990; 1993; Weiß 2009). In that case, reparation cannot proceed and the damage of the object is repeated time and again. In the analysis this may lead to clinical impasse where the ego is caught up with its damaged objects, which are unconsciously re-enacted in the transference and counter-transference. In the case I am going to describe, this evoked feelings of irritation and resignation in me, so that my capacity for reparation was also undermined and I found it difficult to maintain an attitude of unprejudiced understanding.

Clinical material

Mr. B. is a 30-year-old employee, who had grown up in a family from a culturally completely different background. His parents had moved to Germany before his birth and as a child he was often picked on and teased because of his foreign origins. Together with his parents' pressure to conform and their traditional authoritarian style of child education, this became associated with the repeated experience of being humiliated, isolated and ashamed. He attempted to overcome these handicaps by doing well at school and subsequently acquiring detailed knowledge of the financial markets. Through clever transactions, this accrued him a fortune of several million dollars by the age of 21. He resigned from his job in an insurance company after feeling wrongly criticized by a superior and decided to study economics with the aim of becoming a fund manager in an international stock exchange. In order to devote all his time to his studies, he entrusted the administration of his fortune to his father. When his father did not act fast enough during a crisis in the financial markets, most of the fortune was lost in a short time.

Mr. B.'s ensuing depression and feelings of quarrel made it difficult to study. He failed his exams narrowly several times, changed the place where he studied and eventually gave up after the death of an idealized professor. After that, he withdrew from the world and was full of resentfulness and contempt. He blamed his father's 'stupidity' for his failure and refused to try a new start in life. Instead, he expected to be reimbursed for his unjust losses.

Thus he lived at home and tyrannized his parents, whom he accused of living in derelict squalor because they had not followed his 'instructions'. He had only once been able to voice his feelings towards a young woman and had never been able to cope with her rejection. In the same year, he witnessed the terror attack of the World Trade Center in New York. In my view, in terms of unconscious phantasy, the collapse of the Twin Towers represented the collapse of his self-confidence, as well as his murderous rage against his parents. So he spent most of his time in financial analyses in front of the computer, occasionally self-harmed and let his parents feel his resentment. After several suicide threats, he started a psychoanalytic treatment, which he experienced as a humiliating confirmation of his condition, as well as a futile effort to give him back his pride, success and financial independence.

Already during one of our first sessions Mr. B. mentioned that he could not imagine that a human being had ever been so unjustly humiliated as he had and that he was not sure whether he might put a knife to his heart. I was alarmed but also angered by his attack and interpreted that he was putting a knife to my chest and giving me the responsibility if things did not go the way he wanted.

In the subsequent long period of his analysis, Mr. B. was almost exclusively preoccupied with the past. All my attempts to look at his current state were rejected by him. For instance, he described in minute detail the ups and downs of the share prices in 2001, the failures of his father at that time, the unjustified criticism from his course leader, the refusal to acknowledge a previous attendance at a course, which led to him to not being accepted to take an exam seven years ago. When he filled the session with monotonous accusations like this, I felt I could not reach him. I often felt tired, hopeless or annoyed, while my futile efforts to establish emotional contact were ignored with charitable negligence. For Mr. B. it was clear that this treatment came 'too late' and that his misery was *not* my fault.

Many months passed in this tug of war. While I was trying to bring him into the 'here and now', he kept ignoring my interpretations and drew me back into the 'there and then' (O'Shaughnessy 2013). I could sense a powerful grievance and wrath. The only 'solution', the only form of 'reparation' he could imagine, he said, was a return to the state prior to the loss of his fortune and the failure of his studies. As he well knew that I would not be able to bring about this state, my interpretations were experienced as irrelevant or as taunts, which left me with feelings of rejection and anger. In particular, when he presented his father as simple, lazy and useless, I was more than once provoked into getting carried away, pointing out that he was unbearably arrogant. Such 'rebuke', as he called it, hurt him, but he did not let on.

Nevertheless his condition stabilized after about two years and he tried to rebuild his fortune by skillful financial investments. He continued to refuse to seek regular employment and experienced it as a 'punishment of fate to have such incompetent parents as his'. On the surface of it I was excluded from this accusation, but experienced myself as incapable and without success in relation to the patient. Repeatedly, Mr. B. gave me to understand that he experienced 'relationships with people' as disappointing, and it seemed clear to me that the relationship with me could only be another disappointment.

At a time when the conflicts with his parents were coming to a head, he contemptuously said that he wanted 'no more to do with this world'.

Then he created the picture of a desolate island, onto which he had retreated and from which he kept people off with a large sign 'No trespassers'. From this island, he was going to follow the worldwide stock exchanges in the hope of reconstructing his former wealth through clever investments and thus be able to live a life of independence and abundance. While no one was allowed to come close to the island, I was permitted to land from time to time in a small boat to bring him provisions. But even I was not permitted access to the 'darker areas' inside the island.

To me, this picture seemed as much descriptive as provocative. While I was trying to interpret his self-righteous wrath, he made me feel that I did indeed not have access to these 'darker areas' in his internal world. A kind of helplessness spread in me, which went as far as catching myself one day carefully checking the share prices in the mad hope that if they rose, my patient would get better. . . .

It seemed that I had lost all confidence in my ability to help him, as if I had become identified with his omnipotent belief system. I thought the 'provisions'

I was allowed to deliver to the island were upholding the status quo without finding real access to his internal world.

There were times, however, when there was better contact between us. When he once again began by saying 'In the year 2000. . .', and I expected him to continue with his usual complaints about his father's failure, he continued by saying 'In 2000 I would not have understood your interpretations'. To my surprise, he added that, if he understood me correctly, his greatest problem was his attitude of all or nothing and thus he was his worst enemy. And after a short break, he let me know that he was invited to visit friends in Switzerland who organized white water rafting tours for tourists with expert guides from New Zealand.

I had the impression that he expressed an appetite for life in this idea and said that it seems like he considers trusting my guidance and coming from his desolate island into rough waters.

He responded that someone who has never had the experience of failure would probably never understand him, and immediately I had the impression that I was receiving another lesson in failure and misunderstanding.

But it was difficult for Mr. B. to feel understood by me. From his point of view, I was in an ideal position, equipped with all the attributes he longed for: money, prestige, academic achievement and a family. This made him envious, and although he acknowledged my 'analyses' as 'correct', he was insistent that I could never empathize with him.

In this way, Mr. B. 'understood' my interpretations, but could not really take them in and make use of them. His problem was that he had no capacity for *reparation*. Instead of acknowledging the damage he inflicted on others, he was preoccupied with the injustice done to him. He projected his wish for reparation onto others and demanded reparation from them to return to him what was rightfully his and was unjustly kept from him, in particular, money, success and respect. For this reason, in his unconscious phantasy, reparation meant *concrete restitution* rather than making amends.

Thus Mr. B. experienced life and his analysis as constant humiliation. He despised dependency and sought to recreate an illusory state in which everything belonged to him and he was not dependent on anyone. He *tolerated* treatment from his solitary island as long as this provided food for his illusions and his campaign of revenge. However, he seemed to reject analysis, whenever it was likely to get him in touch with the reality of mourning and loss.

In this hopeless situation, time passed by without any prospect of change. It became increasingly clear how much Mr. B. was dominated by a cruel superego organization, which either forced him into a stance of moral superiority or absolute obedience. He claimed the higher moral values for himself and explained his withdrawal from other people in this way, not without regretting not having been able to have a relationship with a woman.

Feelings of humiliation could quickly flip into states of wrath, where he looked down on people. He complained endlessly about the 'stupidity' of his parents and their numerous shortfalls. He could spend whole sessions in disdain about his mother, who had used a fork in a Teflon frying pan despite his 'warn-ings' and his father, who had no table manners, drove like an idiot, did not use his hearing aid and generally did not follow his advice and 'instructions'. And this was why he had stopped talking to him. Talking like this, his voice got louder and louder and he worked himself into an excited rage. He described his parents as 'hopeless cases' and asked himself how much longer he would be 'patient with them'.

In turn, I increasingly experienced *him* as a hopeless case and frequently felt like losing patience with him. He indulgently ignored my attempts to interpret his accusations as directed towards me. If he experienced my comments as criti-cism, he either submitted obediently or stopped talking to me and at times this led to forceful and even loud confrontations in which I found myself carried away into reproaching him, although I had meant to avoid this.

In the case of the scratched Teflon pan, he had accused his mother of 'poison-ing' the food, while I accused him of not wanting to see that he was poisoning other people's food with his angry accusations.

There followed a long silence until he got back into his reproachful and hurt manner of talking about his mother's misdemeanors. I interpreted that he had experienced my comment as a sharp fork, which had scratched his thin internal protective layer and thus poisoned his food.

Although he seemed to experience this interpretation as far-fetched, he lis-tened carefully. In a more lively and engaged way, he protested against my view of his moral superiority by saying that he had a right to think like this. But then his protest flipped to indignation and he declared: 'Because of my failures and unjust humiliations I have developed a strict moral code. And if you think that I have an attitude of moral superiority or you think that an attitude of 'laissez faire' towards my parents would be a better solution, I am definitely of a differ-ent opinion.'

This indignation could rapidly flip into wrath and then his contempt and hatred assumed self-destructive proportions. In wrath, reparation can be thought of only as *mercy*, and this is exactly why it makes the idea of reconciliation nearly impossible.

In the transference, I seemed either identified with the contemptible parents or with a vengeful super-ego, with him imagining that *I* felt in possession of higher moral standards in my omnipotent belief that *I* could change him. Evi-dently, I had to admit to the failure of my own ambitions in order to take on some of his helplessness and distress. After his self-righteous moral declaration, he felt alone and let me know after a long weekend that he felt worse without his sessions. On this occasion, a more desperate sadness and clinginess became apparent that had not been there previously.

Nevertheless, the conflict with the parents escalated when they accepted an invitation to a wedding abroad. He had declined to accompany them and despised them for having accepted that the relatives would pay for their travel costs. With 'absolute obedience' he drove the parents to the airport, but did not speak a word with them and did not look at them when they took their leave. At home, he unplugged the phone that he could not be reached by them. They should remain in doubt about his welfare, while suicidal fantasies and projections of responsibility and guilt dominated his ideation.

This situation was mirrored in treatment, when he said that he would 'advise anyone' not to contact him. He said he was on 'the path to self-destruction', the coldness inside himself was coming to a head and he was capable of doing to himself what others had done to him previously.

I interpreted that here too he had unplugged, sent me warning signals and let me know that nobody could prevent him from doing harm to himself.

He reacted with angry bouts of rage, saying that he was pleased that his parents were away at last and claimed that only he could help himself by rebuilding his fortune. Otherwise, life was meaningless for him.

I attempted to help him understand that he regarded my endeavors as pretty useless, felt terribly lonely and doubted that anyone could understand his despair. In doing so, I had little hope of being able to reach him and was close to giving up.

It was at moments like this that Mr. B. occasionally got into a state of deep sadness. Then, his superiority and rage collapsed and he became completely desperate and helpless. I feared that he would harm himself at the point of relinquishing the dominance of his destructive internal organization and said that he attempted to hold himself together through holding grudges, arrogance and rage in order not to be overwhelmed by sadness, dependency and guilt. He replied that he agreed with my 'analysis', but he *just could not forgive.*

Much to my surprise, he told me in the last session before the Christmas break that he had replied to Christmas cards for the first time in years and was planning to visit friends. After he had said his good-byes and wished me a good Christmas, he turned round and said with tears in his eyes: 'And thank you very much for being always here for me in the past year!'

Such moments could be moving and gave a glimpse of a capacity for gratitude, which had been hidden for a long time. Mr. B. worried that he might not be able to finance the four-times-a-week sessions once the health insurance stopped paying, although I had indicated that I was prepared to make financial accommodations for him. He wanted to know whether he was allowed to return to the analysis at a later date and whether I was prepared to have him back, and he announced that if he were to make money on the stock exchange, he would invest it in his analysis. His mother had said to him that he should not worry so much about his future and he had begun to talk more with his father.

These movements made me feel hopeful, but could easily be destroyed again when humiliation and shame predominated. Then, his accusations and rage grew to monstrous proportions and he retreated into his grievance and rage-fuelled defensive system, where he 'ordered about' his parents like unruly children and wished them dead. At such times, he spoke of his three 'basic premises' for any kind of possible change. Firstly, he had to get back his lost fortune, secondly, others were the guilty ones and they had to change first, and thirdly, the clock had to be turned back and the bad experiences of his childhood had to be undone.

Conclusions

Mr. B.'s three anti-therapeutic 'basic premises' illustrate the foundation of his defensive system. Because of his professional failure and the demeaning experiences of his childhood, he felt humiliated and demanded that others took responsibility for this. The persistence of his grievance and the omnipotence of his wrath made any attempt at reparation impossible for a long time. His way of dealing with a primitive super-ego was to identify with its ideal, omnipotent aspects as well as its cruel and paranoid ones. In this way, he felt superior to his parents and seemed entitled to look down on them and to humiliate them.

In the analysis, both these sides were projected onto me so that I was either an ideal object, which constantly evoked his envy, or a cruel object, who demanded 'absolute obedience', put him down and relentlessly rebuked him with 'sharp criticisms'.

For a long time, there seemed to be no way out of this situation, especially when I did not feel able to tolerate my own sense of failure and disappointment. Then, I would put the blame on him and demand that *he* change. In this, I seemed identified with my patient in dealing with my failure by projecting it into him. So, we got into a situation *where each demanded that the other change*, a dead end that facilitated the thriving of grievance and feelings of revenge, but made reparation very difficult.

Nevertheless, unconscious reparative attempts were not entirely absent. They became noticeable when Mr. B.'s mood became more mournful and he felt helpless and could not see a way out. However, those movements evoked such a degree of despair in him that I feared that any kind of progress in analysis would possibly lead him to kill himself. Thus, when anxiety and guilt became unbearable, he often retreated into his defensive organization once again.

I think of *grievance* as a state in which the wounds are kept open and the wish for reparation is projected onto an object whose every wish for reparation will be denied (Weiß 2008). On the other hand, in his *wrath* Mr. B seemed identified with a morally superior position, where at times he felt like a god and that the world was not good enough to deserve his love. In such a position, reparation is possible only in the form of *mercy.*

Both states of mind, *grievance* and *rage,* render the processing of guilt extremely difficult. Instead of enabling reparation, they trigger feelings of humiliation and contrition, nourish feelings of revenge and thus endlessly continue the damage of the internal objects. Mr. B. was well able to see this cycle and he agreed with my 'analyses' in this regard, but, as he added, he just *could not forgive.*

I believe, though, that genuine *understanding* is bound up with the possibility of reparation. While humiliation and shame require *immediate relief* (Steiner

2006), reparation requires *time*. When this cannot be tolerated and the path to reparation fails, the repetition compulsion takes over, which may not account just for the individual, but also for certain historical and social developments.

I would like to conclude with a consideration that R. Money-Kyrle (1956) indicated in his early paper on counter-transference. There, he argues that the patient comes to stand for the analyst's own damaged internal objects. There-fore, true understanding goes along with the analyst's capacity for reparation. In the treatment of Mr. B., I'd reached more than once a point where I lost all hope that change would be possible. At times, I projected this helplessness and impotence back onto him and held him responsible for my failing.

Only in those moments when I had to acknowledge the limits of my capacity to tolerate and understand, which brought me close to giving up, it became pos-sible for Mr. B. to admit to himself how lonely and desperate he actually was. It seemed as though both analyst and patient had to experience the collapse of their omnipotence in order to recognize the limits of what is achievable and to devise realistic goals (Steiner 2011).

In the case of Mr. B. that meant, as he once put it, that the 'breaking waves' against his lonely island were getting softer, and he could ask me whether he might be able to return. I think that this question contained an expression of his uncertainty as to whether I would be able to forgive him. The possibility to for-give is in turn linked to the possibility of being able to imagine to be forgiven (Rey 1986). In this sense, I thought, the analysis of Mr. B. could not solve his problems, but it might at least have helped him to live with them.

Note

1 In her 1958 paper '*On the Development of Mental Functioning*', M. Klein introduced the idea that the archaic super-ego initially functions as a kind of 'bad bank' which later on devel-ops into a 'container' and eventually into an *agency which allows the ego to make reparation*. It is, in her view, the co-evolution of ego- and super-ego structures in exchange with the early environment that enables psychic growth and development (O'Shaughnessy 1999). These processes and exchanges remain, of course, to a large extent unconscious. Perhaps, in a simple way, one could say that so as to make reparation, four basic requirements are necessary: (1) the integration of hate and love towards the same object, (2) the development of a super-ego that is able to contain the ensuing feelings of mourning and guilt, (3) an acceptance of time and transience, and (4) the endorsement by a third object which helps to repair symbolically what has become damaged and lost in phantasy and reality.

References

Klein, M. (1958). On the development of mental functioning. In: *The Writings of Melanie Klein* (vol. 3, pp. 236–246. London: The Hogarth Press 1975).

Money Kyrle, R. (1956). Normal countertransference and some of its deviations. In: Meltzer, D. & O'Shaughnessy, E. (eds.), *The Collected Papers of Roger Money-Kyrle* (pp. 330–342. Strath Tay, Perthshire: Clunie Press 1978).

O'Shaughnessy, E. (1999). Relating to the superego. *Int. J. Psycho-Anal.* 80, 861–870.

O'Shaughnessy, E. (2013). Where is here? When is now? *Int. J. Psycho-Anal.* 94, 7–16.

Rey, H. (1986). Reparation. *J. Melanie Klein Soc.* 4, 5–35.

Segal, H. (1964). *Introduction to the Work of Melanie Klein.* London: Random House.

Segal, H. (1978). *Delusion and Creativity and Other Psychoanalytic Essays.* London: Free Associations Books.

Segal, H. (1991). *Dream, Phantasy and Art.* London: Routledge.

Steiner, J. (1990). Pathological organizations as obstacles to mourning: The role of unbearable guilt. *Int. J. Psycho-Anal.* 71, 87–94.

Steiner, J. (1993). *Psychic Retreats: Pathological Organizations in Psychotic, Neurotic and Borderline Patients.* London: Routledge.

Steiner, J. (2006). *Narzißtische Einbrüche: Sehen und Gesehenwerden. Scham und Verlegenheit bei pathologischen Persönlichkeitsorganisationen* (Hg. Weiß, H., Frank, C.). Stuttgart: Klett-Cotta.

Steiner, J. (2011). Helplessness and the exertion of power in the analytic session. *Int. J. Psycho-Anal.* 92, 135–147.

Weiß, H. (2008). Groll, Scham und Zorn. Überlegungen zur Differenzierung narzisstischer Zustände. *Psyche – Z Psychoanal.* 62, 866–886.

Weiß, H. (2009). *Das Labyrinth der Borderline-Kommunikation. Klinische Zugänge zum Erleben von Raum und Zeit.* Stuttgart: Klett-Cotta.

Part II

Scientific perspectives from psychoanalysis and cognitive neuroscience

Chapter 6

The unconscious in cognitive science

A few suggestions for psychoanalysis

Carlo Semenza

PADUA

Psychoanalysis and cognitive neuroscience share an interest in consciousness. Each discipline has, in virtue of its methodology and educated observations, uncovered several truths about how mental processes occur in a more or less conscious fashion. Cross-fertilization between the two domains, although obviously desirable, has been so far extremely limited, however. The attention of scholars has been in fact heavily biased by the nature of their interests and aims.

The aim of this essay is, after examining some difficulties intrinsic to the concept of consciousness that contribute to limiting cross-talk between psychoanalysis and cognitive neuroscience, to provide some example of how progress in the direction of a profitable interaction may be accomplished. Some progress, it will be argued, will be made by considering the implications of neuropsychological cases that show a dissociation within consciousness at various levels. These dissociations reflect the relatively modular organization of the brain and, as a consequence, of the cognitive system. By considering the particular properties of these different, relatively independent, brain networks and portions of our mental apparatus, psychoanalysis may find interesting suggestions on what and how to investigate certain psychodynamic processes with its own proper methods.

Consciousness in neuroscience

What is consciousness and from where does it origin? Nowadays, both philosophers and neuroscientists seem to share the belief that consciousness is a function of the brain: "(consciousness is) a real, natural, biological phenomenon literally located in the brain" (Revonsuo, 2001), "consciousness is entirely caused by neurobiological processes and realized in brain structures" (Changeux, 1983).

We all agree that consciousness refers to conscious mental states, feelings, and a sense of self. The definition of consciousness is not at all simple, however. The context of consciousness is broad and diverse and the issues often muddled. According to some people there is no such thing as a unitary consciousness: specific consciousness systems would be there for each given cognitive function.

Consciousness has, moreover, several aspects. For the sake of clarity, it is useful to distinguish the concepts and the terms describing these aspects. The content of consciousness refers to the specific information one is aware of at a given moment. "Conscious access" is the process by which a piece of information becomes a conscious content. "Conscious processing" refers to the various operations that can be applied to a conscious content. "Conscious report" is the process by which a conscious content can be described, verbally or otherwise. One can report something if and only if one is aware of it. "Self-consciousness" is a particular instance of conscious access, whereby the focus of consciousness is one's internal state. The state of consciousness associated with wakefulness or vigilance refers to the ability to entertain a stream of conscious contents.

Importantly, consciousness is highly dependent on attention. Attention, the function allowing stimulus selection within perception, plays a pivotal role in access to consciousness. It is, in turn, sustained by a complex and multifaceted system: "diffuse attention" and "selective attention" and "bottom up" and "top down" processes are just examples of different aspects of attention that may be eventually recruited in service to psychoanalysis.

In Dehaene and Naccache's (2001) words, the cognitive neuroscience of consciousness aims at determining whether there is a systematic form of information processing and a reproducible class of neuronal activation patterns that systematically distinguish mental states that subjects label as "conscious" from other states.

Understanding the neuronal mechanisms of consciousness is a major challenge for cognitive neuroscience, however, and many people have approached the issue from different perspectives. It is thus hard to compare various theories and empirical data coming from different, hardly communicating, sources. Several theoretical models of consciousness have in fact been proposed in recent years within neuroscience. An exhaustive description of these models is not within the aims of this essay. Rather than reporting a comprehensive review of research on consciousness in neuroscience and the theories inspiring and built upon empirical investigations, this essay will consider only some examples. The aim of these examples will be to show the limits of these models in helping psychoanalytic theory and practice.

An example of a model able to reconcile many observations has been proposed by Dehaene and colleagues (Dehaene and Changeux, 1997; Dehaene and Naccache, 2001; Dehaene, 2008; Dehaene, Charles, King and Marti, 2014). The core concept in this model is that of a "global neuronal workspace". This system would correspond to distributed neurons with long-distance connections, dense in prefrontal, cingulate, and parietal regions. These neurons would be capable of interconnecting multiple specialized processors (that work independently and unaware of each other) and to broadcast signals at the brain scale in a spontaneous and sudden manner. This so-called "global neuronal workspace" would break the modularity of the nervous system and allow the broadcasting of information to multiple neural targets. This broadcasting would create a global availability that is experienced as consciousness. During nonconscious processing, in contrast, evidence would be accumulated locally within specialized sub-circuits, but would fail to reach the threshold needed for global ignition and, therefore, conscious reportability.

In the working of the global neuronal workspace, a distinction is made among "subliminal processing", "preconscious processing" and "conscious processing". In subliminal processing, activation propagates but remains weak and quickly dissipates in 1–2 seconds. A continuum of subliminal states can exist, depending on top-down attention, instructions, etc. In preconscious processing, activation can be strong, durable, and can spread to multiple specialized sensori-motor areas; when attention is oriented away from the stimulus, activation is blocked from accessing higher parieto-frontal areas and establishing long-distance synchrony. Finally, in fully conscious processing, activation invades a parieto-frontal system, can be maintained ad libidum in working memory, and becomes capable of guiding intentional actions including verbal reports. The transition between preconscious and conscious processing may be sharp and sudden.

Why does some knowledge remain permanently inaccessible? The global neuronal workspace hypothesis stipulates that information is consciously accessible if it is explicitly coded in the firing of groups of excitatory neurons with bidirectional links to a distributed network of workspace neurons. Information might remain permanently non-conscious for at least three reasons: 1) It is not encoded in neuronal firing; 2) It is not represented in explicit firing form; 3) It is coded by neurons functionally disconnected from the workspace. In summary, non-conscious stimuli do not seem to reach a stage of processing at which information representation enters into a deliberation process that supports voluntary action with a sense of ownership.

This description is admittedly very sketchy. It is sufficient, however, to observe here that the model based on the global neuronal workspace hypothesis has at least one broad similarity with the model held by Meynert and the Vienna school of neurology in the second part of the 19th century. The strength of unconscious processes does not seem to be considered enough. Unconscious processes, in Meynert's conception, would not become conscious because of their weakness. As argued by Solms and Saling (1986), Freud rejected Meynert's model, widely accepted in the Viennese environment, in favor of the model proposed by Hughlings Jackson (1931). According to Jackson's model, very strong processes originating from sub-cortical areas would be actively maintained out of consciousness by the inhibiting action of cortical areas. For this reason, Jackson's model was more compatible with the line of thought that ultimately led to psychoanalysis. Thus, whatever its merits, the global neuronal workspace hypothesis does not seem to have much to say of specific interest for psychoanalysis: nothing seems to be actively kept out of consciousness.

Another model is that recently proposed by Rizzolatti, Semi and Fabbri-Destro (2014). It stands as an exception with respect to other models, insofar it represents the joint effort of neuroscientists and a psychoanalyst. Their theoretical work has a different perspective and deals with different aspects of consciousness with respect to other authors. The authors' main concern is to explore the utility of re-thinking neuro-physiological data and models through the theoretical construct of ego as elaborated by Freud. They argue that the systems underlying the organization of action and conscious perception are both mediated by a cortical motor network formed by parieto-frontal circuits. The activity of this network has, according to the authors, strong similarities to that postulated by Freud for the conscious part of ego. They also propose that the "default-mode network" might represent that part of ego that is mostly involved in unconscious processes. The default-mode network is a network of regions that show high activity at rest, but which "deactivates" during goal-directed cognition (Raichle et al., 2001). The most important components of this system are the medial prefrontal cortex, medial temporal lobe structures, and the posterior cingulate. Rizzolatti et al. (2014) go further in proposing that, in order both to act coherently and to have a basic understanding of the behavior of others, it is necessary to posit the existence of a neurophysiological "motor" ego similar to the "rider" in the metaphor used by Freud (the ego is the rider who drives the horse – the id – and governs motor behavior). A critical component of the neurophysiological motor ego would be the system, mainly located in the fronto-parietal regions, constituted by mirror neurons; these neurons, by automatically reacting to actions performed by others, would sustain identification processes.

The description of Rizzolatti's et al. (2014) theory largely exceeds the aim of this essay. Here one can just observe, once again, that the emphasis on fronto-parietal structures as critical for consciousness is strongly reminiscent of the global neuronal workspace theory mentioned above. As in the case of the global neuronal workspace theory, however, there is no account of how something can be actively kept out of consciousness.

One theory that needs to be mentioned here because, while getting little if any place within cognitive neuroscience, it has been popularized among psychoanalysts, is that proposed by Edelman (2004). Edelman indeed explicitly rejects cognitive neuroscience. According to his theory, in the constitution of consciousness, two main kinds of signals are critical: those originating from the self, constituting value systems and regulatory elements of the brain and body, and those originating from nonself, i.e. signals from the world that are transformed through global mappings. Signals related to value and categorized signals from the outside world would be correlated and lead to memory (conceptual categorization). This value-category memory is linked by "reentrant paths" to the current perceptual categorization of world signals. The concept of "reentrant signalling" between neuronal groups is defined as the ongoing recursive dynamic interchange of signals that occurs in parallel between brain maps and that continuously interrelates these maps to each other in time and space. Reentry thus depends for its operations on the intricate networks of massively parallel reciprocal connections within and between neuronal groups. According to Edelman, this reentrant linkage is the critical evolutionary development that results in primary consciousness.

When it occurs across many modalities (sight, touch, and so forth), primary consciousness can connect objects and events through the memory of previous value-laden experiences. The activity of the underlying reentrant neural systems results in the ability to carry out high-level discriminations. This ability would enhance survival value.

Edelman's theory has been often used with reference to psychoanalysis in very vague, generic ways by both Edelman and psychoanalysts, often leading, unfortunately, to sweeping remarks and gross mistakes (e.g., in interpreting what cognitive science says about memory, or even for rejecting some of Chomsky's ideas). With this proviso, one can only point out here that, contrary to what Edelman apparently believed, the functioning of long-term memory he supported is not incompatible with current thought in cognitive neuroscience, without adding much indeed. He claimed that in cognitive theories long-term memory is isomorphic with, and therefore just directly reflects, experience, hence the superiority of his views – a gross misunderstanding. According to cognitive science, long-term memory is indeed continuously changed and shaped by incoming as well by past experience. As Freud's theory of "Nachträglichkeit" would maintain.

It is finally worth mentioning a set of studies that are interesting for psychoanalysis because they deal with the issue of free will. These studies, pioneered by Libet (1985), were able to detect brain activity related to a decision to move (Soon, Brass, Heinze and Haynes, 2008; Bode, Bogler and Haynes, 2013). This activity appears occur briefly before people become conscious of it. At least some actions – like moving a finger – are initiated unconsciously at first, and enter consciousness a few seconds afterwards. It is thus possible, on the basis of a subject's brain activity, as shown on fMRI, to predict the action (e.g., the choice of a button, left or right) before the subject experiences the conscious decision to perform the action. The brain regions involved in this prediction included the anterior medial prefrontal cortex and the medial parietal cortex (precuneus/ posterior cingulated). Such findings cast doubts on the very concept of free will. These studies are highly controversial, however, and there is no consensus among researchers about the interpretation of findings. Further empirical research is required.

Consciousness may not be unitary:
The modular brain

The models briefly described in the preceding section are just some (important) examples. They hardly account for the variety of different phenomena one can observe, however. There are several additional neural models of consciousness that cannot even be mentioned here. Each one of these models takes a different perspective about how something is or is not experienced as conscious.

There are indeed many ways to (un)consciousness. This essay aims at driving the attention of psychoanalysts to one aspect of consciousness that has not been so far considered in all its potential implications: as somebody put it, consciousness may not be "unitary". This means here that our mind works in relatively independent compartments that are unaware of each other. Psychoanalysts may want to know about the working of these compartments, as learned from clinical neuropsychology, and use this knowledge for their own purposes.

A fundamental concept, critical to the understanding of what will be later dealt with, is that of modularity of mind. This has been a highly debated issue in the past (see Fodor, 1983; Semenza, Bisiacchi and Rosenthal, 1988; Shallice, 1988; Semenza, 1996; Coltheart, 1999), but, for the purpose of the present proposal, just a few relatively uncontroversial notions need to be grasped. A "modular" organization implies the fact that some parts of the brain (and of the mind) act and pursue their purposes with some degree of independency. This is the result of an evolutionary process that has both advantages and disadvantages. Advantages include more rapid and easy evolution (advantageous mutations can modify parts of the system without repercussions on other portions where they might be disadvantageous) and fastest speed of processing (relatively independent systems are not slowed down by others; fixed, mandatory ways of processing avoid ambiguity). Disadvantages include isolation of systems (that may be unaware of each other) and costs of communication among systems (extra energy needs to be devoted to functionally connect portions that usually work in full independence).

The brain (as the cognitive system) is thus, to a certain extent, organized in a modular way. As a consequence, some parts of the brain may not know what the other parts do. This fact is reflected in surprising experimental findings and clinical phenomena due to brain damage that show dissociations within the awareness system.

Disconnections within the brain: Neuropsychological syndromes

The following is a by no means exhaustive, but sufficient, description of some examples of clinical syndromes that suggest the degree of modularity of the brain. In particular, each of these syndromes, provoked by selective brain damage, represents an instance of relative dissociation of conscious information. A clear dissociation can be demonstrated, in these patients, between information that they can consciously process (explicit knowledge) and information that they can only unconsciously process (implicit knowledge). One portion of the brain (and of the mind) thus behaves as if unaware of another portion. The working of one portion of the system in isolation reveals interesting properties of that portion that would be harder to appreciate in a flawlessly working brain. Overall, neuropsychological syndromes seem to support non–unitary theories of consciousness. They are seen to reflect disconnection between single modules and their corresponding consciousness centers.

The "split brain" ("the left hand should not know what the right hand does . . .")

A well-known, paradigmatic condition is that of patients with a so-called split brain (Gazzaniga, 1967; Sperry, 1968). In these relatively rare cases, the corpus callosum, the main connection between the two hemispheres, is partially or totally interrupted. This results in loss of communication between the two cerebral hemispheres. The best-known cases are those resulting from a total surgical resection, in the attempt to reduce the severity of otherwise intractable epileptic seizures.

These patients show very interesting phenomena. Typical examples are the inability to retrieve with one hand an object palpated with the other or the inability of right-handers to name or describe an object in the left hand (this information goes to the right hemisphere, but naming takes place on the left), even when it is being appropriately manipulated. Sometimes the two hands conflict with each other: one hand undoes what the other hand has done, or actively contrasts its action. The two hemispheres seem thus to work independently and independently deal with stimuli presented to each hemisphere.

Split-brain patients have been thus described as having "two minds" and two consciousness systems. In ordinary social situations, however, split-brain patients are indistinguishable from non brain-damaged people, except for certain memory problems. Importantly, they seem to have a unitary sense of themselves and of their mental life. Gazzaniga believes that the working of the left hemisphere is responsible for this sense of unity. The left hemisphere would act as an "interpreter" of what happens and have, in this sense, the last word. Similarly, Morin (2001) suggested that split-brain patients exhibit two uneven streams of self-awareness; a "complete" one in the left hemisphere (the hemisphere where language is processed, at least in right-handers) and a "primitive" one in the right hemisphere.

Blindsight and Anton's syndrome

"Blindsight" (Weiskrantz, Warrington, Sanders and Marshall, 1974; Cowey, 2004) is the phenomenon whereby people who are cortically blind (due to lesions in their primary visual cortex) are able to respond to visual stimuli that they do not consciously see. The patient can thus "guess" above chance level the position and other features (color, shape, movement . . .) of stimuli that he/ she is not conscious of projected in the hemianopsic field.

An anatomical explanation is generally accepted for this finding. The patient "sees" the stimulus, not with the genicolo-cortical pathway (which leads to the primary visual cortex), but with the tecto-cortical pathway, which does not reach primary visual areas. The stimulus, therefore, does not reach consciousness; information, nonetheless, reaches the cortex in a way that can be used unconsciously.

Similar phenomena have been observed in the auditory and tactile modality. Blindsight and related phenomena challenge the common-sense belief that perceptions must enter consciousness to affect our behavior. One can be guided by sensory information of which one has no conscious awareness.

Patients with Anton's syndrome behave as if they can see, despite their full cortical blindness, consequent to total loss of primary visual areas. This syndrome may thus be viewed as a converse of blindsight. These patients confabulate about what they pretend to see.

Unilateral spatial neglect

Unilateral spatial neglect (often referred to, for short, just as "neglect") is the inability to attend or recognize anything placed in the hemi-space contralateral to the lesion. This symptom is not due to a lack of sensation. In most cases, the lesion is located in the posterior right areas; thus, the ignored side is most often the left side. People affected by neglect would not attend the side contralateral to the lesion, even if invited to do so, and would keep ignoring anything placed in that side. They may claim there is nothing there. The syndrome has many varieties and not all phenomena happen in every case.

In a number of cases, people with neglect would not just ignore the site of real space opposite to their brain lesion. In a number of cases, affected by what is called "representational neglect", patients would likewise ignore the site of space of an imagined scene. Thus, the patient reported by Bisiach, Luzzatti and Perani (1979) accurately described the buildings (e.g., the Royal Palace) on the right side of Duomo (the main church) Square in Milan when asked to pretend to be at the end of the square opposite to the church. He would claim that there was nothing of importance on the left side. In contrast, at a later time, when asked to pretend to be exiting from the church, he could again correctly describe the buildings on the right side of this perspective (e.g., the "Galleria"), but he ignored the buildings on the left side.

Neglect may also encompass a delusional state ("somatoparaphrenia"), where the patient denies ownership of a limb or of an entire side of his/her own body. One common phenomenon is the attribution of the limb to the examiner ("It is your arm, doctor!"). A neglected limb may be the object of aggression, whereby the patient may intentionally hurt him/herself.

A number of phenomena related to neglect show how unconsciously perceived, segregated information may influence the processing of other information. For instance, words presented in the neglected visual field make reading easier in the healthy field. Interference ("Stroop" effect) from stimuli in the neglected visual field (not seen consciously!) may affect processing in the healthy field.

Paradoxically, patients affected by personal neglect, even with somatoparaphrenia, may self assess their deficit correctly. For example, in a questionnaire, they may assign a score of 2/10 to their own ability to perform an action like lifting a glass and yet display the false belief that there is nothing wrong with their limb!).

Neglect is one of the most studied neuropsychological syndromes, also in consideration of the implications it has for understanding consciousness and its relation with attention. Conscious processing, this phenomenon suggests, may take place at different levels of integration. Brain injury may result in the isolation of processes that were previously integrated in larger-scale networks. This would have as a consequence the loss of the emergence of a conscious correlate. Within this pathological, acquired modularity, conflict may arise between processes that are not anymore integrated.

Alien hand

In the "alien hand" syndrome, involuntary movements of a limb are experienced by the patient in conjunction with a feeling of estrangement from and personification of the limb itself. The patient regards it as foreign, unwilled, strange, uncooperative. For instance, the patient would put on clothes with the right hand and pull them off with the left hand. Or, when thirsty, fill a glass with one hand and pour it out with the other. While the right hand pays for an item in a store, the left withdraws the money. Hands may be actively fighting each other: holding an envelope, each hand independently and simultaneously tries to hold and to release it, for as long as ten minutes.

The limb is thus perceived as having a will of itself: it seems to act on its own, outside the patient's control. It may actively contradict or oppose the other limb. Ownership is seldom denied, however.

Alien-hand phenomena have been reported to result from two varieties: anterior and posterior. In the anterior variety, the damage is to the left frontal lobe and anterior corpus callosum or corpus callosum alone. The posterior variety may result instead from corticobasal degeneration or posterior vascular damage in the parietal areas, also on the right side only.

Prosopagnosia and Capgras's delusion

Prosopagnosia is the inability to recognize faces while other aspects of visual processing (e.g., object recognition) and memory are spared. It results from damage to posterior areas (inferior occipital areas, fusiform gyrus, anterior temporal cortex) in the right or in the left hemisphere.

One interesting feature of prosopagnosia is that it suggests both a conscious and unconscious aspect to face recognition. Normal people can accurately tell whether given faces are known or unknown; people with prosopagnosia may be unable to successfully identify the people in the pictures or make a simple familiarity judgment (familiar/unfamiliar?). However, when a measure of emotional response is taken (typically a measure of skin conductance), just as happens in normal people, there may be a greater response to familiar faces, even though no conscious recognition takes place.

Capgras's delusion may be considered the reverse of prosopagnosia. The patient believes that familiar people (and/or places, in this case it goes under the name of "reduplicative paramnesia") have been substituted by similar entities. The patient is conscious of physical alikeness but not conscious of identity. They do not seem to feel emotions that would normally be connected with the familiar person (or place). They thus may believe that their relative or spouse has been replaced by an impostor.

An anatomical interpretation of this phenomenon has been proposed. The right amygdala, distinguishing new from old and connecting incoming information to emotions, would be disconnected by brain damage from the frontal lobe and emotional pathways (Ellis and Young, 1990; Hirstein, 2010). The patient would thus be puzzled by the recognition of a familiar face or place without the emotion that he/she is accustomed to experience in relation to such recognition. The delusion (it looks like but it is not) would result from the unconscious attempt to make sense out of this conflicting information.

Amnesia and Claparède's phenomenon

Loss of episodic/autobiographical memory results from bilateral damage to the hippocampus and the amygdala or to the anterior nuclei of the thalamus, the mammillary bodies and the connections between these structures. The patient does not remember episodes and cannot learn any new facts explicitly. In this condition, semantic memory (i.e., conceptual knowledge and words), another component, with episodic memory, of explicit, declarative (conscious!) memory, is preserved. Semantic memory is in fact stored in different brain areas, mostly in the left temporal lobe. Importantly, implicit (procedural) memory is also spared. Implicit memory works mostly unconsciously.

Sparing of implicit memory in amnesia is at the basis of Claparède's phenomenon. Claparède greeted every day an amnesic woman recovered in his ward, but each time she could not remember his face at all. One day, Claparède hid a pin in his hand and shook the woman's hand, pricking her. The next day she still did not remember him. But when Claparède offered his hand to shake, she hesitated and retracted her own hand, as if recognizing a threat. Thus, while she had trouble learning anything explicitly via her episodic memory, she could nonetheless unconsciously learn via implicit memory.

Claparède's phenomenon has been the object of deep investigations of amnesic patients. Thus, in 1962 Milner made the further discovery that even though her amnesic patient HM (arguably the most famous and most investigated patient in the history of neuropsychology) had no conscious recall of new memories about people, places, and objects, he was nonetheless capable of learning new perceptual and motor skills (see Squire and Wixted, 2011, for a relatively recent review). Many additional observations followed in later years, showing how implicit memory could be fully preserved when explicit memory is dramatically disrupted.

Isolation of individual semantics

Isolation of individual semantics is a type of neuropsychological dissociation that has been reported by Semenza, Zettin and Borgo (1998). Their patient featured a very peculiar pattern of dissociation. Impaired functions included: person naming in any conditions, semantic information – face matching, retrieval of person-specific information when proper names are not provided. In contrast, the same patient had intact linguistic functions and memory, face recognition, familiarity judgments, retrieval of person-specific information when proper names were provided. Thus, the patient could not retrieve the name and any other information about a famous person he found nonetheless familiar. But when provided with the name of the person, he then could remember all sorts of biographical information about that person. For instance, when presented with a picture of Luciano Pavarotti, he, an opera fan, would claim that he knew the person but could not remember anything about him. When, however, the examiner suggested that the name of the person was Pavarotti, the patient said: "Yes! This is Luciano Pavarotti, the most famous tenor in the world." He continued providing information he could not previously retrieve, like: "He was the first to get an encore at the Met. He often sings holding a white scarf in his hand, because he is superstitious. He recently left his wife for a younger woman". This last bit of biographical information, interestingly, reflected an event that happened in time after the patient had acquired his brain lesion (in the posterior part of the left hemisphere).

Biographical information, in this condition, appeared to be encapsulated and inaccessible in the patient's brain. The only way to access it was via the key constituted by the personage's name. This can happen, Semenza et al. (1998) argued, only if person-related individual semantic information is relatively separate in the brain from general semantics (a detailed model accounting for this dissociation is reported in Semenza, 2009).

Dissociations in memory: Some suggestions for psychoanalytic theory and practice

The description of the above reported clinical conditions mainly had the aim of drawing attention to the phenomenon of anatomical and functional dissociation in some aspects of consciousness. Portions of the brain are shown to act unawares of other portions. The claim is made here that this fact, once considered by psychoanalysts, may lead to important developments of psychoanalytic theory and practice.

The implications of clinical neuropsychological phenomena would be at least as useful as those of models of consciousness originated in non-clinical neuroscience described above. In order to support this statement, the example will be used here of the dissociation between explicit and implicit memory. Working out the consequences of the distinct properties of these two types of memory, as suggested by neuropsychological research, may lead to progress in some domains of interest in psychoanalysis.

Implicit memory encompasses, by definition, a series of unconscious processes. These processes are implemented in portions of the brain that are different from those sustaining explicit memory. The functioning of explicit memory, as revealed by lesions found in "classic amnesia" and in Korsakoff's syndrome, depends on the medial temporal lobes, including the hippocampuses and the amygdalas, and on the diencephalic midline (including the anterior nuclei of the thalamus, the mammillary bodies, and the connection between these structures). Implicit memory, instead, mainly depends on subcortical structures, the basal ganglia and the cerebellum; only in some cases, like for some memories of visual content, it depends on cortical areas, e.g., the right occipital lobe. In a different perspective, the cortical underpinning of implicit/procedural memory is generally located in the right hemisphere, in contrast with explicit/declarative memory, located in the left hemisphere. Selective lesions to these anatomical systems allowed cognitive neuroscientists to distinguish the two aspects of long-term memory and to better understand their specific properties.

Implicit memory, as said before, works mostly unconsciously or at a subliminal level of awareness. It also matures earlier than declarative memory (even before birth! see Brazelton, 1992) and is clearly operative at birth. Implicit memory contains motor, perceptual (thus corporeal) as well as cognitive abilities, acts in conditioning, on non-associative learning (habituation), and on perceptual facilitation. Crucially, it may also act unconsciously on acquisition of semantic information, and modifies one's judgment and preferences. It does not require focal attention for encoding. One other important property is that implicit memory takes time to establish itself. In contrast, it takes time to fade away: it is very resistant and hard to modify! It is established non-verbally, by imitation, most of the times unconsciously, perhaps through identification and similar mechanisms.

A special sub-category of memory involving the implicit (mostly unconscious) learning and storage of information about the emotional significance of events is called "emotional memory". This memory is supported by the amygdala and its connections. LeDoux (1996) distinguishes between emotional memory and the declarative memory of an emotional situation. Declarative memory entails facts of the situation; emotional memory refers to emotional responses during the event. A declarative memory may or may not trigger an emotional memory.

Psychoanalysis, for a long time, considered only explicit (declarative) memory. Part of the treatment is aimed at favoring the emergence of such memory through so-called "talk therapy". Only relatively recently has attention been focused on the working of implicit (procedural) memory in relation to psycho-analytic processes.

Important contributions by a neuroscientist, Nobel laureate Eric Kandel (1999), and by a number of psychoanalysts also practicing cognitive psychol-ogy or neuroscience (e.g., Fonagy, 1999; Mancia, 2006), started illustrating how implicit memory implies processes that are indeed of direct relevance to psy-choanalysis. This pioneering work constituted the starting point of very fruitful theoretical and empirical work. A number of people followed in contribut-ing in various ways along these lines of thought. Reporting in detail what has been done so far in understanding the implications of the distinction between explicit and implicit memory is beyond the aims of this essay (a good review of some of the most important works can be found in Fosshage, 2005). Only a few examples will thus be reported, along with some suggestions for further work. Before illustrating such examples, however, it is worth recalling why people started thinking that paying attention to implicit memory might be important for psychoanalysis.

It is in fact important to distinguish apparent loss of memory due to repres-sion and apparent loss of memory due to the fact that some memory remains unconscious because in the implicit memory system. This memory may cor-respond to the area of the unconscious ego that is not subject to repression (Hartman, 1939). This area is supposed to be free of conflicts. It is the domain of functions that are present from birth – motility, perception, association – and that mature independently of drives.

It contributes to formation of the self (e.g., Siegel, 1999; Semenza, Costantini and Mariani, 2005). The internal sense of who one is results not only from what one can explicitly recall, but also from implicit recollections. Such recollections create one's mental models and internal subjective experience of psychic con-tents (like images, sensations, emotions) and influence behavioral responses and (Goldberger, 1996) moral development.

Things may go wrong: absence of empathy or excessive intrusiveness may determine as an adaptive, initially useful, isolation (encapsulation) in procedural memory of these ill-represented or non-represented memories. These memo-ries (see also the concepts expressed by Bollas, 1987, who spoke of "unthought known", and Stern, 1998, who spoke of "unformulated experience"), often associated with (micro)traumas, may emerge as physical sensations, nightmares, somatic diseases, acting out, character features, ways and styles of acting, primi-tive defenses, and difficult relations (in particular, once in analysis, with the analyst). For example, consider the following scenarios. A schizoid mother may misinterpret "procedural" signals (equivalent to innate "social releaser" behav-iors, cf. Bowlby, 1998) given by a newborn and provide inconsistent responses. Likewise, a depressed mother may not trust her own ability to respond to her newborn's signals. Repeated exposure to these inadequate signals may shape one's self to one's disadvantage. Furthermore, absence of empathy or exces-sive intrusiveness might determine, as an adaptive and initially useful response, isolation in procedural memory of these ill-represented (or non-represented) memories. Procedural memories present, in fact, some advantage: they allow one to act quickly and automatically, on reflex: as such they can be easily recruited as an efficient, although primitive, way to face what may be felt as a danger.

The intrinsic properties of implicit memory make disadvantageous psychic contents, shaped over time in disadvantageous conditions and (macro- as well micro-) traumas, very resistant to change and hardly accessible to external influence and consciousness. Less primitive, yet hardly accessible, procedural/implicit memories may establish themselves as action patterns later in life through the process of identification. These memories may never become verbal. None of them have ever been repressed.

In reference to these memories, Semenza (2001; 2004) used the term "encapsulated". This term, borrowed from Fodor's theory about the modularity of mind (Fodor, 1983), was meant to stress the inaccessibility and relative isolation, together with the automatic unconscious emergence. This functioning looks just like that of Fodor's modules, triggered by environmental stimuli and daily life occurrences. Changing (and even observing) such a way of operating is a very hard task. The general resistance to change of negative, encapsulated memories emerges out of the primary adaptive function of the implicit/nondeclarative memory system. When disadvantageous, encapsulated memories cannot thus be treated with verbal therapy. They require time (any procedural memory is resistant to oblivion) and technical modifications. Only some will eventually access consciousness.

Working out how encapsulated memories might interfere with transference (and counter-transference) can lead to important theoretical progress. Thus Sanders (1998), Stern (1998), and their colleagues in the Boston Change Process Study Group, a group of infant researchers and psychoanalysts, have developed the idea that there are moments in the interaction between patient and therapist which represent the achievement of a new set of implicit memories that permit the therapeutic relationship to progress to a new level. This progression would not depend on conscious insights. Several further suggestions have been put forward in Fosshage's (2005) review. Fosshage (see also Lichtenberg, Lachmann and Fosshage, 1996) observes how a patient approaches the analytic session with expectancies and selectively attends to and attributes meaning to particular cues that confirm those expectancies. He/she then interpersonally interacts in a way that tends to elicit responses from the analyst that confirm his/her expectancies. These processes thus shape ongoing experience based on previously established implicit memory models. It is crucial, in order to change them, to become aware of these continuously replicating patterns. Modifications can then occur with time and slow change of relational patterns.

One particular field where the above-mentioned concepts may induce a considerable progress may be the study of procedural memory mechanisms working in institutions. In particular, as far as psychoanalysis is concerned, what may be of interest is to gain theoretical insights, such as those just briefly reported, on how institutions taking care of psychiatric patients work. Psychiatric care in hospitals, including outpatient services, surely has aspects where the working of mechanisms proper of implicit memory becomes conspicuous.

One simple starting point may be that there is a rough but fundamental distinction between work based on explicit memory and work based on implicit mechanisms. Thus, psychiatrists, when they do not just limit themselves to pharmacological treatment, do use "talk therapy", and therefore a therapy mostly based on explicit memory functioning. This treatment, administered to individual patients or in small groups, is limited in time. In contrast, the institution apparatus, mostly but not only with the mediation of nursing personnel, takes care of patients virtually full time. It mainly uses a complex set of often unspoken rules and ways of functioning that may remain entirely unconscious. This "treatment" may be no less important in view of a patient's recovery than the "talking" and the pharmacological treatment, with which it may interact in positive or in negative ways.

It is not the aim of this essay to speak at length about psychiatric institutions. It should be recalled, however, that such institutions, whatever their organization, have been shown, from a psychoanalytic perspective, to defend themselves the same way as individuals (Sacerdoti, 1966). Moreover, their defenses are likely to be of primitive order, hard to spot, and resistant to change. How these defenses interact with and may make use of implicit memory mechanisms is of the utmost interest. Borrowing some concepts developed within cognitive neuroscience by considering once again the properties of implicit memory may allow some serious progress.

A few words about repression

One cannot but observe that what has been said about consciousness within the interaction between neuroscience and psychoanalysis has seldom dealt with repression. But repression, (unconscious) active removal of memory material from consciousness, is one of the major discoveries of psychoanalysis! It may be most of what psychoanalytic sessions are about. Neither neuroscience models, such as those described above, or neuropsychological dissociations seem to offer much in helping to understand the nature of the mechanism, however. How repression occurs in the brain is still unknown.

In fact, it is safe to say that attempts to capture repression experimentally did not lead to uncontroversial results. Interesting experiments have been conducted, however (see, for example, Shevrin, Bond, Brakel, Hertel and Williams, 1996; Anderson and Green, 2001; Schnider, 2003; Anderson et al., 2004, and a recent review by Anderson and Hanslmayr, 2014). Anderson et al. (2004), for example, used functional magnetic resonance imaging to identify the neural systems involved in keeping unwanted memories out of awareness. Controlling unwanted memories was associated with increased dorsolateral prefrontal activation, reduced hippocampal activation, and impaired retention of those memories. Prefrontal cortical and right hippocampal activation predicted the magnitude of forgetting. Later, in Anderson and Hanslmayr's (2014) review, emerging behavioral and neuroimaging evidence is reported showing that suppressed awareness of an unwelcome memory is achieved by inhibitory control processes in the lateral prefrontal cortex. These mechanisms would interact with neural structures representing experiences in memory, disrupting traces that support retention. Such results seem to confirm the existence of active forgetting processes and, according to the authors, establish a neurobiological model for guiding inquiry into motivated forgetting.

Rather than fully reviewing similar attempts here, some considerations about what may make things hard for experimenters is offered. Whether and to what extent these active forgetting processes can be likened to repression in the psychoanalytic sense is a matter of debate, however. Unconscious repression does not seem to be captured. But the mechanisms highlighted in these studies may indeed contribute to repression. Capturing (how?) neural changes while repression establishes itself seems very hard indeed. Methods other than neuroimaging did not go very far as well. Surely one misleading assumption has been made. Repression has been considered to work more on unpleasant rather than pleasant memories. Such a distinction is tricky, as psychoanalysts know. Threatening is not the same as unpleasant. And, even if one could distinguish, pleasantness is not the whole point. Thus, contrasting retrieval of pleasant and unpleasant memories is not bound to give results, and it did not (as reported in Baddeley, 1997). Moreover, generating in memory something linked to an emotion and not liking it are different processes, as Lambie and Marcel (2002) have observed. What we do not remember is part of our imagination. What is repressed are rather not events, but affects linked to the same events.

A fundamental difficulty may come from the fact that repression may not be a single mechanism or a unitary phenomenon (Modell, 2003). It may include several components. Besides low-level (subcortical) mechanisms, more linked to drives, a readjustment of meaning may make recollection more acceptable. This mechanism, Modell (2003) argues, may be analogous to metaphor generation. To capture this mechanism in terms of neuroscience may be a very hard task.

A preliminary analysis of the phenomenon in terms of subcomponents, much in the spirit of cognitive neuroscience (Semenza, Bisiacchi and Rosenthal, 1988), would be mandatory, however, and may eventually lead to better experiments. Solms's (2000) suggestion that, in Korsakoff's syndrome, the lack of inhibition mechanisms makes the functioning of the unconscious transparent, through confabulation, may indeed reveal some subcomponent of the repression mechanism. In Korsakoff's syndrome, in fact, a lesion of the thalamic/hypothalamic system provokes amnesia; in addition, possibly a disconnection of these structures from the frontal lobe gives rise to confabulation, whereby previously repressed unconscious contents may emerge. Mental contents revealed by confabulation may not be so transparent, however, and what mechanism and structures had made them inaccessible to consciousness (if they are, indeed, inaccessible) are still unknown.

Conclusions

Psychoanalysis may profit from notions in neuroscience, while pursuing its own aims. There is no theory of consciousness in neuroscience terms at the present time, however, that psychoanalysis can easily use. What aspects of current models could be useful for psychoanalysis still needs to be fully understood. In waiting for more complete and powerful models, some important advances, it is contended here, may come from considering the implications of clinical phenomena observed in neuropsychology.

Neurocognitive syndromes show counterintuitive phenomena that must be taken into account in any possible theory of consciousness. In the first place, they suggest that consciousness may not be a unitary phenomenon. This should eventually be reconciled with our intuition that consciousness is unitary. But dissociations within consciousness are indeed possible and often explainable in neural terms. Considering them may be useful for psychoanalysis.

An example of a domain where progress may be made is that of memory, a domain where neuropsychology has crucially helped in making important distinctions. Properties of different types of memory may be taken into account in order to better understand phenomena related to consciousness. The differences between explicit and implicit memory have indeed been recently exploited in understanding some psychoanalytic phenomena. Further progress seems possible in several directions.

Repression, the active removal from consciousness discovered by psychoanalysis, is still elusive. But its functioning and neural underpinnings must be highlighted sooner or later. It may be useful, as a strategic starting point, to follow Modell's (2003) suggestion that repression may not be a single mechanism or a unitary phenomenon. Of course, unaware of neural mechanisms allowing active removal from consciousness, psychoanalysts will continue to deal with repression, more than often effectively helping their patients. One can only recall that, as in cognitive neuropsychology, many things about behavior may be understood well before neural mechanisms are discovered. As Semenza (2001) observed, Mendel understood the laws of genetic transmission without knowing about chromosomes, let alone about DNA. But in later times, the functions of such structures, the chromosomes, and of such molecules, DNA, became understandable because Mendel's laws were known. Careful observations and stringent theory thus eventually lead to further discovery.

References

Anderson, M.C. & Green, C. (2001). Suppressing unwanted memories by executive control. *Nature*, 410, 366–369.

Anderson, M.C. & Hanslmayr, S. (2014). Neural mechanisms of motivated forgetting. *Trends in Cognitive Science*, 18(6), 279–292.

Anderson, M.C., Ochsner, K.N., Kuhl, B., Cooper, J., Robertson, E., Gabrieli, S.W., Glover, G.H. & Gabrieli, J.D.E. (2004). Neural systems underlying the suppression of unwanted memories. *Science*, 303, 232–235.

Baddeley, A. (1997). *Human Memory: Theory and Practice*. Revised Edition. Hove: Psychology Press.

Bisiach, E., Luzzatti, C. & Perani, D. (1979). Unilateral neglect, representational schema and consciousness. *Brain*, 102(3), 609–618.

Bode, S., Bogler, C. & Haynes, J.D. (2013). Similar neural mechanisms for perceptual guesses and free decisions. *NeuroImage*, 65, 456–465.

Bollas, C. (1987). *The Shadow of the Object: Psychoanalysis of the Unthought Known*. New York: Columbia University Press.

Bowlby, J. (1998). *A Secure Base: Clinical Applications of Attachment Theory*. London/New York: Routledge.

Brazelton, T.B. (1992). *Touch and the Fetus*. Miami, FL: Presented to Touch Research Institute.

Changeux, J.P. (1983). *L'homme Neuronal*. Paris: Fayard.

Coltheart, M. (1999). Modularity and cognition. *TICS*, 3(3), 115–120.

Cowey, A. (2004). Fact, artefact and mith about blindsight. *Quarterly Journal of Experimental Psychology*, 57A, 577–609.

Dehaene, S. (2008). Conscious and Nonconscious Processes: Distinct Forms of Evidence Accumulation? In Engel, C. & Singer, W. (Eds). *Better Than Conscious? Decision Making, the Human Mind, and Implications for Institutions*. Cambridge, MA: MIT Press, pp. 21–50.

Dehaene, S. & Changeux, J.P. (1997). A hierarchical neuronal network for planning behavior. *Proceedings of the National Academy of Sciences of the United States of America*, 94, 13293–13298.

Dehaene, S., Charles, L., King, J.R. & Marti, S. (2014). Toward a computational theory of conscious processing. *Current Opinion in Neurobiology*, 25, 76–84.

Dehaene, S. & Naccache, L. (2001). Towards a cognitive neuroscience of consciousness: Basic evidence and a workspace framework. *Cognition*, 79, 1–37.

Edelman, G. (2004). *Wider Than the Sky: The Phenomenal Gift of Consciousness*. New Haven, CT: Yale University Press.

Ellis, H.D. & Young, A.W. (1990). Accounting for delusional misidentifications. *The British Journal of Psychiatry*, 157(2), 239–248.

Fodor, J. A. (1983). *The modularity of mind: An essay on faculty psychology*. MIT press.

Fonagy, P. (1999). Memory and therapeutic action. *International Journal of Psychoanalysis*, 80, 215–223.

Fosshage, J.L. (2005). The implicit and explicit domains in psychoanalytic change. *Psycho-analytic Inquiry*, 25(4), 516–539.

Gazzaniga, M. (1967). The split brain in man. *Scientific American*, 217(2), 24–29.

Goldberger, M. (1996). *Daydreams: Even More Secret Than Dream*. In *The Secret of Dreams*. Symposium conducted at the meeting of the Western New England Psychoanalytic Society, Yale University, New Haven, CT.

Hartmann, H. (1939). *Ego Psychology and the Problem of Adaptation*. New York: International Universities Press.

Hirstein, W. (2010). The misidentification syndromes as mindreading disorders. *Cognitive Neuropsychiatry*, 15(1), 233–260.

Jackson, J.H. (1931). On Affectations of Speech from Disease of the Brain. In *Selected Writings of Hughlings Jackson 2*. London: Hodder and Stoughton, pp. 155–204.

Kandel, E.R. (1999). Biology and the future of psychoanalysis: A new intellectual framework for psychiatry revisited. *American Journal of Psychiatry*, 156(4, April), 505–524.

Lambie, J.A. & Marcel, A. (2002). Consciousness and the varieties of emotion experience. *Psychological Review*, 109(2), 219–260.

LeDoux, J.E. (1996). *The Emotional Brain: The Mysterious Underpinnings of Emotional Life.* New York: Touchstone.

Libet, B. (1985). Unconscious cerebral initiative and the role of conscious will in voluntary action. *The Behavioral and Brain Sciences,* 8, 529–566.

Lichtenberg, J., Lachmann, F. & Fosshage, J. (1996). *The Clinical Exchange: Technique from the Standpoint of Self and Motivational Systems.* Hillsdale, NJ: The Analytic Press.

Mancia, M. (2006). *Psychoanalysis and Neuroscience.* Milan: Springer.

Milner, B. (1962). Les troubles de la mémoire accompagnant les lésions hippocampiques bilatérales. In Passouant P. (Ed). *Physiologie de l'hippocampe.* Paris: Centre National de la Recherche Scientifique, pp. 257–272.

Modell, A.H. (2003). *Imagination and the Meaningful Brain.* Cambridge, MA: MIT Press.

Morin, A. (2001). The split-brain debate revisited: On the importance of language and self-recognition for right hemispheric consciousness. *Journal of Mind and Behavior,* 22(2), 107–118.

Raichle, M.E., MacLeod, A.M., Snyder, A.Z., Powers, W.J., Gusnard, D.A. & Shulman, G.L. (2001). A default model of brain function. *Proceedings of the National Academy of Sciences of the United States of America,* 98, 676–682.

Revonsuo, A. (2001). Can functional brain imaging discover consciousness in the brain? *Journal of Consciousness Studies,* 8, 3–50.

Rizzolatti, G., Semi, A. A., & Fabbri-Destro, M. (2014). Linking psychoanalysis with neuro-science: The concept of ego. *Neuropsychologia,* 55, 143–148.

Sacerdoti, G. (1966). *Denial of illness: Its relation to mental institutions.* Proceedings of the Fourth World Congress of Psychiatry, Madrid.

Sanders, L. (1998). Introductory comment. *Infant Mental Health Journal,* 19, 280–281.

Schnider, A. (2003). Spontaneous confabulation and the adaptation of thought to ongoing reality. *Nature Neuroscience,* 4, 662–672.

Semenza, C. (1996). Methodological Issues. In Beaumont, J.G., Kenealy, P.M. & Rogers, M.J.C. (Eds). *The Blackwell Dictionary of Neuropsychology.* Oxford, UK: Blackwell, pp. 478–487.

Semenza, C. (2001). Psychoanalysis and cognitive neuropsychology: Theoretical and meth-odological affinities. *Neuro-Psychoanalysis,* 3(1), 3–10.

Semenza, C. (2004). Unconscious how? *Neuro-Psychoanalysis,* 6(1), 87–89.

Semenza, C. (2009). The neuropsychology of proper names. *Mind & Language,* 24(4), 347–369.

Semenza, C., Bisiacchi, P. & Rosenthal, V. (1988). A Function for Cognitive Neuropsychol-ogy. In Denes, G., Semenza, C. & Bisiacchi, P. (Eds). *Perspectives on Cognitive Neuropsychol-ogy.* Howe and London: LEA, pp. 2–30.

Semenza, C., Costantini, M.V. & Mariani, F. (2005). Types of Memory in Psychoanalysis. In Minkovitz, H. (Ed). *Neuroscientific and Psychoanalytic Perspectives on Memory.* International Neuro-Psychoanalysis Congress Proceedings. London: The International Neuro-Psychoanalysis Centre, pp. 133–140.

Semenza, C., Zettin, M. & Borgo, F. (1998.) Names and identification: An access problem. *Neurocase,* 4, 45–53.

Shallice, T. (1988). *From Neuropsychology to Mental Structure.* Cambridge: Cambridge Uni-versity Press.

Shevrin, H., Bond, J., Brakel, L., Hertel, R. & Williams, W. (1996) *Conscious and Unconscious Processes: Psychodynamic, Cognitive and Neurophysiological Convergences.* New York: Guildford.

Siegel, D. (1999). *The Developing Mind: Toward a Neurobiology of Interpersonal Experience.* New York: Guilford Press.

Solms, M. (2000). Psychoanalytic perspective on confabulation. *Neuro-Psychoanalysis*, 2, 133–138.

Solms, M. & Saling, M. (1986). On psychoanalysis and neuroscience: Freud's attitude to the localizationist tradition. *International Journal of Psychoanalysis*, 67, 397–416.

Soon, C.S., Brass, M., Heinze, H.J. & Haynes, J.D. (2008). Unconscious determinants of free decisions in the human brain. *Nature Neuroscience*, 11(5), 543–545.

Sperry, R.W. (1968). Mental Unity Following Surgical Disconnection of the Cerebral Hemispheres. In *The Harvey Lectures*. Series 62, New York: Academic Press, pp. 293–323.

Squire, L.R. & Wixted, J.T. (2011). The cognitive neuroscience of human memory since H.M. *Annual Review Neuroscience*, 34, 259–288.

Stern, D. (1998). The process of therapeutic change involving implicit knowledge: Some implications of developmental observations for adult psychotherapy. *Infant Mental Health Journal*, 19, 300–308.

Weiskrantz, L., Warrington, E.K., Sanders, M.D. & Marshall, J.C. (1974). Visual capacity in the hemianopic field following a restricted cortical ablation. *Brain*, 97, 709–728.

Chapter 7

I am therefore I think

Karl Friston

LONDON

Introduction

> *How can the events in space and time which take place within the spatial boundary of a living organism be accounted for by physics and chemistry?*
>
> Erwin Schrödinger (1944)

How does Schrödinger's question touch on philosophical propositions, such as René Descartes' famous proposition *Cogito ergo sum* ('I think, therefore I am'). This article tries to cast thinking in terms of probabilistic beliefs and thereby link consciousness to probabilistic descriptions of self-organization – of the sort found in statistical physics and dynamical systems theory. This agenda may sound ambitious, but it may be much easier than at first glance. The trick is to associate philosophical notions – such as 'I think' and 'I am' – with formal constructs, such as probabilistic inference and the implications of existing over extended periods of time. In brief, we start off by considering what it means for a system, like a cell or a brain, to exist. Mathematically, this implies certain properties that constrain the way the states of such systems must change, such as ergodicity, i.e., any measurement of such systems must converge over time (Birkhoff, 1931). Crucially, if we consider these fundamental properties in the context of a separation between internal and external states, one can show that the internal states minimize the same quantity minimized in Bayesian statistics. This means one can always interpret a system that exists and as making probabilistic inferences about its external milieu. Formally, this turns Descartes' proposition on its head; suggesting that 'I am [ergodic], therefore I think'. However, if a system 'thinks' – in the sense of updating probabilistic beliefs – then what does it believe?

We will consider the only self-consistent (prior) belief, which is 'I think, therefore I am [ergodic]'. This prior belief is formally equivalent to minimizing uncertainty about the (external) causes of sensory states that intervene between external and internal states. This is precisely the imperative that drives both scientific hypothesis testing and active perception (Gregory, 1980; Helmholtz, 1866/1962; O'Regan & Noë, 2001; Wurtz, McAlonan, Cavanaugh, & Berman, 2011). Furthermore, it provides a nice perspective on the active sampling of our sensorium that suggests that perceptual processing can be associated with

Bayesian belief updating (Dayan, Hinton, & Neal, 1995) – a dynamic that can therefore be derived from the basic principles of self organization. To make these arguments more concrete, we will consider an example of the ensuing active inference, using simulations originally described in (Friston, Adams, Perrinet, & Breakspear, 2012).

This article comprises three sections. The first section draws on two recent developments in formal treatments of self-organization. The first is an application to Bayesian inference and embodied perception in the brain (Friston, Kilner, & Harrison, 2006). The second is an attempt to understand the nature of self-organization in random dynamical systems (Ashby, 1947; Haken, 1983; Maturana & Varela, 1980; Nicolis & Prigogine, 1977; Schrödinger, 1944). This material has been presented previously (Friston, 2013) and, although rather technical, has some relatively simple implications. Its premise is that biological self-organization is (almost) inevitable and manifests as a form of active Bayesian inference. We have previously suggested (Friston, 2013) that the events '*within the spatial boundary of a living organism*' (Schrödinger, 1944) may arise from the very existence of a boundary or blanket – and that a (Markov) blanket may be inevitable under local coupling among dynamical systems. We will see that the very existence of a Markov blanket means we can interpret the self-organization of internal states in terms of Bayesian inference about external states.

The second section looks more closely at the nature of Bayesian inference, in terms of prior beliefs that might be associated with a system that minimizes the dispersion (entropy) of its external states through action. We will see that these prior beliefs lead to a pre-emptive sampling of the sensorium that tries to minimize uncertainty about hypotheses encoded by the internal states.

The final section illustrates these ideas using simulations of saccadic searches to unpack the nature of active inference. This section contains a brief description of an agent's prior beliefs about the causal structure of its (visual) world and how that world would be sampled to minimize uncertainty. Finally, the results of simulated saccadic eye movements and associated inference are described, with a special emphasis on the selection of beliefs and hypotheses that are entertained by our enactive brain.

I am therefore I think

This section covers the basic theory behind the self-organization of (weakly mixing ergodic) random dynamical systems to show that they can always be interpreted in terms of active modelling or inference. This is important because it leads to conclusions that are exactly consistent with the good regulator theorem (every good regulator is a model of its environment) and related treatments of self-organization (Ashby, 1947; Maturana & Varela, 1980; Nicolis & Prigogine, 1977; van Leeuwen, 1990). It also means that there is a direct Bayesian interpretation of any self-organized dynamics in a system that exists in the ergodic sense. What follows is a summary of the material in (Friston, 2013).

Ergodic densities and flows

We start by considering any (weakly mixing) ergodic random dynamical that can be described by stochastic differential equations of the following form:

$$\dot{x} = f(x) + \omega \qquad\qquad 1$$

Here, the flow of states $f(x)$ is subject to random fluctuations ω. Because the system is ergodic (and weakly mixing) it will, after a sufficient amount of time, converge to an invariant set of states called a *pullback* or *random global attractor* (Crauel, 1999; Crauel & Flandoli, 1994). The associated ergodic density $p(x \mid m)$ for any system or model m is the solution to the Fokker-Planck equation (Frank, 2004) describing the time evolution of the probability density over states

$$\dot{p}(x \mid m) = \nabla \cdot (\Gamma\nabla - f)p \qquad\qquad 2$$

Here, the diffusion tensor Γ is the half the covariance (amplitude) of the random fluctuations. Equation 2 shows that the ergodic density depends upon flow, which can always be expressed in terms of curl-free and divergence-free components. This is the Helmholtz decomposition (a.k.a. the fundamental theorem of vector calculus) and can be formulated in terms of an anti-symmetric matrix $Q(x) = -Q(x)^T$ and a scalar potential $L(x)$ that plays a role of a Lagrangian (Ao, 2004)

$$f(x) = (Q - \Gamma)\nabla L(x) \qquad\qquad 3$$

Using this standard form (Yuan, Ma, Yuan, & Ping, 2010), it is straightforward to show that $p(\tilde{x} \mid m) = \exp(-L(x))$ is the solution to the Fokker Planck equation above (Friston & Ao, 2012). This means one can express the flow in terms of the ergodic density:

$$f(\tilde{x}) = (Q - \Gamma)\nabla \ln p(x \mid m) \qquad\qquad 4$$

This is an important result because it shows the flow can be decomposed into a component that flows towards regions with a higher ergodic density (the curl-free or irrotational component) and an orthogonal (divergence-free or solenoidal) component that circulates on isocontours of the ergodic density. These components are like walking uphill and walking around the base of the hill respectively. In summary, any ergodic random dynamical system can be formulated as a circuitous ascent on the log likelihood over the states it visits. Later, we will interpret this likelihood in a statistical sense and see that any random dynamical system can be interpreted as performing some form of inference on itself.

Systems and Markov blankets

When we talk about a system that exists in a way that can be separated from its environment, we implicitly call on the notion of a Markov blanket. A Markov blanket is a set of states that separates two other sets in a statistical sense. The term Markov blanket was introduced in the setting of Bayesian networks or graphs (Pearl, 1988) and refers to the children of a set (the set of states that are influenced), its parents (the set of states that influence it) and the parents of its children.

A Markov blanket induces a partition of states into *internal states* and *external* states that are hidden (insulated) from the internal (insular) states by the Markov blanket. For example, the surface of a cell may constitute a Markov blanket separating intracellular (internal) and extracellular (external) states (Auletta, 2013; Friston, 2013). Statistically speaking, external states can only be seen vicariously by the internal states, through the Markov blanket. The Markov blanket can itself be partitioned into two sets that are, and are not, children of external states. We will refer to these as surface or *sensory states* and *active states* respectively. Put simply, the existence of a Markov blanket $S \times A$ implies a partition of states into external, sensory, active and internal states: $x \in X = \Psi \times S \times A \times R$ as in Figure 7.1.

External states cause sensory states that influence − but are not influenced by − internal states, while internal states cause active states that influence − but

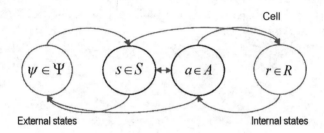

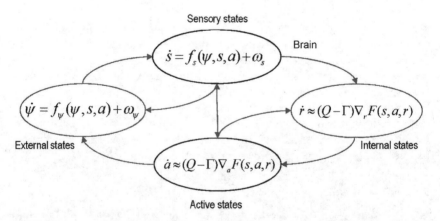

Figure 7.1 Markov blankets and the free energy principle. (See p. 135 for more on this figure.)

are not influenced by – external states. Crucially, the dependencies induced by Markov blankets create a circular causality that is reminiscent of the perception and action cycle (Fuster, 2004). This circular causality means that external states cause changes in internal states, via sensory states, while the internal states couple back to external states through active states.

Equipped with this partition, we can now consider the dependencies among states implied by the Markov blanket, in terms of their flow above. The flow through any point *(s, a, r)* in the state space of the internal states and their Markov blanket is (Friston, 2013):

$$f_r(s,a,r) = (\Gamma - Q)\nabla_r \ln p(s,a,r \mid m)$$
$$f_a(s,a,r) = (\Gamma - Q)\nabla_a \ln p(s,a,r \mid m)$$

5

This shows that the flow of internal and active states performs a circuitous gradient ascent on the *marginal* ergodic density over internal states and their Markov blanket. It is a marginal density because we have marginalized over the external states. This means the internal and active states behave as if they know the distribution over external states that would be necessary to perform the marginalization. In other words, the internal states will appear to respond to sensory fluctuations based on (posterior) beliefs about underlying fluctuations in external states. We can formalize this notion by associating these beliefs with a probability density over external states $q(\psi \mid r)$ that is encoded (parameterized) by internal states:

Lemma (free energy): *for any random dynamical system with a Markov blanket and Lagrangian $L(x) = -\ln p(\psi, s, a, r)$, there is a free energy $F(s,a,r)$ that describes the flow of internal and active states in terms of a generalized descent*

$$f_r(s,a,r) = (Q - \Gamma)\nabla_r F$$
$$f_a(s,a,r) = (Q - \Gamma)\nabla_a F$$

6

$$F(s,a,r) = E_a[L(x)] - H[q(\psi \mid r)]$$

This free energy is a functional of a variational) density $q(\psi \mid r)$ – parameterized by internal states – that corresponds to the expected Lagrangian minus the entropy of the variational density.

Proof: using Bayes rule, we can rearrange the expression for free energy in terms of a Kullback-Leibler divergence (Beal, 2003)

$$F(s,a,r) = -\ln p(s,a,r \mid m) + D_{KL}[q(\psi \mid r) \mid\mid p(\psi \mid s,a)]$$

7

When $q(\psi \mid r) = p(\psi \mid s,a)$, the divergence term disappears and we recover the ergodic flow in Equation 5:

$$f_r(s,a,r) = (\Gamma - Q)\nabla_r \ln p(s,a,r \mid m)$$
$$f_a(s,a,r) = (\Gamma - Q)\nabla_a \ln p(s,a,r \mid m)$$

8

In other words, the ergodic flow ensures the variational density is the posterior density, such that the variational density represents the hidden states in a Bayes-optimal sense

Remarks: all this proof says is that if one interprets internal states as parameterizing Bayesian beliefs about external states, then the dynamics of internal and active states can be described as a gradient descent on a variational free energy function of internal states and their Markov blanket. Variational free energy was introduced by Feynman to solve difficult marginalization problems in path integral formulations of quantum physics (Feynman, 1972). This is also the free energy bound that is used extensively in *approximate Bayesian inference* (e.g., variational Bayes) (Beal, 2003; Hinton & van Camp, 1993; Kass & Steffey, 1989). The expression for free energy in Equation 7 discloses its Bayesian interpretation: the first term is the negative log evidence or *marginal likelihood* of the internal states and their Markov blanket. The second term is a *relative entropy* or Kullback-Leibler divergence (Kullback & Leibler, 1951) between the variational density and the posterior density over external states (i.e., the causes of sensory states). Because this divergence cannot be less than zero, the internal flow will appear to have minimized the divergence between the variational and posterior density. In other words, the internal states will appear to have solved the problem of Bayesian inference by encoding posterior beliefs about the causes of its sensory states – under a generative model provided by the Lagrangian. This is known as *exact* Bayesian inference because the variational and posterior densities are identical. Later, we will consider approximate forms (under the Laplace assumption) leading to *approximate* Bayesian inference. In short, the internal states will appear to engage in Bayesian inference, but what about action?

Because the divergence in Equation 7 can never be less than zero, free energy is an upper bound on the negative log evidence. Now, because the system is ergodic we have

$$F(s,a,r) \geq -\ln p(s,a,r \mid m)$$

$$\Rightarrow$$

$$E_t[F(s,a,r)] \geq E_t[\underbrace{-\ln p(s,a,r \mid m)}_{\text{expected surprise}}] = \underbrace{H[p(s,a,r \mid m)]}_{\text{entropy}} \qquad 9$$

This means that action will (on average) appear to place an upper bound on the entropy of the internal states and their Markov blanket. Together with the Bayesian modelling perspective, this is consistent with the good regulator theorem (Conant & Ashby, 1970) and related accounts of self-organization (Ashby, 1947; Friston & Ao, 2012; Nicolis & Prigogine, 1977; Pasquale, Massobrio, Bologna, Chiappalone, & Martinoia, 2008; van Leeuwen, 1990). These treatments emphasize the homoeostatic nature of self-organization that maintains internal states within physiological bounds. This characteristic resistance to the dispersion of internal states underlies the peculiar ability of animate systems to resist the second law of thermodynamics – or more precisely the fluctuation theorem (Evans &

Searles, 1994). Furthermore, as shown elsewhere (Friston, 2010; Friston, 2012) free energy minimization is consistent with information-theoretic formulations of sensory processing and behaviour (Barlow, 1961; Bialek, Nemenman, & Tishby, 2001; Linsker, 1990). Finally, Equation 7 shows that minimizing free energy entails maximizing the entropy of the variational density (or posterior uncertainty) in accord with the maximum entropy principle (Jaynes, 1957). Maximizing posterior uncertainty may seem odd, but it is a vital part of Bayesian inference – that is closely related to the Laplace's principle of indifference and Occam's razor.

One interesting feature of the free energy formulation is that internal states encode beliefs about the consequences of action. In other words, internal states can infer action only through its sensory consequences – in the same sense that we are not aware of our movements *per se*, only their sequelae. This creates an important distinction between action and (approximate posterior) beliefs about its consequences encoded by internal states.

From our current (existential) perspective, this statistical interpretation of ergodic behavior has something quite profound to say: because internal states encode probabilistic beliefs, the free energy *function* of internal states now becomes a free energy *functional* (function of a function) of a probability distribution. This is remarkable because the flow of (material) states therefore becomes a functional of (immaterial) probabilistic beliefs. This links the physical (states or *res extensa*) to the mindful (beliefs or *res cogitans*) in an interesting way. Another perspective on this bridge over the Cartesian divide is that the free energy Lemma above provides a (wide sense) realization relationship (Gillett, 2002; Wilson, 2001). In other words, the implicit process of inference affords a unique mapping between biophysical states (internal states) and the properties (probabilistic beliefs) they realize (c.f., Bechtel and Mundale, 1999). See Figure 7.2.

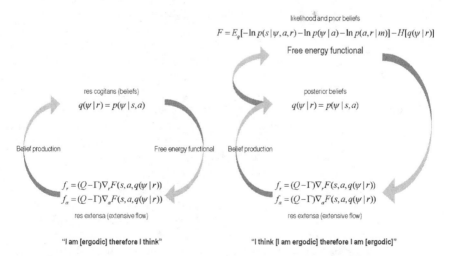

likelihood and prior beliefs
$$F = E_q[-\ln p(s\,|\,\psi,a,r) - \ln p(\psi\,|\,a) - \ln p(a,r\,|\,m)] - H[q(\psi\,|\,r)]$$
Free energy functional

res cogitans (beliefs)
$$q(\psi\,|\,r) = p(\psi\,|\,s,a)$$

posterior beliefs
$$q(\psi\,|\,r) = p(\psi\,|\,s,a)$$

Belief production   Free energy functional   Belief production

$$f_r = (Q-\Gamma)\nabla_r F(s,a,q(\psi\,|\,r))$$
$$f_a = (Q-\Gamma)\nabla_a F(s,a,q(\psi\,|\,r))$$
res extensa (extensive flow)

$$f_r = (Q-\Gamma)\nabla_r F(s,a,q(\psi\,|\,r))$$
$$f_a = (Q-\Gamma)\nabla_a F(s,a,q(\psi\,|\,r))$$
res extensa (extensive flow)

"I am [ergodic] therefore I think"   "I think [I am ergodic] therefore I am [ergodic]"

Figure 7.2 Material and immaterial aspects of ergodic dynamics. (See pp. 135–6 for more on this figure.)

In the next section, we consider the nature of these beliefs in a bit more detail and work towards a more explicit realization of beliefs in the context of active inference and Bayesian belief updating.

I think therefore I am

The previous section established that (ergodic) systems with measures that converge over time are, in some sense, equipped with probabilistic beliefs that are encoded by their internal states. However, there is nothing in this formulation that differentiates between the sorts of systems (or their Markov blankets) that emerge over time – or the nature of the attracting set of states that endow them with a recognizable phenotype. This attracting set or random dynamical attractor can be highly structured and space-filling but retain a low volume or entropy (Freeman, 1994) – like the cycle of states we seek out in our daily routine. Conversely, the attracting set could encompass a large number of states with an amorphous (high volume or entropy) attractor. In this section, we try to explain the emergence of structured attracting sets that are characteristic of animate systems – like ourselves – by exploiting the modelling interpretation of ergodic flows. The argument goes as follows:

Lemma: *the internal states of any ergodic system that is equipped with a Markov blanket and a low measure attracting set (or low entropy ergodic density) must believe they have a low measure attracting set.*

Proof: the proof is by *reductio ad absurdum*. The free energy Lemma demonstrates the existence of a Lagrangian that plays the role of a probabilistic generative model of a system's external states. This model entails (prior) beliefs of the system that determine its action, where action constitutes the flow described by the Lagrangian. Now, if the beliefs entailed by the Lagrangian do not include a low measure attracting set, then any action that preserves a low measure attracting set cannot be described by the Lagrangian. This means that the system cannot be ergodic (because it violates free energy Lemma) and will dissipate after a sufficient period of time.

Remarks: this argument rests upon the circular causality inherent in the mapping between probabilistic descriptions (beliefs) and biophysical dynamics (flows). In other words, action is a component of flow that induces an ergodic probability density with an associated Lagrangian. This Lagrangian entails beliefs that describe action. Put simply, the physical behaviour of an ergodic system must be consistent with its beliefs. This means that it is entirely tenable to regard the internal states (encoding beliefs) to be the authors of their own existence – where these beliefs are fulfilled by action. Clearly, this rests on a permissive environment that allows itself to be sampled in a way that renders the beliefs a veridical description of that sampling. This permissive aspect emphasizes the co-evolution of agents and their (sampled) environments, which are forever locked in an existential alliance.

In what follows, we will work through this argument in more detail, looking at the beliefs that systems or agents might entertain. In the current setup, beliefs are probability distributions that specify the free energy, which describes the flow of internal states and action (Equation 6). We have seen that posterior beliefs are encoded by the internal states. However, free energy is also defined by the Lagrangian or probabilistic generative model. We can unpack this model in terms of its likelihood and priors in the following way:

$$F = E_q[-\underbrace{\ln p(\tilde{s} \mid \tilde{\psi}_v, \tilde{\psi}_u, \tilde{a}, \tilde{r})}_{\text{likelihood}} - \underbrace{\ln p(\tilde{\psi}_v \mid \tilde{\psi}_u)}_{\text{empirical priors}} - \underbrace{\ln p(\tilde{\psi}_u \mid \tilde{a})}_{\text{empirical priors}} -$$

$$\underbrace{\ln p(\tilde{a}, \tilde{r} \mid m)}_{\text{full priors}}] - \underbrace{H[q(\tilde{\psi} \mid \tilde{r})]}_{\text{posterior uncertainty}}$$

10

Here, the external states $\Psi = \Psi_v \times \Psi_u$ have been separated into *hidden* and *control states*. Control states are the consequences of action and − in the generative model − determine the evolution of hidden states. Equation 10 also introduces a ~ over states to denote their motion, acceleration and so on, such that $\tilde{x} = (x, x', \ldots)$. This allows us to consider probabilities over the flow or trajectories of states as opposed their instantaneous value.

As above, the free energy is the expected Lagrangian (energy) minus the entropy of the posterior beliefs. However, here the Lagrangian has been factorized into likelihood, empirical and full priors. The likelihood is simply the probability of some sensory states given their causes, while empirical priors are probability distributions over the hidden states, given control states and control states, given action. The full priors are over action and internal states and will not play a role in what follows. Empirical priors are a technical term denoting components of a (hierarchical) generative model that are 'sandwiched' between the likelihood and full priors.

These components of the generative model are implicit in the system dynamics; in other words, they constitute the Lagrangian whose expectation, under posterior beliefs, produces the marginal density describing flow in Equation 5. In this sense, the generative model embodies prior beliefs about the evolution of hidden and control states and how these states create the sensorium in a probabilistic sense. The prior beliefs concern the consequences of action and − through the minimization of free energy by action − constitute self-fulfilling beliefs about the consequences of behavior. So what form might these beliefs take?

If we consider any system or agent that has adapted to (or has adapted) its environment, then its ergodic density will have low entropy, which is upper bounded by the measure or volume of its random dynamical attractor (Friston, 2012). In other words, it will engage with its environment in a structured and organized fashion, revisiting attracting sets of states time and time again in an itinerant fashion. In computational biology and physics, this is known as a nonequilibrium steady-state (Jarzynski, 1997; Tomé, 2006). One can express the entropy of the ergodic density in terms of the entropy of sensory states (and their Markov blanket) and an equivocation or conditional entropy:

$$H(\Psi, S, A, R) = H(S, A, R \mid m) + H(\Psi \mid S, A)$$
$$= \underbrace{E_t[-\ln p(\tilde{s}, \tilde{a}, \tilde{r} \mid m)]}_{\text{expected surprise}} + \underbrace{E_t[H(\Psi \mid S = \tilde{s}, A = \tilde{a})]}_{\text{expected uncertainty}} \qquad 11$$

Because the system is ergodic, these two components correspond to the expected surprise and posterior uncertainty over time. Surprise is just the negative log marginal density or Bayesian model evidence that is implicitly minimized by ergodic flow, while the expected uncertainty is the entropy of the posterior distribution over external states. Although these expressions may look complicated, they say something quite intuitive; namely, agents that have adapted to (or have adapted) their environment are generally not surprised about their sensory samples and are confident about the causes of those samples. However, there is a problem here.

Recall from the previous section that the ergodic flow suppresses only surprise or its free energy bound (Equation 9). This means that there is no guarantee that the causes of sensations will have low entropy. Indeed, we saw in the previous section that action only suppresses the entropy of sensory states and their Markov blanket – it does not affect the entropy of external states. In other words, ergodic systems could, in principle, have high entropy and dissipate themselves over large volumes of state space. So what properties (or beliefs) must low entropy systems possess?

One simple answer is to appreciate that external states depend on action. This means that it is sufficient for the agent to have prior beliefs (entailed in its kinetics, wiring or functional architecture) that the consequences of action will create a low-entropy environment. Put simply, external states depend on action but action only minimizes surprise. Therefore, agents with low entropy ergodic densities must find high-entropy distributions surprising. We can express this formally as follows:

$$-\ln p(\tilde{\psi}_u \mid \tilde{a}) \underbrace{}_{\text{prior surprise}} \propto \underbrace{E_t[H[p(\tilde{\psi}_v \mid \tilde{s}, \tilde{a})]]}_{\text{posterior uncertainty}} = \underbrace{E_\tau[H[q(\tilde{\psi}_v(t + \tau) \mid \tilde{r}_v(t), \tilde{\psi}_u)]]}_{\text{expected uncertainty}} \qquad 12$$

This expression says that the most likely control states are those that minimize posterior entropy or uncertainty about hidden states in the future. In other words, inherent in the generative model of a low-entropy system, there are prior beliefs that control states are unlikely to engender posterior uncertainty. The second equality uses the fact that the variational density is the posterior density over hidden states. This means that its time average can be approximated by evaluating the entropy of hidden states in the future, for any given trajectory of control states.

There are three interesting technical points about this inherent optimism. First, notice that while prior beliefs speak to a minimization of uncertainty under posterior beliefs (Equation 12), the posterior beliefs *per se* are trying to maximize posterior uncertainty (Equation 6). This creates a dialectic that can be resolved only by sampling the sensorium in a way that minimizes uncertainty subject to Laplace's principle of indifference. Second, notice that the posterior uncertainty is about future states. This immediately brings active inference into the realm of anticipation and planning, which we will see illustrated below in terms of anticipatory eye movements. Finally, we have a rather unique probabilistic construction in which prior beliefs are a functional of posterior beliefs, where posterior beliefs depend upon prior beliefs. This circular dependency is illustrated in the right panel of Figure 7.1 and underwrites the (mindful) control of external states.

The prior beliefs above are functions of control states and functionals of beliefs about future hidden states. The uncertainty or entropy that quantifies these prior beliefs can be regarded as the *salience* of fictive outcomes, where a salient outcome resolves uncertainty (entropy) associated with posterior beliefs about the causes of sensations. In the illustrations below, salience will be a function of where a visual image could be sampled: $\sigma(\tilde{\psi}_u) = -H[q(\tilde{\psi}_v(t + \tau) \mid \tilde{r}_v(t), \tilde{\psi}_u)]$. This leads to the notion of a salience map that constitutes prior beliefs about the outcomes of visual palpation.

In summary, we have seen that agents can be the authors of their own phenotype – if we interpret the Lagrangian that underwrites their dynamics in terms of beliefs: in particular, prior beliefs about how the sensorium will be sampled. In practical terms, this means one can simulate self-organization in one of two ways. First, one could write down some equations of motion and examine the emergent (nonequilibrium steady-state) behavior – that could be described with a Lagrangian or ergodic density. Alternatively, one can write down the Lagrangian and simulate the same behavior using a gradient ascent on the ensuing free energy. The crucial difference is that one can prescribe behavior in terms of a Lagrangian that describes the flow – as opposed to describing the flow that prescribes a Lagrangian. It is in this sense – of prescribing behavior in terms of Lagrangians based on prior beliefs – that we can regard agents as the autopoietic scribes of their embodied exchange with the world. In the final section, we will try to illustrate this in terms of active sampling of the visual world and demonstrate some phenomena that come close to unconscious and possibly conscious inference.

Simulating saccadic searches

This section reproduces the simulations of sequential eye movements described in (Friston, Adams, Perrinet, & Breakspear, 2012) to illustrate the theory of the previous section. Saccadic eye movements are a useful vehicle to illustrate active inference because they speak directly to visual search strategies and a wealth of psychophysical, neurobiological and theoretical study; e.g., (Bisley & Goldberg, 2010; Ferreira, Apel, & Henderson, 2008; Grossberg, Roberts, Aguilar, & Bullock, 1997; Shires, Joshi, & Basso, 2010; Srihasam, Bullock, & Grossberg, 2009;

Tatler, Hayhoe, Land, & Ballard, 2011; Wurtz, McAlonan, Cavanaugh, & Berman, 2011). Having said this, we will focus on the basic phenomenology of saccadic eye movements to illustrate the key features of the active inference scheme described above. This scheme can be regarded as a formal example of active vision (Wurtz, McAlonan, Cavanaugh, & Berman, 2011), sometimes described in enactivist terms as visual palpation (O'Regan & Noë, 2001). People interested in the neurobiological aspects of active inference will find accessible introduction to predictive coding in Bastos, Usrey, Adams, Mangun, Fries and Friston (2012).

This section first describes the production of visual signals and how they are modelled. We focus on a fairly simple paradigm – the categorization of faces – to illustrate the behavior induced by prior beliefs that constitute a generative model. Specifying a generative model allows us to simulate self-organized behavior by specifying the dynamics of external states, internal states and their Markov blanket in terms of a Lagrangian that entails prior beliefs about minimizing uncertainty. In other words, we will integrate the equations of motion in Equations (1) and (6) and interpreting the resulting dynamics (see Figure 7.3 for the form of these equations):

$$\dot{\tilde{x}} = f(\tilde{x}) + \omega : \quad f(\tilde{x}) = \begin{cases} f_{\psi}(\tilde{\psi}, \tilde{s}, \tilde{a}) \\ f_{s}(\tilde{\psi}, \tilde{s}, \tilde{a}) \\ (Q - \Gamma)\nabla_{\tilde{r}}F(\tilde{s}, \tilde{a}, \tilde{r}) \\ (Q - \Gamma)\nabla_{\tilde{a}}F(\tilde{s}, \tilde{a}, \tilde{r}) \end{cases} \qquad 13$$

Clearly, to perform the simulations we have to specify the equations of motion for external and states. This corresponds to specifying the nature of the processes generating sensory samples. In addition, we have to specify the Lagrangian $L(\tilde{x})$ that determines the free energy and subsequent dynamics of perception and action.

In what follows (and generally), the divergence free component of flow is chosen to simply update the (generalized) states, given their generalized motion: $Q\nabla_{\tilde{x}}F = D \cdot \tilde{x}$, where $D \cdot \tilde{x} = (x', x'', \dots)$ is a derivative operator (Friston, Stephan, Li, & Daunizeau, 2010). One interesting issue that will emerge from these simulations is that the external states generating sensations are not necessarily the states assumed by a generative model.

The generative process

In these simulations, sensory signals are generated in two modalities – proprioception and vision. Proprioception reports the centre of gaze as a displacement from the origin of some extrinsic frame of reference. The visual input corresponds to an array of sensory channels sampling a two-dimensional image or visual scene $I : \mathbb{R}^2 \to \mathbb{R}$. This sampling uses a grid of 16×16 channels that samples a small part the image – like a foveal sampling. To make this sampling

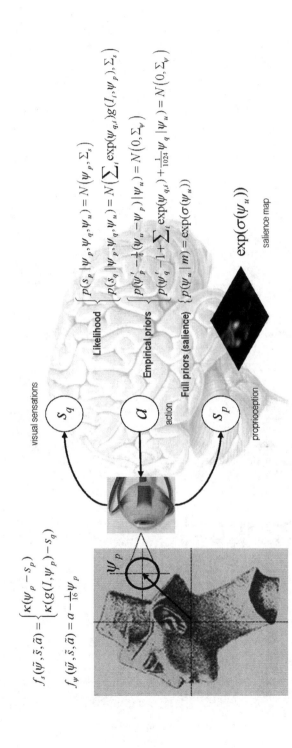

External and sensory states   Generative model of external and sensory states

Figure 7.3   Generative models of visual search. (See p. 136 for more on this figure.)

more biologically realistic, each visual channel was equipped with a center-surround receptive field that reports a local weighted average of the image.

The only changing external state $\psi \in \mathbb{R}^2$ describes the center of oculomotor fixation, whose motion is driven by action (and decays with a time constant of 16 time bins of 12 ms). This external state determines where the visual scene is sampled (foveated). The proprioceptive and visual signals were effectively noiseless, where there random fluctuations had a log precision of 16. The motion of the fixation point was subject to low amplitude fluctuations, with a log precision of eight. This completes our description of the process generating proprioceptive and visual signals. We now turn to the model of this process that generates action.

The generative model

As in the generative process, proprioceptive signals are just a noisy mapping from external proprioceptive states encoding the direction of gaze. Visual input is modelled as a mixture of images sampled at a location specified by the hidden proprioceptive state. This hidden state decays with a time constant of four time bins (48 ms) towards a hidden control state. In other words, the hidden control determines the location that attracts gaze – in a way not dissimilar to the equilibrium point hypothesis for motor reflexes (Feldman & Levin, 1995). Crucially, in the model, visual input depends on a number of hypotheses or internal images $I_i : \mathbb{R}^2 \rightarrow \mathbb{R} : i \in \{1,...N\}$ that constitute the agent's prior beliefs about what could cause its sensations. The input encountered at any particular time is a weighted mixture of these internal images, where the weights correspond to hidden perceptual states. The dynamics of these perceptual states implement a form of dynamic softmax, in the sense that the solution of their equations of motion ensures the weights sum to one. This means that we can interpret the (hidden) perceptual states as the (softmax) probability that the i-th internal image or hypothesis is the cause of visual input.

In summary, given hidden proprioceptive and perceptual states, the agent can predict its proprioceptive and visual input. The generative model is specified by these predictions and the amplitude of the random fluctuations that determine the agent's prior certainty about sensory inputs and the motion of hidden states. In the examples below, we used a log precision of eight for proprioceptive sensations and let the agent believe its visual input was fairly noisy, with a log precision of four. All that now remains is to specify prior beliefs about the hidden control state attracting the center of gaze.

Priors and saliency

To simulate saccadic eye movements, we integrated the active inference scheme for 16 time bins (196 ms) and then computed a map of salience to update the prior expectations about the hidden control states that attract the centre of gaze.

This was repeated eight times to give a sequence of eight saccadic eye movements. The salience was computed for $1024 = 32 \times 32$ locations distributed uniformly over the visual image or scene according to Equation 11 (where the expected uncertainty was evaluated at the location prescribed by the control state). In other words, salience was evaluated under current (posterior) beliefs about the content of the visual scene for all allowable points of fixation. The ensuing salience over the 32×32 locations constitutes a salience map whose peak drives the next saccade (by reflexively engaging action through the proprioceptive consequences of the most likely control state). Notice that salience is a function of, and only of, fictive beliefs about the state of the world and essentially tells the agent where to sample (look) next.

Figure 7.4 provides a simple illustration of salience based upon the posterior beliefs or hypothesis that local (foveal) visual inputs are caused by an image of Nefertiti. The right panel summarizes the classic results of the Yarbus (Yarbus, 1967) in terms of an image and the eye movements it elicits. The left panels depict visual input after sampling the image on the right with center-surround receptive fields. Note how the receptive fields suppress absolute levels of luminance contrast and highlight edges. It is these edges that inform posterior beliefs about both the content of the visual scene and where it is being sampled. This information reduces posterior uncertainty and is therefore salient. The salient features of the image (middle panel) include the ear, eye and mouth. The location of these features and a number of other salient locations appear to be consistent with the locations that attract saccadic eye movements (as shown on the right). Crucially, the map of salience extends well beyond the field of view (circle on the picture). This reflects the fact that salience is not an attribute of what is seen, but what might be seen under a particular hypothesis about the causes of sensations.

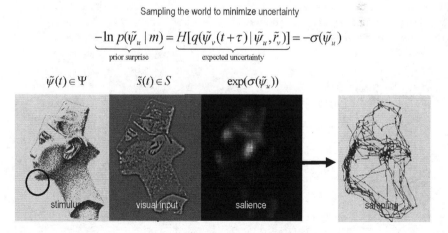

Sampling the world to minimize uncertainty

$$-\ln p(\tilde{\psi}_u \mid m) = \underbrace{H[q(\tilde{\psi}_v(t+\tau) \mid \tilde{\psi}_u, \tilde{r}_v)]}_{\text{expected uncertainty}} = -\sigma(\tilde{\psi}_u)$$

$\underbrace{\phantom{-\ln p(\tilde{\psi}_u \mid m)}}_{\text{prior surprise}}$

$\tilde{\psi}(t) \in \Psi$ $\tilde{s}(t) \in S$ $\exp(\sigma(\tilde{\psi}_u))$

Figure 7.4 Salience and visual searches. (See p. 136 for more on this figure.)

To make the simulations a bit more realistic, we added a further prior implementing inhibition of return (Itti & Koch, 2001; Wang & Klein, 2010). This involved suppressing the salience of locations that had been recently foveated. The addition of inhibition of return ensures that a new location is selected by each saccade and can be motivated ethologically by prior beliefs that the visual scene will change and that previous locations should be revisited.

In summary, we have described the process generating sensory information in terms of a visual scene and hidden states that specify how that scene is sampled. We have described both the likelihood and priors that together comprise a generative model. The special consideration here is that these priors are based upon beliefs that agents will sample salient sensory features based upon its current posterior beliefs about the causes of those features. We are now in a position to look at the sorts of behavior this model produces.

Simulating saccadic eye movements

We conclude with a realization of visual search under the generative model described above. Our purpose here is to illustrate the nature of active inference, when it is equipped with priors that maximise salience or minimise uncertainty. Figure 7.5 shows the results of a simulation, in which the agent had three internal images or hypotheses about the scene that it might sample (an upright face, an inverted face and a rotated face). The agent was presented with an upright face and its posterior expectations were evaluated over 16 (12 ms) time bins, after which salience was evaluated. The agent then emitted a saccade by foveating the most salient location during the subsequent 16 time bins. This was repeated for eight saccades.

The upper row shows the ensuing eye movements as red dots at the fixation point of each saccade. The corresponding sequence of eye movements is shown in the insert on the upper left, where the red circles correspond roughly to the agent's field of view. These saccades were driven by prior beliefs about the direction of gaze based upon the salience maps in the second row. Note that these maps change with successive saccades as posterior beliefs about the hidden perceptual states become more confident. Note also that salience is depleted in locations that were foveated in the previous saccade – this reflects the inhibition of return. Posterior beliefs about hidden states provide visual and proprioceptive predictions that drive eye movements. Oculomotor responses are shown in the third row in terms of the two hidden proprioceptive states corresponding to vertical and horizontal eye displacements. The portions of the image sampled (at the end of each saccade) are shown in the fourth row. The penultimate row shows the posterior beliefs in terms of their posterior expectations and 90% confidence interval about the true stimulus. The key thing to note here is that the expectation about the true stimulus supervenes over its competing representations and, as a result, posterior confidence about the stimulus category increases (the posterior confidence intervals shrink to the

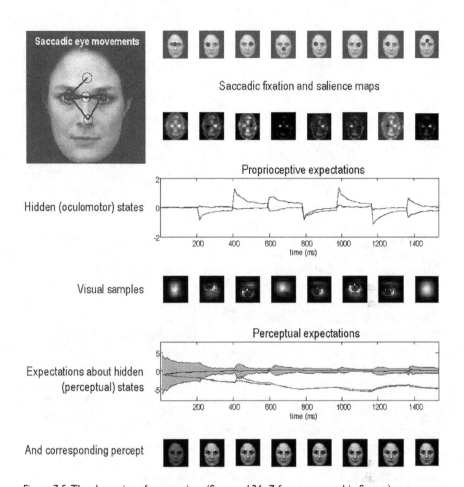

Figure 7.5 The dynamics of perception. (See pp. 136–7 for more on this figure.)

expectation): see (Churchland, Kiani, Chaudhuri, Wang, Pouget, & Shadlen, 2011) for an empirical study of this sort of phenomenon. The images in the lower row depict the hypothesis selected, where their intensity has been scaled to reflect conditional uncertainty, using the entropy (average uncertainty) of the softmax probabilities.

This simulation illustrates a number of key points. First, it illustrates the nature of evidence accumulation in selecting a hypothesis or percept the best explains sensory data. One can see that this proceeds over two timescales, both within and between saccades. Within-saccade accumulation is evident even during the initial fixation, with further stepwise decreases in uncertainty as salient information is sampled. The within-saccade accumulation is formally related to evidence accumulation as described in models of perceptual discrimination (Churchland, Kiani, Chaudhuri, Wang, Pouget, & Shadlen, 2011; Gold & Shadlen, 2003). This is meant in the sense that the posterior expectations about perceptual states are driven by sensory information. However, the accumulation here rests explicitly on the priors implied by the generative model. In this case, the prevalence of any particular perceptual category is modelled as a dynamical process that has certain continuity properties. In other words, inherent in the model is the belief that the content of the world changes in a continuous fashion. This is reflected in the progressive elevation of the correct perceptual expectation above its competitors and the consequent shrinking of the posterior confidence interval. The transient changes in the posterior beliefs, shortly after each saccade, reflect the fact that new data are being generated as the eye sweeps towards its new target location. It is important to note that the agent is not just modelling visual contrast, but also how contrast changes with eye movements – this induces an increase in conditional uncertainty during the fast phase of the saccade. However, due to the veracity of the posterior beliefs, the posterior confidence shrinks again when the saccade reaches its target location. This shrinkage is usually to a smaller level than in the previous saccade.

This illustrates the second key point; namely, the circular causality that lies behind perceptual sampling. Put simply, the only hypothesis that can endure over successive saccades is the one that correctly predicts the salient features that are sampled. This sampling depends upon action or an embodied inference that speaks directly to the notion of visual palpation (O'Regan & Noë, 2001). This means that the hypothesis prescribes its own verification and can survive only if it is a correct representation of the world. If its salient features are not discovered, it will be discarded in favor of a better hypothesis. This provides a nice perspective on perception as hypothesis testing (Gregory, 1980; Kersten, Mamassian, & Yuille, 2004), where the emphasis is on the selective processes that underlie sequential testing. This is particularly pertinent when hypotheses can make predictions that are more extensive than the data available at any one time.

Finally, although the majority of saccades target the eyes and nose, as one might expect, there is one saccade to the forehead. This is somewhat paradoxical, because the forehead contains no edges and cannot increase posterior confidence about a face. However, this region is highly informative under the remaining two hypotheses (corresponding to the location of the nose in the inverted face and the left eye in the rotated face). This subliminal salience is revealed through inhibition of return and reflects the fact that the two competing hypotheses have not been completely excluded. This illustrates the competitive nature of perceptual selection induced by inhibition of return and can regarded, heuristically, as occasional checking of alternative hypotheses. This is a bit like a scientist who tries to refute his hypothesis by acquiring data that furnish efficient tests of his competing or null hypotheses.

Conclusion

In conclusion, starting with some basic considerations about the ergodic behavior of random dynamical systems, we have seen how inference could be construed as emergent property of any weakly mixing (random dynamical) system – and how it can be described in terms of a generalized descent on variational free energy. Using this formalism, we have been able to address some fairly abstract issues in the philosophy of realization and the Cartesian divide between the material (ergodic flow) and the immaterial (beliefs entailed by the flows Lagrangian). Some relatively simple (*reductio ad absurdum*) arguments about the Lagrangian of ergodic systems lead to the notion that any autopoietic or self-organizing system implicitly entertains prior beliefs that they will sample the sensorium to minimize their uncertainty about its causal structure. These somewhat abstract arguments were unpacked using simulations of saccadic searches, which have been previously reported to illustrate the computational anatomy of embodied (active) perceptual inference.

The take-home message of this work is that the process of unconscious – and indeed conscious inference – may conform to the same basic principles that underlie self-organization in any system with coupled dynamics. The emergence of intentional phenomena rests upon the notion of a Markov blanket that separates internal states from external states. The very presence of this separation implies a generalized synchrony (Hunt, Ott, & Yorke, 1997; Huygens, 1673) between external (e.g., environmental) and internal (e.g., neuronal) states that will appear to be lawful – in the sense that internal states minimize the same free energy functional used for Bayesian inference. This lends a quintessentially inferential or predictive aspect to internal states that has many of the hallmarks of cognition and consciousness, particularly when one considers that the agent is the author of its behavior.

Crucially, this inference or assimilation is active, in the sense that the internal states affect the causes of sensory input vicariously through action. The resulting circular causality between perception and action fits comfortably with many formulations in embodied cognition and artificial intelligence: for example, the perception action cycle (Fuster, 2004), active vision (Shen, Valero, Day, & Paré, 2011; Wurtz, McAlonan, Cavanaugh, & Berman, 2011), the use of predictive information (Ay, Bertschinger, Der, Güttler, & Olbrich, 2008; Bialek, Nemenman, & Tishby, 2001; Tishby & Polani, 2010) and homeokinetic formulations (Soodak & Iberall, 1978). Furthermore, it connects these perspectives to more general treatments of circular causality and autopoiesis in cybernetics and synergetics (Haken, 1983; Maturana & Varela, 1980). Remarkably, these conclusions were articulated by Helmholtz over a century ago (von Helmholtz, 1971):

> *Each movement we make by which we alter the appearance of objects should be thought of as an experiment designed to test whether we have understood correctly the invariant relations of the phenomena before us, that is, their existence in definite spatial relations.*
>
> Herman von Helmholtz (1878) p.384

Acknowledgments

KJF is funded by the Wellcome trust (Ref: 088130/Z/09/Z). This paper was prepared for a presentation at the Joseph Sandler Psychoanalytic Research Conference 2014.

References

Ao, P. (2004). Potential in stochastic differential equations: novel construction. *J. Phys. A: Math. Gen.*, *37*, L25–30.

Ashby, W. R. (1947). Principles of the self-organizing dynamic system. *J. Gen. Psychology.*, *37*, 125–8.

Auletta, G. (2013). Information and metabolism in bacterial chemotaxis. *Entropy*, *15* (1), 311–26.

Ay, N., Bertschinger, N., Der, R., Güttler, F., & Olbrich, E. (2008). Predictive information and explorative behavior of autonomous robots. *Eur. Phys. J. B*, *63*, 329–39.

Barlow, H. (1961). Possible principles underlying the transformations of sensory messages. In W. Rosenblith (Ed.), *Sensory Communication*. Cambridge, MA: MIT Press, pp. 217–34.

Bastos, A. M., Usrey, W. M., Adams, R. A., Mangun, G. R., Fries, P., & Friston, K. J. (2012). Canonical microcircuits for predictive coding. *Neuron*, *76* (4), 695–711.

Beal, M. J. (2003). Variational algorithms for approximate bayesian inference. PhD Thesis, University College London.

Bechtel, W., & Mundale, J. (1999). Multiple realizability revisited: Linking cognitive and neural states. *Philosophy of Science*, 175–207.

Bialek, W., Nemenman, I., & Tishby, N. (2001). Predictability, complexity, and learning. *Neural Computat.*, *13* (11), 2409–63.

Birkhoff, G. D. (1931). Proof of the ergodic theorem. *Proc. Natl. Acad. Sci. U.S.A.*, *17*, 656–60.

Bisley, J. W., & Goldberg, M. E. (2010). Attention, intention, and priority in the parietal lobe. *Annu. Rev. Neurosci.*, *33*, 1–21.

Churchland, A. K., Kiani, R., Chaudhuri, R., Wang, X. J., Pouget, A., & Shadlen, M. N. (2011). Variance as a signature of neural computations during decision making. *Neuron*, *69* (4), 818–31.

Conant, R. C., & Ashby, R. W. (1970). Every good regulator of a system must be a model of that system. *Int. J. Systems Sci.*, *1* (2), 89–97.

Crauel, H. (1999). Global random attractors are uniquely determined by attracting deterministic compact sets. *Ann. Mat. Pura Appl.*, *4* (176), 57–72.

Crauel, H., & Flandoli, F. (1994). Attractors for random dynamical systems. *Probab. Theory Relat. Fields*, *100*, 365–93.

Dayan, P., Hinton, G. E., & Neal, R. (1995). The helmholtz machine. *Neural Comput.*, *7*, 889–904.

Evans, D. J., & Searles, D. J. (1994). Equilibrium microstates which generate second law violating steady states. *Phys. Rev. E*, *50* (2), 1645–8.

Feldman, A. G., & Levin, M. F. (1995). The origin and use of positional frames of reference in motor control. *Behav. Brain Sci.*, *18*, 723–806.

Ferreira, F., Apel, J., & Henderson, J. M. (2008). Taking a new look at looking at nothing. *Trends Cogn. Sci.*, *12* (11), 405–10.

Feynman, R. P. (1972). *Statistical Mechanics*. Reading, MA: Benjamin.

Frank, T. D. (2004). *Nonlinear Fokker-Planck Equations: Fundamentals and Applications. Springer Series in Synergetics*. Berlin: Springer.

Freeman, W. J. (1994). Characterization of state transitions in spatially distributed, chaotic, nonlinear, dynamical systems in cerebral cortex. *Integr. Physiol. Behav. Sci.*, *29* (3), 294–306.

Friston, K. (2010). The free-energy principle: a unified brain theory? *Nat. Rev. Neurosci.*, *11* (2), 127–38.

Friston, K. (2012). A free energy principle for biological systems. *Entropy*, *14*, 2100–21.

Friston, K. J. (2013). Life as we know it. *Royal Soc. Interf.*, 10(86), 20130475.

Friston, K., Adams, R. A., Perrinet, L., & Breakspear, M. (2012). Perceptions as hypotheses: saccades as experiments. *Front Psychol.*, *3*, 151.

Friston, K., & Ao, P. (2012). Free-energy, value and attractors. *Comput. Math. Methods Med.*, *2012*, 937860.

Friston, K., Kilner, J., & Harrison, L. (2006). A free energy principle for the brain. *J. Physiol. Paris*, *100* (1–3), 70–87.

Friston, K., Stephan, K., Li, B., & Daunizeau, J. (2010). Generalised filtering. *Math. Probl. Eng.*, *vol.*, *2010*, 621670.

Fuster, J. M. (2004). Upper processing stages of the perception-action cycle. *Trends Cogn. Sci.*, *8* (4), 143–5.

Gillet, H. (2002). Differential algebra–a scheme theory approach. In L. Guo, P. J. Cassidy, W. F. Keigher, W. Y. Sit (Eds.), *Differential algebra and related topics*. River Edge, NJ/London: World Scientist, pp. 95–123.

Gold, J. I., & Shadlen, M. N. (2003). The influence of behavioral context on the representation of a perceptual decision in developing oculomotor commands. *J. Neurosci.*, *23* (2), 632–51.

Gregory, R. L. (1980). Perceptions as hypotheses. *Phil. Trans. R Soc. Lond. B*, *290*, 181–97.

Grossberg, S., Roberts, K., Aguilar, M., & Bullock, D. (1997). A neural model of multimodal adaptive saccadic eye movement control by superior colliculus. *J. Neurosci.*, *17* (24), 9706–25.

Haken, H. (1983). *Synergetics: An Introduction. Non-equilibrium Phase Transition and Self-organisation in Physics, Chemistry and Biology* (3rd ed.). Berlin: Springer Verlag.

Helmholtz, H. (1866/1962). Concerning the perceptions in general. In *Treatise on Physiological Optics* (J. Southall, Trans., 3rd ed., Vol. III). New York: Dover.

Hinton, G. E., & van Camp, D. (1993). Keeping neural networks simple by minimizing the description length of weights. *Proc. COLT-93*, 5–13.

Hunt, B., Ott, E., & Yorke, J. (1997). Differentiable synchronisation of chaos. *Phys. Rev. E*, *55*, 4029–34.

Huygens, C. (1673). *Horologium Oscillatorium*. France: Parisiis.

Itti, L., & Koch, C. (2001). Computational modelling of visual attention. *Nat. Rev. Neurosci.*, *2* (3), 194–203.

Jarzynski, C. (1997). Nonequilibrium equality for free energy differences. *Phys. Rev. Lett.*, *78*, 2690.

Jaynes, E. T. (1957). Information theory and statistical mechanics. *Phys. Rev. Ser. II*, *106* (4), 620–30.

Kass, R. E., & Steffey, D. (1989). Approximate bayesian inference in conditionally independent hierarchical models (parametric empirical Bayes models). *J. Am. Stat. Assoc.*, *407*, 717–26.

Kersten, D., Mamassian, P., & Yuille, A. (2004). Object perception as Bayesian inference. *Annu. Rev. Psychol.*, *55*, 271–304.

Kullback, S., & Leibler, R. A. (1951). On information and sufficiency. *Annals Math. Stat.*, *22* (1), 79–86.

Linsker, R. (1990). Perceptual neural organization: some approaches based on network models and information theory. *Annu. Rev. Neurosci.*, *13*, 257–81.

Maturana, H. R., & Varela, F. J. (1980). Autopoiesis: the organization of the living. In V. F. Maturana, H.R. & Varela, F. J. (Eds.), *Autopoiesis and Cognition*. Dordrecht, Netherlands: Reidel, pp. 63–140.

Nicolis, G., & Prigogine, I. (1977). *Self-organization in Non-equilibrium Systems*. New York: John Wiley.

O'Regan, J. K., & Noë, A. (2001). A sensorimotor account of vision and visual consciousness. *Behav. Brain Sci.*, *24* (5), 939–73.

Pasquale, V., Massobrio, P., Bologna, L. L., Chiappalone, M., & Martinoia, S. (2008). Self-organization and neuronal avalanches in networks of dissociated cortical neurons. *Neuroscience*, *153* (4), 1354–69.

Pearl, J. (1988). *Probabilistic Reasoning in Intelligent Systems: Networks of Plausible Inference*. San Fransisco, CA: Morgan Kaufmann.

Schrödinger, E. (1944). *What Is Life?: The Physical Aspect of the Living Cell*. Dublin: Trinity College, Dublin.

Shen, K., Valero, J., Day, G. S., & Paré, M. (2011). Investigating the role of the superior colliculus in active vision with the visual search paradigm. *Eur. J. Neurosci.*, *33* (11), 2003–16.

Shires, J., Joshi, S., & Basso, M. A. (2010). Shedding new light on the role of the basal ganglia-superior colliculus pathway in eye movements. *Curr. Opin. Neurobiol.*, *20* (6), 717–25.

Soodak, H., & Iberall, A. (1978). Homeokinetics: a physical science for complex systems. *Science*, *201*, 579–82.

Srihasam, K., Bullock, D., & Grossberg, S. (2009). Target selection by the frontal cortex during coordinated saccadic and smooth pursuit eye movements. *J. Cogn. Neurosci.*, *21* (8), 1611–27.

Tatler, B. W., Hayhoe, M. M., Land, M. F., & Ballard, D. H. (2011). Eye guidance in natural vision: reinterpreting salience. *J. Vis.*, *11* (5), 5.

Tishby, N., & Polani, D. (2010). Information theory of decisions and actions. In V. Cutsuridis, A. Hussain, & J. Taylor (Eds.), *Perception-reason-action Cycle: Models, Algorithms and Systems*. Berlin: Springer, pp. 601–636.

Tomé, T. (2006). Entropy production in nonequilibrium systems described by a Fokker-Planck equation. *Braz. J. Phys.*, *36* (4A), 1285–9.

van Leeuwen, C. (1990). Perceptual-learning systems as conservative structures: is economy an attractor? *Psychol. Res.*, *52* (2–3), 145–52.

von Helmholtz, H. (1971). The facts of perception (1878). In R. Karl (Ed.), *The Selected Writings of Hermann von Helmholtz*. Middletown, CT: Wesleyan University Press, pp. 366–408.

Wang, Z., & Klein, R. M. (2010). Searching for inhibition of return in visual search: a review. *Vision Res.*, *50* (2), 220–8.

Wilson, R. A. (2001). Two views of realization. *Philosophical Studies*, 104(1), 1–31.

Wurtz, R. H., McAlonan, K., Cavanaugh, J., & Berman, R. A. (2011). Thalamic pathways for active vision. *Trends. Cogn. Sci.*, *5* (4), 177–84.

Yarbus, A. L. (1967). *Eye Movements and Vision*. New York: Plenum.

Yuan, R., Ma, Y., Yuan, B., & Ping, A. (2010, Dec 13). Constructive Proof of Global Lyapunov Function as Potential Function. Retrieved from: *http://arxiv.org/abs/1012.2721v1*

Figure legends

Figure 7.1: Markov blankets and the free energy principle. These schematics illustrate the partition of states into internal states and external states that are separated by a Markov blanket – comprising sensory and active states. The upper panel shows this partition as it might be applied to a cell: where the internal states can be associated with the intracellular states of a cell, while sensory states become the surface states or cell membrane overlying active states (e.g., the actin filaments of the cytoskeleton). The lower panel shows the same dependencies but rearranged so that they can be related to action and perception in the brain: where active and internal states minimize a free energy functional of sensory states. The ensuing self-organization of internal states then corresponds to perception, while action couples brain states back to external states. See main text for details and Table 7.1 for a definition of the variables.

Figure 7.2: Material and immaterial aspects of ergodic dynamics. Left panel: This schematic highlights the relationship between the (ergodic) flow of biophysical states described by a free energy functional of a probability density. This (variational) density corresponds to posterior beliefs over the external states causing sensory states. The important point illustrated here is that there is a lawful coupling between the (material) flow and the (immaterial) beliefs that are realised by (caused by) and realise (cause) the flow. Right panel: the same scheme has been unpacked to highlight the fact that the free energy functional depends upon both posterior beliefs and prior beliefs inherent in the generative model (or flow's Lagrangian). Furthermore, these prior beliefs are themselves predicated on posterior beliefs (through their uncertainty or entropy) adding an extra layer of probabilistic bootstrapping. The key distinction between right

Table 7.1 Definitions of the tuple $(\Omega, \Psi, S, A, R, p, q)$ underlying active inference

---

- *A sample space* Ω from which random fluctuations $\omega \in \Omega$ are drawn

- *External states* $\Psi : \Psi \times A \times \Omega \rightarrow \mathbb{R}$ – states of the world that cause sensory states and depend on action

- *Sensory states* $S : \Psi \times A \times \Omega \rightarrow \mathbb{R}$ – the agent's sensations that constitute a probabilistic mapping from action and external states

- *Action states* $A : S \times R \times \Omega \rightarrow \mathbb{R}$ – an agent's action that depends on its sensory and internal states

- *Internal states* $R : R \times S \times \Omega \rightarrow \mathbb{R}$ – representational states of the agent that cause action and depend on sensory states

- *Ergodic density* $p(\psi, s, a, r \mid m)$ – a probability density function over external $\psi \in \Psi$, sensory $s \in S$, active $a \in A$ and internal states $r \in R$ for a system or model denoted by m

- *Variational density* $q(\psi \mid r)$ – an arbitrary probability density function over external states that is parameterized by internal states

---

and left panels is that the (material) flow of the system is now prescribed by (immaterial) prior beliefs about the nature of this flow and, in this sense, suggests one can interpret the dynamics of animate systems as predicated upon beliefs about their own behavior.

Figure 7.3: Generative models of visual search. This schematic (left panel) provides the equations of motion generating sensory states (in proprioceptive and visual modalities). Visual input is generated from an image that can be sampled locally by foveating a particular point – an external state of the world. The generative model (right panel) is provided in terms of likelihood, empirical prior and full prior densities. The proprioceptive likelihood is based on a noisy version of the expected eye position, while the visual input is generated from a number of potential images or hypotheses. Their relative weights are (non-negative) perceptual hidden states, whose dynamics ensure they always sum to unity. The full priors are determined by a map of salience that approximates the posterior confidence in the inferred hidden states (here, the perceptual states encoding the competing images). See main text and (Friston, Adams, Perrinet, & Breakspear, 2012) for further details.

Figure 7.4: Salience and visual searches. This schematic provides an illustration of salience based upon the posterior beliefs or hypothesis that local (foveal) visual inputs are caused by an image of Nefertiti. The right panel summarizes the classic results of Yarbus – in terms of a stimulus and the eye movements it elicits. The left panels depict visual input after sampling the image on the far right (using conventional centre surround receptive fields) and the associated saliency map based on a local sampling of 16-x-16 pixels (using the generative model described in the main text). The size of the field of view, in relation to the visual scene, is indicated by the circle on the left image. The key thing to note here is that the salient features of the image include the ear, eye and mouth. The locations of these features appear to be consistent with the locations that attract saccadic eye movements (as shown on the right).

Figure 7.5: The dynamics of perception. This figure shows the results of a simulation, in which a face was presented to an agent whose responses were simulated using the inference scheme described in the main text. In this simulation, the agent had three internal images or hypotheses about the stimuli it might sample (an upright face, and inverted face and a rotated face). The agent was presented with an upright face and its posterior expectations were evaluated over 16 (12 ms) time bins until the next saccade was emitted. This was repeated for eight saccades. The ensuing eye movements are shown as red dots at the end of each saccade in the upper row. The corresponding sequence of eye movements is shown in the insert on the upper left, where the red circles correspond roughly to the proportion of the image sampled. These saccades are driven by prior beliefs about the direction of gaze based upon the saliency maps in the second row. Note that these maps change with successive saccades as posterior beliefs about the hidden states become more confident. These posterior beliefs provide both visual and proprioceptive predictions that drive eye movements. Oculomotor responses are shown in the third row in terms of the two hidden oculomotor (proprioceptive) states corresponding to vertical and horizontal displacements. The associated portions of the image sampled (at the end of each saccade) are shown in the fourth row. The penultimate row shows the posterior beliefs in terms of their sufficient statistics, namely posterior expectations and the 90% confidence interval about the true stimulus (grey area). The final row shows the percept that is implicitly selected (weighted by its uncertainty).

Chapter 8

Struggling with unconscious, embodied memories in a third psychoanalysis with a traumatized patient recovered from severe poliomyelitis

A dialogue between psychoanalysis and embodied cognitive science

Marianne Leuzinger-Bohleber

FRANKFURT

Rolf Pfeifer

ZÜRICH/SHANGHAI

Introduction

One aim of this volume is to illustrate how fruitful the interdisciplinary dialogue between psychoanalysts and contemporary scientists from the broad field of neuroscience can be for both sides.

As mentioned in the introduction to this book, it is interesting from a perspective of the history and sociology of science that since the 1990s many different scientific disciplines have intensified their interest in the so-called mind-body-problem: psychoanalysis, philosophy, academic psychology, cognitive science and modern neurosciences. In cognitive science, e.g., 20 years ago some kind of a revolution took place: from the "Classical to Embodied Cognitive Science".[1] The conceptualization of how the mind works has changed completely and, as will be shown in this chapter, has great implications for clinical psychoanalytical practice as well as for theorizing in contemporary psychoanalysis. The question how unrepresented, unconscious meanings can be discovered, remembered and worked through is and has been, as is well known, one of the central topics of psychoanalysis (see, e.g., Levine, Reed & Scarfone, 2013).

In this chapter we will concentrate on one example of a contemporary interdisciplinary dialogue, the dialogue between psychoanalysis and the so-called Embodied Cognitive Science. This dialogue is relatively new and not yet very well known in the psychoanalytical world. The two authors of this chapter have been involved in this dialogue for nearly four decades (see, e.g., Pfeifer & Leuzinger-Bohleber, 1986, 1991, 1992, 1995; Leuzinger-Bohleber & Pfeifer, 1998, 2002a, b,

2004, 2006, 2013a, b; Leuzinger-Bohleber, Henningsen & Pfeifer, 2008), an inspiring experience for both of them (see Leuzinger-Bohleber, 2015). In this paper, we focus on one aspect of this dialogue: the illustration of how this inter-disciplinary dialogue may inspire the clinical psychoanalytical practice. Accord-ing to our experiences, it opens the mind of the psychoanalysts to understand unconscious processes in the transference/countertransference situation in a new and, as we think, innovative way. This is particularly true for working with severely traumatized patients, as we will try to illustrate. Understanding their unconscious "embodied memories" may lead to a structural change in their feelings, cognitions and behavior – which, for Mrs. B., had an existential dimen-sion for her life and the life of her whole family (see section 3).

Memory has always been a central issue in psychoanalytic theory and prac-tice. Many authors engaged in current debates on so-called false memories in the context of sexual abuse claim that observing "procedural memories" in the psychoanalytic situation opens a window for "stored knowledge" of experiences during the first years of life. Procedural memories, defined on a descriptive level as a specific form of long-term memory, cover mechanical and bodily skills (like eating with a knife and fork). As will be discussed in this chapter: in contrast to "procedural memory", the concept of "embodied memories" is much more specific, and offers a more precise understanding of the so-called sensory-motor coordination of the traumatized patient in the psychoanalytic relationship. This unconsciously – in very specific situations – leads to the precise re-construction of the bodily sensations, affects and fantasies that match the original traumatic interaction. Their intensity and quality prove to be inappropriate in the present, new relationship with the analyst. For the patient, it is essential to decode in detail the specific (sensory-motor) stimuli that, because of their precise analo-gies, trigger the "embodied memories" of the traumatic experiences. We will try to illustrate that this means more than just "understanding procedural mem-ories" and refer to the concept of "embodied memories", which has been dis-cussed it in detail in other publications (see, e.g., Leuzinger-Bohleber & Pfeifer, 2002a, b, 2006, 2013a; Leuzinger-Bohleber, 2015).

To briefly summarize: Recent developments in cognitive science and the neu-rosciences suggest that traditional notions of memory based on stored structures that are also often underlying psychoanalytic thinking cannot account for a number of fundamental phenomena and thus need to be revised. In this chapter, we suggest that memory be conceived as

- a theoretical construct explaining current behavior by reference to events that have happened in the past.
- Memory is not to be conceived as stored structures but as a function of the whole organism, as a complex, dynamic, re-categorizing and interactive process, which is always "embodied".
- Memory always has a subjective and an objective side. The subjective side is given by the individual's history, the objective side by the neural patterns

generated by the sensory motor interactions with the environment. This implies that both "narrative" (subjective) and "historical" (objective) truth have to be taken into account in achieving stable psychic change. We will illustrate this thesis by extensive clinical materials from the case of a polio patient, which were already published in a different version earlier (Leuzinger-Bohleber, 2015, p.104–120), because in this third psychoanalysis with a severely (organically) traumatized patient we can discuss in detail how understanding and working through embodied memories proves to be indispensable for a sustainable psychic transformation of severely traumatized patients (section 3).

A new understanding of unconscious memories: Some theoretical remarks

Many memory researchers have postulated in recent years that declarative (autobiographic) and procedural (implicit) memory must be distinguished (cf. e.g. Milner, Squire & Kandel, 1998). On a descriptive level, this differentiation makes sense: in the declarative memory, we store verbal, visual and symbolic memories; in the procedural memory, we store memories of physical processes that cannot become conscious in later periods of time. A gifted Swiss skier, who is engaged in skiing competitions, for instance, remembers being held by her father when learning to ski at the age of three. However, it is almost impossible for her as a young adult to remember the exact motor skills she learned then and still (unconsciously) performs. Declarative memory does not develop until the third or fourth year of life. Some analysts, e.g., Fonagy and Target (1997), conclude from this that declarative, autobiographic memories do not go back to the first three years of life, which means that "historical truths" of this period of life cannot be psychoanalytically grasped. They write in their summary: ". . . whether there is historical truth and historical reality is not our business as psychoanalysts and psychotherapists" (p. 216). As we have discussed in several papers, in our view these conclusions are based on a major categorical mistake: the differentiation between declarative and procedural memory refers to the *descriptive level of memory performances and not to processes in the brain* that enable remembering. Even if the region of the hippocampus is not fully developed until the third or fourth year of life, experiences are stored in the brain structures before then, even in their entirety and not just in a single, specific brain region (e.g. Leuzinger-Bohleber & Pfeifer, 2013a).These experiences are physical (sensorimotor) memories that become – unconsciously – manifest, as for instance in Mrs. B.'s enactments in the psychoanalytical sessions (described in section 3) and, to express this phenomenon in psychoanalytic terms – led to the striking (physical) countertransference reactions in the psychoanalyst via processes of projective and introjective identifications. The encoding of these unconscious traces in the physical ("embodied") reactions of our patients enables us – this is our thesis – to discover some unconscious fantasies and experiences that date back to pre-speech. It seems to us that the concept of "Embodiment" makes this path of recognition more easily understandable in the analytic relationship, as we want to explain briefly:

Implicitly, the above-mentioned reasoning postulates an outdated memory model that assumes fixed "storage" in the brain from which experiences formed after the fourth year of life can be retrieved. However, memory is not to be conceived as stored structures or "store-house-model" (computer metaphor). This notion is fundamentally incorrect. Human memory is not a hard disk and does not include a long-term store from which the necessary knowledge is transferred to short-term memory in order to be made conscious afterwards. Memory and remembering are functions of the whole organism, as a complex, dynamic, re-categorizing and interactive process, which is always "embodied", in other words, based on sensory-motor experiences and becomes manifest in the behavior of the organism (not just in the brain or a specific region in the brain). This means that memory is not an abstract cognitive function but is always based on actual sensory-motor stimulations which receive and process visual, haptic, auditory and proprioceptive stimuli and, like in earlier situations, actively make up and "produce" out of them analogies between the current and this earlier situation. Thus, "embodied" remembering is not simply "non-verbal" or "descriptively unconscious" but highly constructive, dynamic and historically determined. Therefore, these conceptualizations of Embodied Cognitive Science can well be connected with the psychoanalytic concept of the dynamic unconscious. Moreover, memory is neither located in the hippocampus nor in the neocortex: the brain in its entirety as an information processing system is just as involved in the emergence of memory as the whole organism (which is necessary for the functioning of the brain).

The distinction between the new, biologically inspired and "classical" models of memory becomes very clear in a diagram published by Gerald Edelman in 1992 (cf. also Leuzinger-Bohleber & Pfeifer, 1998, S. 897ff.). In the case of traditional models of memory – analogous to information processing in computers – one assumes a precise storage of knowledge, which is static and unchanging, and thus making transference to new problem solving possible.

By contrast, "knowledge storing" in the dynamic models of embodied cognitive science, though less exact, precisely through this quality enables optimum generalization and adaption to a new situation. In the process, so-called neuronal maps are produced through the functional circulation of the organism's constant interaction with its environment.

> These consist of several 10000s of neurons, which work functionally in one direction. Thus, each system of perception has, e.g. the visual apparatus, the sensuous surface of the skin etc, and a multiplicity of maps which are stimulated by qualitatively different impressions: colour, touch, direction, warmth etc. These maps are connected to one another by parallel and reciprocal fibres, which guarantee the renewed and repeated entry, flow and exchange of signals. If one map is selected by way of the stimulation of

OLD VIEW

Replicative

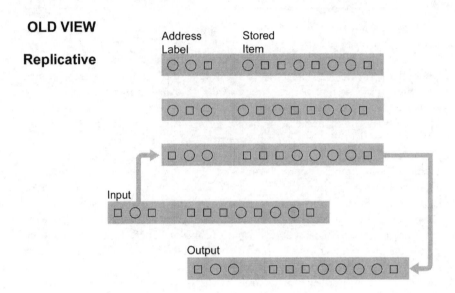

NEW VIEW

Dynamic

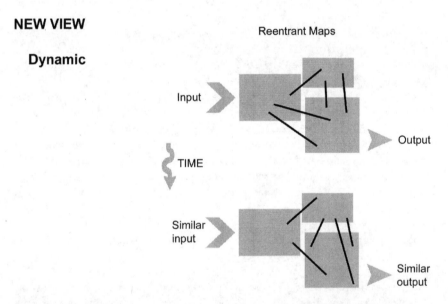

Figure 8.1 A comparison of "classic" and "embodied" memories. Adapted from Gerald Edelman (1992)

groups of neurons, then a stimulation of the maps to which it is connected simultaneously results. Due to the reciprocal connections (›reentry‹), the nerve impulses are returned, whereby the reinforcement or attenuation of synapsis in the neuronal groups occurs in the synapses of each map: the connections of the maps themselves undergo modification. Through this, new selective qualities emerge, in other words, ›automatic‹ re-categorizations of current stimuli from different sense channels

(Leuzinger-Bohleber & Pfeifer, 1998, p. 898f.).

Through such "sensomotoric coordination", which is connected with permanent re-categorizations, the organism ensures a sustained ability to orient itself in the environment, namely, to connect current experience with previous experience whereby, due to the new situation, previous re-categorizations are adapted by way of the retained stimuli.

Hence, due to the above-outlined radical conceptual rethinking, in embodied cognitive science memory is understood as a function of the total organism, the product of complex, invariably "embodied", dynamic re-categorizing and interactive processes (cf. among others, Leuzinger-Bohleber & Pfeifer, 2013b).

Gerald Edelman's (1987) book *Neural Darwinism*, António Damasio's (1994) *Descartes' Error*, Lakoff and Johnson's (1999) *Philosophy in the Flesh: The Embodied Mind and Its Challenge to Western Thought* and Rolf Pfeifer and Josh Bongard's (2006) *How the Body Shapes the Way We Think* are probably the most well-known examples that show that the Cartesian dualism between mind and body must be revised in favor of a radically new perception of an "embodiment" of the psyche in the body.

There exists no Kantian radically autonomous person, with absolute freedom and a transcendent reason that correctly dictates what is and isn't moral. Reason, arising from the body, doesn't transcend the body. What universal aspects of reason there are arise from communalities of our bodies and brain and the environments we inhabit. The existence of these universals does not imply that reason transcends the body. Moreover, since conceptual systems vary significantly, reason is not entirely universal. [. . .] Since reason is shaped by the body, it is not radically free, because the possible human conceptual systems and the possible forms of reason are limited

(Lakoff & Johnson, 1999, p. 5).

Each interaction with the environment changes the organism: A new view to the nature-nurture problem

As indicated above, from the viewpoint of embodied cognitive science, psychic processes are constituted only through the subject's adaptive, re-categorizing interaction with the environment, in which memory is actively constructed.

One further postulate is that the organism finds itself in ongoing transformation. We would also like to give an example of this from epigenetics, a highly interesting research field for psychoanalysis – which, thanks to recent technical advances in molecular genetics, has brought forth a wealth of interesting studies. Furthermore, proven genetic vulnerabilities do not represent the victim's destiny, but first make their appearance where previous, weighty environmental or relationship experiences play a role. Thus, those studies, among others, by Caspi et al. (2003) and Hauser (2008) that were capable of verifying genetic vulnerability by way of the so-called moderated 5 – HHT allel of the serotonin transporter gene were given considerable attention. This proved that people with this genotype only then suffer from depression when subjected to ongoing weighty life circumstances or earlier traumas, such as child abuse. Kaufman et al. (2006) and Goldberg (2009) were also able to show that a responsive, empathetic motherly behavior in the first months of life represents a protective factor, whereby the risk of becoming ill from depression, is also reduced in cases of proven vulnerability (cf. also Suomi, 2010, 2011).

These studies on epigenetics confirm the basic psychoanalytic thesis of an ongoing and determining interaction between genetics and environment, between biology and social experience, especially in early and earliest childhood. The developmental perspectives of embodied cognitive science differentiates these general theses, among others, by empirically showing that the organism's interaction with the environment, as one has imagined for considerable time, is not regulated exclusively by a "genetic program", but by an ongoing dynamic and "embodied" interaction between subject and environment, namely, from the outset. We go on to elaborate this in greater detail in the following.

Embodiment, self-regulation and "learning by doing" (John Dewey)

Just how radically the view of self-regulatory processes of the embodiment concept has called into question our previous understanding of psychically functioning processes is best illustrated by Pfeifer and Bongard's experiment in fundamental research (2006, pp. 177–211):

For the purposes of examining the effects of sensomotoric coordinations and the principle of self-regulation, researchers reconstructed a molecular chain comprising motoric, sensoric elements ("cells") as well as binding elements in an experiment. Through the connection of sensoric and motoric elements, such a molecular chain can set itself in caterpillar-like motion, without thereby following a corresponding (genetic) control program: The sensoric stimulation moves the motoric element, which consequently shifts the sensoric element, etc.

After having left their experiment[2] one evening, researchers were surprised to discover when returning the following morning that a fascinating, complex structure on a new cell structure had developed (first image in figure): this was the fundamental evidence of embodiment, namely, of a self-organizing principle according to "learning by doing" (John Dewey). Without (central) regulation of performing sensomotoric coordination, a cell structure forms. Thus this cell structure is "intelligent" to the extent that it generates self-organized intelligent behavior over the course of time (in the experiment: shifting an obstacle).

What do these experiments show us?

I)   Biological systems are self-organized and develop "intelligent" bodies, namely, structures in which they interact with the environment by way of sensomotoric coordinations without central regulation.

II) In the case of (biological) beings, learning always simultaneously occurs sensomotorically (in the body) and in the brain (in neuronal networks).

III) Learning, problem-solving and memory are thus no longer functions of a "saving in the brain", but invariably the product of complex, self-regulated, sensomotoric coordination.

IV) Psychic processes, such as "unconscious memories" or affects and fantasies evoked in a certain situation are "constructed" between subject and environment in the here and now of a current interaction: consequently, thinking, feeling and action thus arise only interactively: the subject cannot learn in an insular quasi autistic capsule and further develop itself: it requires interaction with the environment.

V)   Similarly, such categories that constitute the basis of all learning and understanding do not develop by retrieval or modification of stored knowledge. They are automatically brought forth by sensomotoric coordination (spontaneously "constructed"). Since this is decisive for our subject of understanding that which is non-represented (unconscious), one further experiment should be cited: if we give a one-year-old child a red rubber ball in one hand and in the other a brown chocolate bar, he will put both in his mouth several times, though he will prefer the chocolate bar after no more than two or three attempts: through sensomotoric coordinations – learning by doing – he has formed categories without an adult having to explain it to him, namely, without the aid of cognitive schema: the brown, long-shaped object tastes good, one can eat it – and although one can bite the round object, it does not taste good, one cannot eat it! And yes, at some point the mother will remark: "and, does the chocolate taste good?" from which point on the child also associates the linguistic concept with his self-constructed categories. As this example indicates, the concept of embodiment provides a solution for one of the central problems of developmental psychology, namely, the early pre-linguistic acquisition of categories and, finally, also symbols and language.

VI) The concept of "embodiment" is thus radically "historical", as psychic processes in the present always take place as the product of sensomotoric coordinations analogous to those in the subject's idiosyncratic past: the past inevitably impacts the present and future – that is, for the most part, unconsciously.

VII)   In that each new experience further develops sensomotoric coordinations, earlier experiences are permanently rewritten. Hence, the "historic truth" can never be reconstructed "one to one" on the basis of specific behavior in the present. Put more bluntly: this is the subjective part of all psychic experience. And yet, in the sensomotoric coordinations, past real experiences are retained "objectively" ("embodied") and can be measured, in principle, with the aid of neurobiological methods. For this reason, psychic experience, such as memory always receive a "subjective" as well as an "objective" side.

"So much pain could have been spared . . ." – clinical observations from a third psychoanalysis

What do these new concepts of "embodied memories" offer to psychoanalytical practice? The following, relatively detailed description of a third psychoanalysis will hopefully illustrate our position that the (mostly unconscious) understanding of memory processes in the back of the analyst's mind indeed does have an essential influence on his understanding of the unconscious dimensions in a patient´s behavior in psychoanalytical sessions as well as in his everyday love relationships, etc.

a) Motivation for a third analysis

Mrs. B., 52 years old, has decided to do another sequence of psychoanalysis, because she still suffers from severe sleeping disorders as well as from apparently psychotic "breakdowns" during conflicts in her relationship with her husband. These unexplainable breakdowns are a heavy burden to herself as well as to the relationship. She has already completed two psychoanalyses, with which by and large she is very content. She initiated the first analysis at the age of 23 after a complete breakdown following the death of her disabled brother. It lasted almost three years. "As soon as I felt better, I jumped up from the couch and tried to do everything by myself again . . .". She thought of the second analysis as a continuation of the first, because the depression and the severe symptoms of exhaustion kept returning and led to serious suicidal attacks. At the age of 29 she initiated her second psychoanalysis, which lasted almost five years. She gives the treatment the credit for her "having had the courage to settle in a new relationship with (another) man and becoming pregnant. My daughter's birth (when she was 33) was a turning point in my life – I have definitely buried suicidal tendencies although suicidal thoughts still come to mind once in a while. Unlike previous times, I am now absolutely sure that I am in control of these impulses, because I am not going to do something like this to my children. For this I am grateful to psychoanalysis". At the age of 38 she gave birth to twins and very much enjoyed experiencing the growing up of her three children "I was so incredibly thankful that my children were healthy, which in contrast to my husband has never been a given for me. I always reckoned with catastrophe and always reacted with panic if one of the children got sick or had a mild accident . . . Because of my psychoanalysis I knew that these events reactivated memories of my childhood catastrophes – I could not do anything about that! Fortunately, my husband was a good counterbalance to those fears, otherwise a lot would have gone wrong . . .".

Mrs. B. has always been employed. She successfully directed a large innovative institution for severely disabled children, has written several books about her work and is an internationally known expert in her field. "I know that to the outside world I represent a model career. I am much admired, because I am able to combine motherhood, marriage and a professional career – but still I cannot get rid of this basic feeling, that I live on the edge of a great abyss. A catastrophe could occur anytime . . . often at night I am convinced, that everything is breaking down around me. Then I lie awake, get a panic attack and hallucinate falling into a deep, black hole. I have to get up each time, otherwise I cannot endure it . . .". The greatest burden is the "sudden breakdowns", which Mrs. B. experiences in conflict situations with her husband. "They occur completely unexpected, mostly at times when I feel very relaxed. Often I suddenly experience my husband as emotionally inaccessible and withdrawn, and am then immediately convinced that he wants to leave me. I panic, I rage and attack him physically, just out of control. My entire body is a single wound – everything hurts – an unendurable state, which I only want to bring to an end. Mostly I am acutely suicidal in this situation and would like to get the whole thing over with. In tears and with the feeling of extreme coldness I finally creep away into a dark corner, cowering like an embryo, usually for hours. – The whole thing is a nightmare. When it is over, I am not at all able to imagine this state. Then I am terribly ashamed. I am terrified that I can be such a different person. It is like a psychosis and for my husband and me a horror over and over again, unbearable. Often I am afraid that because of this the relationship will fall apart . . . neither analysis could change anything about this . . ."

b) Remembering the insights of the former two psychoanalyses: An attempt at integration?

In the first months of treatment (four sessions a week, couch setting), memories of the two psychoanalyses often emerged, with two different analysts, one woman and one man, each of a different theoretical orientation, one with a chiefly modern Anglo-American object-relational approach, the other one seeing himself mainly as a Neo-Kleinian analyst. Telling me these memories seem to me like an attempt at integration. Unconsciously, Mrs. B. seems to want to inform me about the current state of her unconscious fantasies and conflicts. "It is strange how much is coming to my mind about these former treatments. For years I hardly ever thought of them . . .", she once says.

To mention just one example: In the third month of treatment, Mrs. B.'s father dies. Mrs. B. reacts with terrible guilt feelings because she was abroad when he unexpectedly passed away. In the next months, she seems to be para-lyzed in the analytic sessions, unable to feel anything. "I am feeling like a robot – everything has lost its meaning – it is like someone turned off the light." After some months of not being able to reach the mainly silent Mrs. B. emotionally, I am more and more concerned about the state of her patho-logical mourning. I finally dream that my patient is lying in a coffin next to a dead person. It is not clear if she is still alive. "You seem to be paralyzed here on the couch like a severely ill or even dead person. Could it be that you are sacrificing your own life because you feel so guilty at having given a successful speech in Los Angeles while your father was dying?" I ask my patient in the next session. She now remembers her dreadful feelings of guilt during her first analysis after the suicide of her handicapped brother. "For months I was lying on the couch, silently like a dead person . . .". She recalls that she found out in her analysis that the identification with the dead brother also was due to unbearable feelings of hatred and aggression.

For years, the four-year-older, visibly physically disabled brother had been jealous of his younger, healthy and talented sister, who was also the father's favorite child. Many memories had appeared at that time of how her brother had secretly tortured her as an infant, mostly unrecognized by the parents. Mrs. B. now recalls that it was crucial for calming her own depression during her first analysis to work through her own sadistic and aggressive fantasies, which had been overly stimulated through her brother's tortures and had been banished into the unconscious. She didn't allow herself to have such feelings towards her handicapped brother. Instead, the only option was to flee from the relationship. Mrs. B. recalls many scenes of being alone in the woods as a small child, insecure and lonely, occupied with intensive daydreaming.

In the following sessions, we are able to understand that the death of her father had reactivated the traumatic loss of her brother. She now releases herself from her silence and recalls many insights of both her former psychoanalyses. I cannot report any details here, but give only a short summary of her "life nar-rative" due to her psychoanalytic insights:

Because of her high achievements and social behavior, she excelled in school. She was considered as the "integrative element" in her class, mediated conflicts and cared for weak and needy children. As became clear in her first analysis, she had formed an altruistic, beaming, warm-hearted personality, which was yet imprinted at its core by profound loneliness, "somehow fundamentally unconnected with the close supporting figures." She felt loved and respected only when she was able to be there for others. These "truths" had especially become clear in the transference with the first analyst: often she had the fan-tasy that the analyst was happy if a session could not take place and she only received the fees.

Her first loving relationship had also followed the same pattern: She uncon-sciously searched for a needy partner, whom she could care for and nurse. Another central insight of the first analysis evolved around her narcissistic fantasies of omnipotence, of her being able to soothe or heal disabled persons. The brother's suicide revealed the omnipotence fantasies, another trigger for the depressive breakdown. The analytic work also dealt with Oedipal fantasies and wishes, such as her feelings of guilt, that she had preferred the lively father as opposed to the depressed mother. Three years of analytical work led her out of her depression: Mrs. B. was able to take up and successfully complete her studies. The recurring nightmares of being pursued because of a crime, which was unknown to her, disappeared, yet the chronic feelings of exhaustion, as well as the basic feeling of "not really being anchored in this world" remained.

Because she could also profit from psychoanalysis in her professional field, which focused on disability, she decided to continue treatment with another analyst in the city, in which she now lived. As she recalls, the analyst soon realized that she was not able to lie still on the couch, but that she constantly had to move. In this context, memories of her polio infection, shortly after her fourth birthday, appeared for the first time. During this illness it remained uncertain for weeks whether she would live or die. Mrs. B. knew of her infection, but mostly had integrated the feeling of how "lucky" she was that she survived the disease without any visible consequences and that she, in contrast to her handicapped brother, was a healthy, talented and handsome child, "everybody's sunshine", as she had often been called within her family. Her enormous fear of passivity had been connected to the experienced fear of death and this realization finally led to coping better with situations of professional overburdening. The hypothesis about the early interaction with the depressive mother played a great role here. The insufficient empathy for her own body and its state was attributed to insufficient introjection of a caring, empathetic maternal primary object. Because, as it was assumed, the mother did not carry out her holding and containing functions sufficiently, the archaic, and above all aggressive impulses could not be integrated "well enough" and thus led to a severe weakness in the area of stable representations of the self and of others as well as to her severe suicidality. Mrs. B. commented: "Together we found a way out of this horrible dark world, the pathological and aggressive seduction of being united with my dead brother, the unconscious anger and revenge, which was primarily directed towards my mother – but also towards my analyst – and similar terrible and embarrassing fantasies. In the relationship with the analyst I gradually thereafter rediscovered many brighter sides of experiences in the early relationship with my father. I sensed that the analyst liked working with me, was truly interested in me and was able to empathize with me and my despair. Thereby I was again able to believe that my father, and possibly my mother in her sense, loved me." Such insights finally made it possible for her to free herself from a restrictive relationship with a mathematician, in which she felt very lonesome. Thereafter, Mrs. B. fell in love with a man, her future husband, with whom for the first time she experienced a satisfying and fulfilling sexuality.

c) Doubts about the "untreatable early disorder"

In the following months of psychoanalysis, there appeared, among other things, doubts about the hypothesis of an untreatable early disorder:

- Mrs. B. depicted her mother's interaction with the three grandchildren in many different versions. In these situations she experienced her as jovial, humorous and with much empathy and fantasy for the infants. These observations raised doubts about her mother's diagnosis of severe personality disorder. We discussed the question that her former perception of her mother's personality also could have been partially due to her infantile (Oedipal) fantasies and projections onto her primary object.
- The "psychotic states" during Mrs. B.'s breakdowns did not seem to have the character of a psychosis, but rather of a dissociative state as described by recent trauma research. At the time of Mrs. B.'s first two psychoanalyses little psychoanalytic knowledge about trauma was available. Are the "states" an unconscious enactment of traumatic experiences?
- As an analyst, I often noticed the strange way in which Mrs. B. talked about her polio infection. The narration almost had something coquettish. It appeared to be some form of a "wonderful fairy tale of a lucky girl who (just) escaped death", who, thanks to a "lucky star", was able to continue her way of life without restrictions, in contrast to many of her classmates, who bore witness to the epidemic through visible handicaps. In her narration, every record of fright, fear of death and physical pain was missing. Does this express denial of the trauma suffered?
- Both psychoanalysts, as recalled by Mrs. B., seemed to have shown hardly any interest in details of her polio illness. It came to light that even Mrs. B. had almost no medical knowledge about polio, e.g., she did not even know how the disease is transmitted, what its cause is, what types of polio exist, etc. This was extraordinary for an intellectual woman, especially one who is employed in upper management in a home for the disabled.
- Instead, we, more and more understood, that the "psychotic breakdowns" of Mrs. B. were connected to "embodied memories"[3] of the dramatic and traumatic beginning of her polio disease. Which "historical-biographical truths" could be encoded in Mrs. B.'s unconscious enactments in the psychoanalytic process?

d) Approaching the specific "embodied" trauma of the polio infection in the transference: Indispensable for structural change?

"Suddenly everything is different. . . . " dissociation and trauma

The following sessions took place around one year after the beginning of psychoanalysis. After a weekend, Mrs. B. comes to the session in a warm woollen sweater, in spite of the sunny weather. She looks pale and tired, with a frozen expression on her face. "Is she ill?" I ask myself. I notice that she stops several times while walking up the stairs, breathing heavily. This is uncommon behavior for her. I am thinking that I myself had trouble climbing the stairs last week while suffering from a slight infection. Lying on the couch, Mrs. B. is silent for a long time. She lies there in a stiff and frozen position. The longer she is silent, the more intensive my depressive feelings become . . . Suddenly my dream with the two people lying in a coffin comes to my mind (see b). I panic because I suddenly fantasize that someone could close the lid of the coffin in spite of the fact that it is not clear whether the people are really dead. Now I make the association that both of us are wearing warm woollen sweaters in spite of the sunny weather outside. Are we the dying people in the coffin? Mrs. B. does not know that I myself have suffered from polio in my childhood and that I share with her one of the generally unknown long-term symptoms, the difficulty of regulating bodily temperature. I ask myself whether my dream contains not only the issue of the death of Mrs. B.'s father and brother as mentioned above, but also our shared experience of being paralyzed and threatened by death during the polio infection.

Mrs. B. is still silent. Finally, after about half an hour, I break the silence: "Is it difficult for you to talk today? – Where are you with your thoughts?" – "I did not want to tell you what happened during the weekend. I do not want to burden you . . . and, well, psychoanalysis does not change anything anyway . . ." – "Are you afraid I would not be able to cope with your experiences?" I comment (thinking of Mrs. B.'s fantasies about her mother during her polio infection). Finally, Mrs. B. slowly starts to talk:

She had spent the weekend in a holiday house with her husband and their adolescent children. She had looked forward to this event for months, because it would be the first time that the whole family would be reunited again. The "catastrophe" happened during a walk through the sunny meadows. She felt very relaxed and happy, made jokes with her husband and the children. She then told her husband about her plans to celebrate his coming birthday in an idyllic little restaurant close to a lake, which she already had reserved. Her husband did not react with enjoyment, as she had expected, but withdrew, seemingly somehow angry (he told her many days later that he felt overwhelmed and excluded by her plans). Immediately, everything changed: the positive mood collapsed, her body became stiff and "dead", she seemed hardly able to breath. At the same time, she had terrible headaches and a strong impulse to vomit. Her entire body was hurting. Because she was not capable of coping with these painful changes she started – in front of her children – to attack her husband, verbally and even physically. Finally her husband and her children left her, extremely angry. The children went back to their homes. She was in a desperate state. For hours, she sat in a corner of her bedroom in the dark, freezing and in a curled up position like an embryo. "I almost could not bear it – the terrible pains in every part of my body. I only wished that everything would come to an end. . . ." – Her husband found her in this state when he returned in the middle of the night. He tried to talk with her and to take her into his arms. For hours she could not bear the bodily contact and continued to attack him violently. Finally, after many hours cowering in the dark corner in his presence but silent, she calmed down a little and the extreme pains diminished. In the morning, she could finally allow her husband to touch her and to bring her to bed. Exhausted she fell asleep. . . .

Mrs. B. is deeply ashamed and shocked. She suffers from heavy guilt feelings and fears having finally destroyed her relationship with her children. "It is like a nightmare – in this state I am like a different person. Am I crazy or psychotic?" While listening to the patient, I had realized that the topic "polio" had disappeared from our psychoanalytic sessions for about nine months. I comment: "I can imagine how painful and degrading this is for you. You had hoped that the breakdowns would not appear anymore after all these psychoanalytic sessions. It is understandable that you feel doubts whether psychoanalysis will be able to change these terrible states of mind. – I was just thinking that polio as a subject of our work here has disappeared for a long time. Could it be that your "breakdown" unconsciously wants to remind us of this topic? Perhaps your body is expressing some unconscious memories of unbearable physical and emotional pain during the polio infection in this "crazy way", memories which are normally not accessible to you as today in this session." Mrs. B. seems to be touched and starts to cry. "Yes, I have forgotten about all this for a long time again. . . ." she says.

After this session she surfs the Internet. While reading the medical information, she recognizes that she had suffered from *paralytic poliomyelitis with typical symptoms, above all symptoms of palsy*". She remembers that she was playing with her cousin in the garden feeling relaxed and happy in the middle of her summer holiday. All of sudden she felt very ill, and had to throw up. "From that moment on I felt absolutely miserable – my entire body hurt, particularly my head". She phones her mother, requesting more details. She tells her that she had high fever with attacks of shivering. She screamed with pain and would not let anyone touch her, because every single touch hurt. Both legs were paralyzed. She was close to death for several weeks.

In the following sessions, we discover the analogies between her psychic and bodily sensations during her "breakdown", and the beginning of her polio infection. It now seems probable to us that the extreme emotional and physical states during her "breakdown" are specific "embodied memories": the triggering experience of her husband's "sudden", "unexpected" and "abrupt" withdrawal in the trustful, happy situation on the walk, the experience "that from one moment to the next everything is different . . .", as well as the unbearable pain of the entire body bear a striking analogy to her experience at the outbreak of polio.

According to the above summarized concept of "embodied memory" we can explain the "automatically reconstructed" memory of the traumatic experiences in the following way: The perceptions of information in different sensory channels in the triggering situation (the sudden, unexpected changes of the facial expressions of her husband, his gesture and bodily position, his withdrawal, his resistance to holding her hand anymore (while being angry, he does not want to hold her hand) lead to analogous sensory-motor coordination as in the situation of the sudden breakout of the polio in the sunny garden. These sensory-motor coordination "construct" the "embodied memories" on the bodily state (headaches and pains of the entire body, throwing up, despair, changes perception of the surrounding persons etc.)

"The catastrophe – Fear of death and panic"

In one of the following sessions, Mrs. B. tells me one of the few conscious memories of the polio infection:

Beatrice (Mrs. B.) is lying in the darkened room, all by herself, peaceful and wishing her beloved God would take her with him to heaven. . . . In this scene, Beatrice does not feel any physical pain; she is lying there entirely calmly. To us, the picture of peaceful solitude and the childlike wish "that the dear God may take her to him" seem to be an expression of massive denial of the extreme physical pain which accompanies every bodily movement in acute polio, as well as a denial of the perception of being paralyzed and of the massive fear of death.

We finally find the analogies to the traumatic situation in infancy triggering her "embodied memories": In her dissociated states, Mrs. B. tries to get herself into a paralyzed and cringing position in a corner of the (bed)room; she tries not to move at all in order to "freeze" the unbearable storms of affect, the panic and the pain of the entire body. Hours later, she successfully reaches a state of motionless calmness, freedom from pain, and "paralyzation of the feelings", which gives enormous relief. Only when she is able to get herself into this state of emotional peace can she endure her husband physically touching and relieving her. Here she also seems to construct an "embodied memory", an attempt to manage the overwhelming with unbearable pain and vehement affects by "freezing herself".

"It is most bearable, when I am by myself . . ."

In her dissociative state, as just described, Mrs. B. attacks her husband vigorously and sends him away; she cannot bear his physical presence, least of all "his angry-perplexed-fearful face", although simultaneously she panics when he leaves her.

To us, another detail of the memory of the darkened room just described seems to offer the key to understanding this part of the enactment.

Mrs. B. remembers her mother's fearful face. To see her in this state is far more unbearable than lying alone in the darkened room. According to Mrs. B.'s (Oedipal) fantasies, her mother probably could hardly contain the fear that her child might die, or survive even more severely handicapped than the older son. "For years she told me over and over again how many children had died in the village during the epidemic. On Saturdays she often took me with her, and placed flowers on the graves of the polio children". Mrs. B. recalls how she imagined lying in one of these graves herself.

In the session, we assume that Mrs. B. identified with her mother's fantasized wish for death in this situation, perhaps another aspect of her later suicidal tendencies. In any case, she developed a central unconscious conviction that when ill and needy she would become a heavy burden to others so that she had to hide it and "cure herself". I assume that a seed of Mrs. B.'s profound loneliness lies within this unconscious conviction – only her husband, a very much loved child of a physically ill mother, could again and again reach out to her emotionally in her loneliness.

Probably the comforting bodily contact, which each time finally gets her out of her states, is also connected to embodied memories.

She recalls that in the evenings her father used to sit down on her bed and hold her hand – for her a pleasant (maybe also psychologically life saving) experience. Apparently, it was he who was able to control his fears for the child, and therefore also able to communicate to his ill daughter a hopeful, positive bodily experience.

Because of these memories, it is easier for Mrs. B to understand why the very empathetic analyst in the second treatment could lead her out of the severe depressive crisis: presumably she unconsciously connected in the transference such experiences of good object relationship with her father.

Denial of the horror, flight into health as a "sunshine child"

In the following months, Beatrice, having survived the life-threatening disease, fled into healthiness in an impressive way and reinterpreted the fear she had suffered as a remarkable "lucky stroke of fate". Perhaps she had received not enough support from her parents[4] in order to deal with the traumatization. Understandably, both probably were happy and relieved that they had their healthy, uncomplicated and talented child back. Unconsciously, Beatrice experienced herself as positively selected by fate, as a chosen one, who because of her remarkable talent or because of being especially loved by "almighty God" had now received the existential assignment to be there for others, especially for disabled individuals like her brother, in the form of a "sunshine child". She developed into an altruistic personality (see also Anna Freud, 1936). However, the suffered trauma remained unconsciously present influencing, for example, the basic feeling of being alone and lonely, of not deserving her own existence, feeling guilty for the tragic fates of her brother and her polio, and therefore being allowed to exist only as the "Siamese twin of a disabled sibling". The severe depressions and states of exhaustion in her late adolescence seem to be connected to the repressed and not unassimilated fear from the trauma.[5]

The struggle for memory (Bohleber) – The integration of the trauma – And its therapeutic effect

The struggle for understanding of the "embodied memories" lasted months and was characterized by renewed denial and the wish to reestablish the old, seemingly manic, contraphobic defense of the suffered pain and despair. Attempts at flight set in again and again, including thoughts about terminating the analysis before completion. To mention just one example: after being confronted with her renewed denial of her polio traumatization in again not taking notice of her exhaustion and falling into depression, she angrily jumps off the couch and shouts at me: "You want to keep me little. You are envious because of all my activities and successes." In the next session she reports a dream: "A little girl completely dressed in white, with fine white shoes, was climbing up a large mountain of shit. As she arrived at the top she began to sing beautifully . . ." We both have to smile: "Yes, it really is a mountain of shit, this polio. The little girl just does not care about it and is even capable of bringing happiness to the whole world by singing so beautifully. . . ."

We can talk about the temptation of denying the trauma again and again, in order to not have to confront oneself with the horror of the trauma and one's own vulnerabilities. Again and again Mrs. B. tries to prove to herself that "everything is fine – polio has gone away for ever . . .". It is a very painful process for her, that she – physically and emotionally – is still suffering from the consequences of the traumatization and that she will never be able to completely overcome them or to delete all traces of the traumatic memories. She constantly experiences her physical vulnerability as narcissistic defects. She often expresses her sadness because, judging by her dreams, the early traumatization (growing up with a depressed mother and a disabled brother, her polio infection etc.) have influenced her unconscious fantasies so much, a topic which I cannot elaborate further here.[6]

As far as the psychoanalytic technique is concerned, it was difficult not to be blind to Mrs. B.'s repeated denial of the trauma (during the first year of psychoanalysis, see above). She often tried to seduce me with her wish to hear that the trauma – compared, e.g., with the Shoah – had not been so severe and would not have any long-term consequences for her. On the other hand, as we now know, I had to cope with the risk of a re-traumatization if the reactivation of the traumatic experiences in the analytical relationship became too intensive. Many psychoanalytical authors have described that coping with the intensity of the reactivation of trauma in the psychoanalytic process is one of the main difficulties in the analytical work with traumatized patients. The successful navigation of these risks must be linked to a continual processing of the difficult feelings in the countertransference, which is often difficult to manage without supervision. Therefore, I just want to mention how important the containing function of the psychoanalytic relationship was in the psychoanalysis with Mrs. B. I have no doubt that working through the trauma (e.g., the state of extreme helplessness, of despair and unbearable pain, the panic connected with fear of death etc.) in the transference was indispensable for the gradual structural change in Mrs. B.'s personality.

In spite of all defence maneuvers, a gradually increasing integration of the trauma takes place, which manifests itself primarily in Mrs. B.'s altered basic feeling of self, for me an indicator of structural change in her personality. In daily life, she experiences herself as more fearful, more careful and less permanently capable of working intensively, at first experiencing these changes as a threat and as a loss of narcissistic satisfaction. She increasingly feels dependent on interactions with others and on their support in solving problems. At the same time, more confidence in others is gradually appearing and with it a basic feeling of connectedness, of shared responsibility. These emotions are completely new kinds of experience for her. She continues to work a lot, but at the end of the second year of the treatment she notices: "Already for quite some time now my nightmares have disappeared, the expectation of catastrophe has decreased . . . I don't seem to be continuously standing on the edge anymore . . .". It is also important to her that she has a better feeling for her body, especially for reactions of tiredness and that she pays attention to these signals, presumably a reason for her reduced feeling of chronic exhaustion. "I feel more grounded in myself and less absent from reality than before this analysis," she once says. However, it is most important for her that the breakdowns during the conflicts in her marriage rarely reoccur. "For my husband and me it is very important that we increasingly understand what these breakdowns mean and what triggers them. Most of the time I can detect when panic appears and then directly ask my husband if and why he is emotionally withdrawing. I am still incredibly frightened in such situations and I have to deal with the expectation of catastrophes, but I don't break down entirely anymore . . . You probably can't imagine how relieved I am . . .".

In many psychoanalytical sessions, Mrs. B. occupies herself with mourning. Reproaches towards her two former analysts appear. She formulates these very clearly, even harshly, without, however, destroying the aforementioned gratitude that her two psychoanalyses, despite their limitations, had opened many doors for transforming her life.

Conclusion

Centered around the insights from the third psychoanalysis with Mrs. B., we made attempts to verify the hypothesis that the working through in the transference with the analyst of the traumatic experiences, and the reconstruction of the biographical-historical reality of the trauma suffered (emotional as well as cognitive) both proved indispensable for lasting structural change in this severely traumatized patient. As we have tried to illustrate with the clinical material, the traumatic experience had been integrated into Mrs. B.'s basic feeling of identity as an unrecognized source that had largely determined her personality development. Convinced of her selection by the almighty as a "chosen one" and of her "eternal guilt as one who is preferred by fate", she was equally convinced of being under the obligation of sacrificing her own life to the handicapped and to others less privileged. She thus developed a "false self" and a lifestyle of constant exhaustion. Understanding the details of her biographical trauma helped her to modify her core identity and to accept the hidden vulnerabilities of her own body and her dependency on others, particularly her husband. These changes are connected to the disappearance of her nightly panic, her constant "waiting for catastrophe" and her breakdowns, which is a great relief for her and her family. *"So much pain could have been spared to myself, my husband and my children if only I had had the courage to take a close look at my trauma earlier"*, she had once said in an analytic session.

We hope that this case history of Mrs. B. might contribute to the discussion of some technical issues in the treatment of other severely traumatized patients. Many questions still seem to be open: do we have to modify our techniques according to the different kinds of early trauma of our patients? Compared with victims of manmade disasters, it seems to me that patients traumatized through illness develop different kinds of unconscious fantasies in order to explain their survival. As mentioned above, Mrs. B. was unconsciously convinced that she was a "chosen one" who had been positively singled out by God or fate. She also developed specific unconscious body fantasies (being invulnerable etc.). These unconscious fantasies could be connected to the difficulties seen in the "Auserwählten" (Freud, 1916) in really accepting the reality principle (Jacobson, 1959). Therefore, we think that former polio patients could be considered as a specific nosological group from many points of view. They share specific characteristics of the unconscious long-term effects of polio infection, for instance "embodied memories" of the experience of extreme, sudden pain, of being paralyzed, of approaching death, but also of the helplessness of the primary objects and of the doctors who did not have any possibility of treating the illness. Their only hope was that the child's body might be successful in its fight against the illness. It seems most likely that a child suffering from polio would have perceived all these factors, integrating them into the unconscious fantasies of its own body being immortal and no longer vulnerable. Within the framework of this paper, we were not able to deal with the question of whether patients from other nosological groups, e.g., having suffered from other severe illnesses in their first years of life, show different kinds of long-term effects (e.g., a patient of mine from former East Germany with its rigid medical system who suffered from severe encephalitis in her first year of life). We also think that further clinical research on this question is necessary. However, we assume that, also for these other groups of patients severely traumatized through illness, it would prove indispensable to work on the chronic denial of the traumatization again and again in the psychoanalytic process for achieving structural change.

Another topic that needs further discussion is the relationship between "narrative" and "biographical" truth in psychoanalytic treatment. As we hope we were able to illustrate, it seems clear that a largely intellectual reconstruction of biographical facts does not lead to therapeutic change. Only detailed (emotional and cognitive) understanding of the enactment of traumatic events in the therapeutic relationship and in close object relationships (Mrs. B.'s breakdowns), including the scarcely bearable emotional intensity, lead to structural change. Without the holding and containing function of the analyst and the empathetic attitude of trying to understand the not understandable, Mrs. B. would not have had the courage to look at and to withstand the horror of the traumatic events of her life. Without this courage in a sustaining therapeutic relationship, neither understanding nor working through the trauma would have been possible.

We have tried to illustrate that the concept of "embodied memory" might be helpful in understanding that early trauma is remembered by the body in a more specific way than in merely understanding procedural memories (which means mechanical or bodily skills) in the transference, as other authors contend. Trying to understand "embodied memories" means observing in detail the sensory-motor coordination in the analytic relationship. This enables one finally to decode the inappropriate intensity of affects and fantasies that match the original traumatic interaction and not the present, new relationship to the analyst. The reconstruction of the original trauma then helps to understand the "language of the body" and to connect it with visualizations, images and verbalizations.

We mentioned only briefly that the reconstruction of the trauma supported the process of conceptualization, e.g., by empathizing with the intentions of the primary objects during the polio infection. These processes improved the current relationship with the Mrs. B.'s parents, particularly with her mother, because for years the relationship had been dominated by unconscious feelings of revenge and hatred.

Therefore, the discovery of the "biographical-historical truth" of the traumatic experiences, as well as their working through in the psychoanalytic relationship, helped to integrate the trauma into the self and the identity of the patient, which remains one of the main aims of a psychoanalytic treatment with severely traumatized patients.

Notes

1 A change of paradigms is always connected with a change of research methodology. One fundamental criticism of the storehouse metaphor characterizing the so-called Classical Cognitive Science came from biologically oriented memory researchers. From a perspective of adaptive behavior, they argued that living systems could not survive in a constantly changing environment if memory functioned like a computer. Living organisms are forced to adapt constantly to new situations, transferring knowledge gained in past situations to new ones that are never identical. Therefore, constructive, adaptive processes are indispensable. The organisms can be characterized as self-learning and self-regulating systems in constant interaction with environment (see also Leuzinger-Bohleber, 2015, p. 19ff.)
Cognitive Science always had a self-understanding of an interdisciplinary scientific discipline considering in their models of the mind the state of the art in as many different disciplines as Cognitive and Developmental Psychology, Psychoanalysis, Neurosciences, Neurobiology, Developmental and Affective Neurosciences, Linguistics, Informatics, Biology, Genetics, and even Engineering (see Pfeifer & Bongard, 2006).
2 A short film on this experiment can be found at http://www.ifi.unizh.ch/ailab
3 The explanation of the concept of "embodied memories" will not be repeated here.
4 Trying to understand her parents' behavior during her polio was essential for her increasing capacity for understanding more profoundly the intentions and motives of her primary objects. This had an observable effect on her social relationships.

5 After having studied the medical literature, Mrs.B. also asked herself whether the unusual symptoms of exhaustion, which had been the main reason for her earnest suicidal intentions during the second analysis, were related to a post polio syndrom (26 years after the polio infection). The main hypothesis was hardly to be tested a posteriori, mainly because medical information, which assumes episodic but also progressive development of PPS, bore contradictions. Yet it seemed important to her that the analytical treatment, without knowledge of PPS, had made possible better coping with her body: avoidance of extreme muscle exertion, as in the movement and dance groups during the previous years, good phases of relaxation with the infants, less stress, etc. These are all recommendations given to patients of PPS today.

6 To mention just one example: apparently during the polio infection, age-related Oedipal, sexual fantasies had been mixed with a magical processing of the respiratory complaints. She had repeated infantile dreams of anacondas suffocating her (see danger of suffocation during polio) or about poisonous snakes: the venom destroying the body from the inside – this also possibly being a processing of oral fantasies in connection with polio (see also case descriptions of Bierman, Silverstein & Finesinger, 1958). Mrs. B. narrates that unconscious body fantasies played a great role in her second psychoanalysis, triggered by the pregnancy. "That I had such an easy birth and that I could experience my body in a new way as healthy and functioning had also to do with the important processing of my fears that something destructive could be hiding in my body." But apparently the connection to polio was not explicitly recognized back then. In our psychoanalytical work, we still came across more body fantasies: Beatrice attributed surviving polio to her "very special body", a body that could defeat a deadly disease and therefore was immortal, invincible and without boundaries. These body fantasies were probably in part the basis for the aforementioned extraordinary dissimulation of physical states (such as pneumonia) or her pronounced contraphobic behavior (see also Jacobson, 1959).

References

Bierman, J. S., Silverstein, A. B., & Finesinger, J. E. (1958). A depression in a six-year-old boy with acute poliomyelitis. *The Psychoanalytic Study of the Child, 13*, 430.

Caspi, A., Sugden, K., Moffitt, T. E., Taylor, A., Craig, I. W., Harrington, H., McClay, J., Mill, J., Martin, J., Braithwaite, A., & Poulton, R. (2003). Influence of life stress on depression: Moderation by a polymorphism in the 5-HTT gene. *Science, 301* (5631), 386–389.

Damasio, A. R. (1994). *Descartes' error: Emotion, reasoning, and the human brain.* New York: GP Putnam.

Edelman, G. M. (1987). *Neural Darwinism: The theory of neuronal group selection.* New York: Basic Books.

Edelman, G. M. (1992). *Bright air, brilliant fire: On the matter of the mind.* New York: Basic books.

Fonagy, P., & Target, M. (1997). The recovered memory debate. In: Sandler, J., & Fonagy, P. (Eds.): *Recovered memories of abuse: True or false?* London: Karnac Books, 183–217.

Freud, A. (1936). *Das Ich und die Abwehrmechanismen.* Frankfurt am Main: Fischer Taschenbuchverlag, 2006.

Freud, S. (1916). Einige Charaktertypen aus der psychoanalytischen Arbeit. *GW, 10*, 231–253.

Goldberg, D. (2009). The interplay between biological and psychological factors in determining vulnerability to mental disorder. *Psychoanalytic Psychotherapy, 23*, 236–247.

Hauser, S. T. (2008). The interplay of genes, environments, and psychoanalysis. *Journal of the American Psychoanalytic Association, 56*, 509–514.

Jacobson, E. (1959). The "exceptions" – An elaboration of Freud's character study. *Psychoanalytic Study of the Child, 14*, 135–153.

Kaufman, J., Yang, B. Z., Douglas-Palumberi, H., Grasso, D., Lipschitz, D., Houshyar, S., Krystal, J. H., & Gelernter, J. (2006). Brain-derived neurotrophic factor-5-HTTLPR gene interactions and environmental modifiers of depression in children. *Biological Psychiatry, 59*, 673–680.

Lakoff, G., & Johnson, M. (1999). *Philosophy in the flesh: The embodied mind and its challenge to Western thought.* New York, NY: Basic Books.

Leuzinger-Bohleber, M. (2015). Zum Dialog zwischen der Psychoanalyse und den Neurowissenschaften: Trauma, Embodiment und Gedächtnis. Eine Einleitung. In: Leuzinger-Bohleber, M., Fischmann, T., Böker, T., Northoff, G., & Solms, M. (Eds.): *Psychoanalyse und Neurowissenschaften. Chancen – Grenzen – Kontroversen. Reihe Psychoanalyse im 21. Jahrhundert.* Stuttgart: Kohlhammer.

Leuzinger-Bohleber, M., Henningsen, P., & Pfeifer, R. (2008). Die psychoanalytische Konzeptforschung zum Trauma und die Gedächtnisforschung der Embodied Cognitive Science. In: Leuzinger-Bohleber, M., Roth, G., & Buchheim, A. (Eds.): *Psychoanalyse – Neurobiologie – Trauma.* Stuttgart: Schattauer, 157–171.

Leuzinger-Bohleber, M., & Pfeifer, R. (1998). Erinnern in der Übertragung – Vergangenheit in der Gegenwart? Psychoanalyse und Embodied Cognitive Science im Dialog. *Psyche – Z Psychoanal, 52*, 884–919.

Leuzinger-Bohleber, M., & Pfeifer, R. (2002a). Remembering a depressive primary object: Memory in the dialogue between psychoanalysis and cognitive science. *The International Journal of Psychoanalysis, 83*, 3–33.

Leuzinger-Bohleber, M., & Pfeifer, R. (2002b). Embodied Cognitive Science und Psychoanalyse. Ein interdisziplinärer Dialog zum Gedächtnis. In: Giampieri-Deutsch, P. (Ed.): *Psychoanalyse im Dialog der Wissenschaften.* Stuttgart: Kohlhammer, 242–271.

Leuzinger-Bohleber, M., & Pfeifer, R. (2004). Lembrando de um objeto primário depressivo. [Remembering a depressive object, 2002]. *Livro Anual de Psicanálise, 18*, 11–39.

Leuzinger-Bohleber, M., & Pfeifer, R. (2006). Recollecting the past in the present: Memory in the dialogue between psychoanalysis and cognitive science. In: Mancia, M. (Ed.): *Psychoanalysis and neuroscience.* Milano: Springer, 63–97.

Leuzinger-Bohleber, M., & Pfeifer, R. (2013a). Embodiment: Den Körper in der Seele entdecken – Ein altes Problem und ein revolutionäres Konzept. In: Leuzinger-Bohleber, M., Emde, R. N., & Pfeifer, R. (Ed.): *Embodiment – ein innovatives Konzept für Entwicklungsforschung und Psychoanalyse.* Göttingen: Vandenhoeck & Ruprecht, 14–38.

Leuzinger-Bohleber. M., & Pfeifer, R. (2013b). Psychoanalyse und Embodied Cognitive Science in Zeiten revolutionären Umdenkens. Erinnern, Übertragung, therapeutische Veränderung und „Embodied metaphors". In: Leuzinger-Bohleber, M., Emde, R. N., & Pfeifer, R. (Eds.): *Embodiment – ein innovatives Konzept für Psychoanalyse und Entwicklungsforschung.* Göttingen: Vandenhoeck & Ruprecht, 39–74.

Levine, H. B., Reed, G. S., & Scarfone, D. (Eds.) (2013). *Unrepresented states and the construction of meaning: Clinical and theoretical contributions.* London: Karnac Books.

Milner, B., Squire, L. R., & Kandel, E. R. (1998). Cognitive neuroscience and the study of memory. *Neuron, 20*, 445–468.

Pfeifer, R., & Bongard, J. (2006). *How the body shapes the way we think: A new view of intelligence.* Cambridge: The MIT Press.

Pfeifer, R., & Leuzinger-Bohleber, M. (1986). Application of cognitive science methods to psychoanalysis: A case study and some theory. *International Review of Psycho-Analysis, 13*, 221–240.

Pfeifer, R., & Leuzinger-Bohleber, M. (1991). A dynamic view of emotion with an application to the classification of emotional disorders. *ifi des Instituts für Informatik der Universität Zürich*, Nr. 91, 92.

Pfeifer, R., & Leuzinger-Bohleber, M. (1992). A dynamic view of emotion with an application to the classification of emotional disorders. In: Leuzinger-Bohleber, M., Schneider, H., & Pfeifer, R. (Eds.): *"Two butterflies on my head . . ." Psychoanalysis in the interdisciplinary scientific dialogue*. New York: Springer, 215–245.

Pfeifer, R., & Leuzinger-Bohleber, M. (1995). "Ich warf mich voll Angst auf den Boden . . . " (Traumdetail einer Analysandin): Sensomotorische Aspekte des Gedächtnisses. In: Bareuther, H. u.a. (Red.): *Traum und Gedächtnis. Neuere Ergebnisse der psychologischen, psychoanalytischen und neurophysiologischen Forschung*. (Materialien aus dem Sigmund-Freud-Institut, 15). Münster: Lit Verlag, 55–95.

Suomi, S. (2010). *Trauma and epigenetics*. Unpublished Paper given at the 11th Joseph Sandler Research Conference: Persisting Shadows and Later Trauma. Frankfurt am Main, 7 February, 2010.

Suomi, S. J. (2011). Trauma und Epigenetik. In: Leuzinger-Bohleber, M., & Haubl, R. (Eds.): *Psychoanalyse: Interdisziplinär – International – Intergenerationell*. Göttingen: Vandenhoeck & Ruprecht, 295–315.

Part III

Clinical studies

Chapter 9

Trauma, dreams and transformations in psychoanalysis

Combining clinical and extra-clinical research in an EEG/fMRI study

Tamara Fischmann, Michael Russ,
Margerete Schoett, Marianne Leuzinger-Bohleber

FRANKFURT

Introduction[1]

As mentioned in the introduction of the present volume, a growing number of research groups throughout the world have apparently begun to realize that the neurosciences and psychoanalysis could benefit from each other in interesting ways. The neurosciences are now equipped with objective, precise methods for verifying hypotheses on human behavior, while psychoanalysis, based on its rich experience with patients and its unique method of field research, has developed a variety of different models in order to conceptualize the multi-layered and complex observations that derive from the psychoanalytic situation and to test them by means of its specific form of empirical research, namely, clinical psychoanalytical research. The explanatory models and insights developed by psychoanalysis can also be of interest to neuroscientists and raise specific research questions.

At the Sigmund Freud Institute, we consider the results of the dialogue between psychoanalysis and the neurosciences in various ways:

a) As an interdisciplinary framework for reflecting on changes in psychoanalyses and psychoanalytic treatments in clinical papers
b) In theoretical papers discussing different topics of contemporary psychoanalysis (e.g., unconscious fantasies, memory, trauma, symbolization and mentalization)
c) As a theoretical background in the conceptualization of our large empirical studies in the field of psychotherapy research (e.g., the LAC Depression Study) and the projects on early prevention (the EVA Study, the FIRST STEP project etc.)
d) In clinical and empirical studies on the outcome of psychoanalyses and psychoanalytic long-term treatments.

In this chapter, we give a summary of an innovative attempt to combine clinical psychoanalytical studies on changes in the manifest dreams of an analysand treated as part of the LAC depression study and the extra-clinical investigation of the changes of dreams in the sleep laboratory. As discussed in the chapter on epistemological and methodological problems of research in contemporary psychoanalysis, contrasting findings in the genuine psychoanalytical context ("Junktim research", according to Freud) with results obtained by way of more "objective" instruments (investigations in the sleep laboratory) seems both interesting and challenging.

In the introduction, Eric Kandel's position was mentioned, namely, that in the future it will be possible to "prove" the effectiveness of psychoanalyses and psychoanalytic treatments, as well as to apply methods of contemporary neurosciences. As will be shown in the following section, many research groups have sought to realize this vision.

Neuroscientific studies on the outcome of psychoanalysis and psychoanalytic treatment: A short overview

Margerete Schoett, a scientist at the Sigmund Freud Institute, has collected the most important studies in this field in the following overview table:

Table 9.1 Examples of empirical testing of psychoanalytic/psychodynamic psychotherapy using neuroimaging methods

Buchheim, A., Viviani, R., Kessler, H., Kächele, H., Cierpka, M., Roth, G., ... & Taubner, S. (2012)

Objective: Examination of the effects of psychoanalytic psychotherapy on the neural processing of attachment-relevant material in chronic depression.

Patient sample: $N = 31$ (N = 15 chronically depressed (DSM-IV), outpatients, N = 16 healthy controls

Methods: *Intervention:* psychoanalytic psychotherapy (15 month: 90–210 h, 2–4 × weekly sessions); *fMRI-stimuli:* Attachment relevant and not attachment relevant pictures from the *Adult Attachment Projective. Neuroimaging:* fMRI (3-T SIEMENS Magnetom Allegra); *Points of measurement:* pre post

Results: *fMRI:* Assimilation of BOLD activity in patients and healthy controls in the course of the treatment: amygdala (L), anterior hippocampus (BA36), vACC (BA25): Significant correlation with symptomatic burden (GSI und BDI [$p > 0.05$]), medial PFC (BA8–9)

Discussion: Assimilation in brain areas previously associated with depression, anxiety, emotional (dys-) regulation and therapeutic change in patient sample who underwent psychodynamic therapy is discussed to suggest a reduced use of defense mechanisms such as suppression and avoidance.

De Greck, M., Bölter, A.F., Lehmann, L., Ulrich, C., Stockum, E., Enzi, B., & Northoff, G. (2013)

Objective: Examination of the effects of a psychodynamic psychotherapy on neural correlates of empathy and emotional memory in patients with somatoform disorder.

Patient sample: N = 30 (N = 15 inpatients with somatoform disorder (DSM-IV), partially medicated; N = 15 healthy controls (age-matched)

Methods: *Intervention:* multimodal psychodynamic psychotherapy (inpatient setting, 38–80 days); *fMRI-Stimuli:* "Japanese and Caucasian Facial Expressions of Emotion" – battery (JACFEE) and the "Japanese and Caucasian Neutral Faces" – battery (JACNeuF); *Neuroimaging:* 1.5T MR Scanner (General Electric Sigma Horizon), *points of measurement:* pre post (average of 58 days)

Results: *fMRI:* Normalization of former diminished modulation of BOLD response after the treatment in patient sample (in reaction to "anger"): parahippocampal gyrus, putamen (L), postcentral gyrus (L), superior temporal gyrus (L), parahippocampal gyrus, posterior insula (L), cerebellum (L); (decrease in BOLD activity correlated with symptomatic burden)

Discussion: The parahippocampal gyrus is associated with autobiographic, emotional memory. The increased activity in this area is explained by the authors as improved self-perception, which is obtained through psychodynamic psychotherapy. The recognition of emotional states of others can be improved through insight into one's own emotional processes, and thereby be credited as the basis for the improvement of alexithymia and somatic symptoms.

Beutel, M.E., Stark, R., Pan, H., Silbersweig, D., & Dietrich, S. (2010); Beutel, M.E., Stark, R., Pan, H., Silbersweig, D.A., & Dietrich, S. (2012)

Objective: Examination of the effects of a psychodynamic short-term treatment on the neural processing of emotional response inhibition in patients with panic disorder.

Patient sample: N = 27 (N = 9 inpatients with panic disorder (ICD-10), N = 18 healthy controls

Methods: *Intervention:* multimodal, manualized, panic-focused psychodynamic short-term therapy (inpatient setting, 4 weeks); *fMRI-Paradigm:* Emotional, language based go-/no-go-task (valence: neutral, positive, negative); *Neuroimaging:* fMRI (1,5-T SIEMENS Magnetom Symphony)

Results: Assimilation of BOLD activity in patients and healthy controls in the course of the treatment: *"Emotion":* Lateral PFC ↓, supplementary motor area ↑ (in positive and negative emotional stimuli), hippocampus (L) (in negative emotional stimuli). *"Inhibition"* (go vs no-go): amygdala (L) ↑, hippocampus (L) ↑, ventrolateral PFC (L) ↓, lateral OFC (L) ↓. Post treatment patients show increased BOLD activity compared to healthy control in the middle temporal gyrus (emotional context) and Caudate (inhibitory context).

Discussion: According to the authors, the anticipated decrease in the BOLD response in the area of the hippocampus over the course of the therapy mirrors the enhanced handling on negative events, which is also shown in behavioral results. This result supports the assumption of a fronto-limbic network, which participates in emotion regulation in threatening situations. The patterns found in the inhibition task mirror the disturbed behavioral control of patients, which signals either a dysfunction within the DLPFC or a hippocampal hyper activity.

Table 9.2 Examples of ongoing studies examining the efficacy of psychoanalytic/psychody-
namic psychotherapy using neuro imaging methods

The Frankfurter-EEG-fMRI-Depression-Study (FRED)

**Fischmann, T., Russ, M. O., & Leuzinger-Bohleber, M. (2013), Fischmann, T.,
Russ, M., Baehr, T., Stirn, A., & Leuzinger-Bohleber, M. (2012)**

Objective: Examination of the effects of a psychotherapeutic long-term treatment
(psychoanalysis and cognitive behavioral therapy) on the neural reaction to 1. conflict
relevant, individualized stimuli (see Kessler et al., 2011) and 2. memory of individualized
dream material.

Patient sample: N = 33 (N = 15 chronic depressed, out patients; N = 18 healthy controls)

Methods: *Intervention:* Long-term psychotherapy (PSA, CBT), *fMRI Paradigm:* conflict
relevant sentences (from the *Operationalized Psychodynamic* Diagnostics) and neutral
sentences; dream material (single words) and neutral single words; *Neuroimaging:* fMRI
(3-T SIEMENS Magnetom Allegra); *Points of measurement:* begin of psychotherapeutic
treatment (T1), 7 month (T2) and 15 month (T3) after beginning of treatment

Results (single case analysis): differences in activation in reaction to dream words vs.
neutral word vanish in the course of the treatment. Similar tendencies can be seen in
reaction to the conflict related sentences vs. the neutral sentence.

Discussion: The assimilation of neural pattern of reaction to emotional material is
discussed as a reflection of an enhanced processing of conflictuous material in the
course of the psychotherapy. A possible validation of these results and according brain
regions can be conducted in a group comparison of the full sample.

**Böker, H. Himmighofen, H., Richter, A., Ernst, J., Bohleber, L., Hofmann, E., . . . &
Northoff, G. (2013)**

Objective: The effectiveness of an outpatient psychoanalytic treatment of depressed
patients will be assessed with regards to psychodynamic, behavioural and neural change.
The fMRI assessment is currently being conducted using the "Interpersonal relations
picture set (IRPS)".

**Gawrysiak, M. J., Swan, S. A., Nicholas, C., Rogers, B. P., Dougherty, J. H., &
Hopko, D. R. (2013)**

Objective: Examination of the effects of a pragmatic psychodynamic psychotherapy on
neural responses to positive and negative stimuli in a patient with breast cancer (single
case study). *fMRI-Stimuli:* Individualized sequences of music (joyful, neutral). *Results and
discussion:* Increased activation of the VmPFC and oPFC after the treatment is discussed
as an increased capacity to experience pleasure.

Further studies examining psychoanalytic concepts: e.g. Atmaca et al. (2011),
Fan et al. (2011), Gerber & Peterson (2006), Kehyayan et al. (2013), Schmeing
et al. (2013) und Siegel & Peterson (2012).

See Abbass et al. (2014) for a systematic review of psychodynamic psychotherapy neuroimaging studies.

Böker & Seifritz (2012) give the following summary:

Ultimately, we still do not know how substantial the outcome variance for
the effect of psychotherapy by way of a neurobiological perspective will be.

Whereas the answer to immediate leading research has, to date, only been approximate in its initial approach, through inspired perspectives and heuristics, the findings in neuroscientific research have made major contributions to the understanding of mechanisms of action and, no less, to the success of a therapy [. . .]

In sum, neurobiological research will make essential contribution in the future to the discovery of mechanisms of action in specific psychotherapeutic interventions for the identification of predicators of responsiveness in psychotherapy (above all, also in comparison to psychopharmacotherapy) and to obtaining risk indicators for relapse probability

(p. 632).

To illustrate these authors' estimations, we present one of our own studies – the so-called FRED Study.

Changes of dreams: A genuine psychoanalytical indicator for transformations in psychoanalysis with traumatized, chronically depressed patients

As we have discussed in previous papers, within the transference relationship with the analyst it is inevitable to revive the traumatic experience and understand its biographical ("historical") dimension in detail when dealing with severely traumatized, depressive patients (Fischmann, Leuzinger-Bohleber, & Kächele, 2012; Leuzinger-Bohleber, 2015). Only then does trauma in its enclosed, psychic existence become accessible to therapeutic work: the unutterable horror is linked to visualizations, metaphors and eventually to verbalizations. Dreams are often helpful in this context: with many analysands, they convey indicators for an incipient symbolization process and conclusively the onset of "meaning giving" therapeutic coping with the traumatization.

In dream research, dreaming is described as a thought-process where our inner system is engaged to process information (Dewan, 1970). Inner (cognitive) models are constantly being modified in coordination with what is perceived. In contrast to dreaming, reactions to our environment are immediate during the waking state, thus enabling information consolidation into memory only limited by capacity restrictions of the system itself. Nevertheless, consolidation processes do continue during sleep in an "off-line" modus, thus enabling integration into long-term memory here as well (Fosshage, 2007; Stickgold, Hobson, Fosse, & Fosse, 2001).

According to Moser and von Zeppelin (1996)[2] – psychoanalysts and dream researchers at the same time – so-called dream complexes activated by current events process the entirety of information deriving from unsolved conflicts and traumatic situations while dreaming. The dream searches for solutions or rather best possible adaptations for these dream complexes. A dream, which is usually pictorial, consists of at least one situation produced by a "dream-organizer". Dream-organization may be considered, according to Moser, as a bundle of affective-cognitive procedures, generating a micro-world – the dream – and controlling its course of action. Within this system, the "dream-complex" is a template facilitating dream organization.

Thus, it may be assumed that a "dream-complex" originates from one or more complexes stored in long-term-memory, rooted in conflictuous and/or trauma-tizing experiences, which found their condensates in introjects. These introjects are closely related to triggering stimuli from the outside world and structurally similar to stored situations of the complex. The search for solution of the complex is governed by the need for security and the wish for involvement, i.e., the security-principle and the involvement-principle, managing the dream-organization. Wishes within these complexes are links between self- and object-models and RIGs (i.e., Representation Interaction Generalized), which are accompanied by con-victions and a hope for wish fulfillment. Conflictuous complexes are areas of bundled wishes, RIGs and self- and object-models with a repetitive character, thus creating areas of unbound affective information. Affects within such an area are interconnected by k-lines, which are blocked and therefore not locatable. In order to solve these conflictuous complexes, it is necessary to retrieve this affective information into a relational reality in order to make them come alive and locat-able (cf. Figure 9.1). This is attempted in dreams, their function being the search for a solution of the complex. This search for a solution within a dream again is governed by the above-mentioned security-principle and involvement-principle. The following illustration may serve as an elucidation of this model.

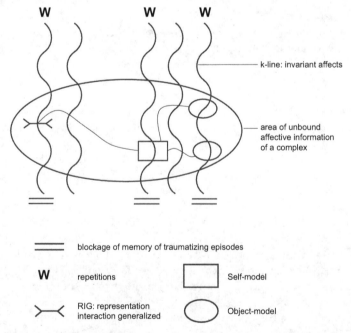

Figure 9.1

The Frankfurt fMRI/EEG depression study (FRED study)[3]

Could the above-mentioned "meaning giving" psychoanalytic processes also become a part of studies based on the new possibilities of neuroimaging studies? As already mentioned: Eric Kandel is convinced that psychoanalysis must apply these new methods in order to prove neurobiologically the sustainability of its results (Kandel, 2009 and verbal accounts). Otherwise, it will vanish from the world of science and be remembered only as a historical relic, a memory attesting to Sigmund Freud's enlightening spirit in the 20th century. In society, it will be marginalized, even though to this day it is the most exciting and complex theory of the human spirit. Although many scientific theoretical and philosophical arguments could be imposed against this point of view, Kandel's assessment is surely correct in the sense that proving the sustainability of psychoanalysis and psychoanalytic therapies with neurobiological methods such as fMRI or EEGs would immediately enhance the acceptance of psychoanalytical procedures within the world of medicine.

Keeping this in mind, we perceived the opportunity of an institutional cooperation with the Max Planck Institute for Brain Research in Frankfurt, a. M. – in order to additionally examine a number of our chronically depressed patients in our LAC study[4] with fMRI and EEGs – as an enormous chance. The FRED study[5] is designed as a replication of the Hanse-Neuropsychoanalysis Study (see Buchheim et al., 2012). The already tested methods of the Hanse-Neuropsychoanalysis Study are implemented here in combination with our sleep-dream-research. This is an ongoing study; therefore, we can only give an account of our attempts to correlate psychoanalytic and neuroscientific methods within this study by presenting a single case study.

FRED[6] (Frankfurt fMRI/EEG Depression Study) is an example of a fruitful combination of the two domains – psychoanalysis and neurosciences. This very ambitious project currently conducted at the Sigmund Freud Institut (SFI) and BIC (Brain Imaging Centre) in cooperation with the MPIH Frankfurt (Max Planck Institute for brain research)[7] seeks to examine changes of brain functions in chronic depressed patients after long-term-therapies, aiming to find multi-modal-neurobiological changes in the course of psychotherapies.

When looking at depression from a brain-physiological angle, some interesting findings have been put forth: for instance, that depression is related to a neurotransmitter disorder, or a frontal lobe dysfunction (cf. Belmaker & Agam, 2008; Caspi et al., 2003; Risch et al., 2009). Northoff and & Hayes (2011) have convincingly put forth that the so-called reward system is disturbed in depression and that there is evidence that deep brain-stimulation can improve severe depression (also see Solms & Panksepp, 2012).

But despite all these findings, no distinct brain-physiological marker for depression has been found so far. It was therefore deemed plausible to pose the research question of whether changes in the course of therapy have brain-physiological correlates, which we are currently investigating in FRED.

Generally speaking, psychotherapists – especially psychoanalysts – work with what can be remembered and with recurring – usually dysfunctional – behaviors and experiences. The assumption is that this has precipitations within the brain, like synapse configuration, priming, axonal budding and more, giving ground to the hypotheses of FRED that (1) psychotherapy is a process of change in encoding conditions of memory and (2) elements of memories can be depicted in fMRI by a recognition experiment of memories related to an underlying conflict. This constitutes the neuro-psychoanalytic aspect of the FRED study, of which some preliminary results will be given in the following. Another aspect of change relevant for the study is that of clinical change found in dreams in the course of psychotherapy. The analysis of dreams with the specific method of Moser and von Zeppelin (1996) – as will be outlined – enables the comparison of empirically elicited findings with clinically reported ones from the therapist.

We will illustrate in the following – in an attempt to combine clinical and extra-clinical (experimental) research – a single case taken from the LAC depression study.[8] We have reported the changes of dreams of a severely traumatized, chronically depressed patient as one indicator for therapeutic changes from a clinical perspective in another paper (Leuzinger-Bohleber, 2013, chapter 5.1). The same patient, part of a subsample of the 408 chronically depressed patients recruited in the LAC depression study, was willing to spend the necessary two nights in the sleep laboratory of the Sigmund Freud Institute, since investigating his severe sleeping disturbances was of clinical importance. The patient's EEG data elicited indeed showed pathological sleep patterns so that he had to be referred to a medical expert for sleeping disturbances. As a result of this "therapeutic intervention" in the sleep laboratory, we were able to compare his dreams obtained in the laboratory with those reported in psychoanalysis, giving us the unique opportunity to compare changes in dreams obtained "naturalistically" in psychoanalytic treatment with those dreams collected in the frame of an experimental sleep laboratory.

In this paper, we can give only a short overview of a model of the generation of dreams developed by Moser and von Zeppelin (1996), which is the theoretical background for our hypotheses looking at changes of dreams in depressed patients and applying a coding system for investigating the manifest dream content based on this model. In the following part of this chapter, we relate these data to neurophysiological measures associated to his dreams elicited from this patient within the FRED study. We then focus on contrasting the experimental findings of the changes in dreams from the sleep laboratory with those reported in psychoanalysis regarding this single case.

Design

The FRED study investigates the hypotheses that (1) psychotherapy is a process of change in encoding conditions of memory and 2) change in memory encoding will precipitate change in brain activation patterns detectable in fMRI scanning. We hypothesized that changes in memory processing during the psychotherapy will impact the processing of trauma-related memories. In the FRED study, we aimed at highlighting changes in memory processing during the psychotherapy, scanning depressed patients during a recognition task involving stimuli related to an underlying conflict, at the beginning of the psychotherapy and 7 and 15 months later. With such a paradigm, we predicted that the contrast [recognition of trauma-related words/sentences vs. control conditions] will highlight brain regions known to be involved in processing self-relatedness and the retrieval of autobiographical memory and/or emotional memory (emotional memory; amygdala, hippocampus, prefrontal cortex, see Buchanan, 2007; episodic memory and processing self-relatedness: medial prefrontal cortex, parietal cortex, temporal poles, see Legrand & Ruby, 2009; autobiographical memory: medial frontal cortex and hippocampus, see Maguire et al., 2001) and that such a pattern of activation will change across time and in the course of psychotherapy. Our predictions for the session effects are as follows: In successfully treated psychotherapy subjects, the patterns of activation are changing from Time 1 to Time 3, therefore producing significant session effects in statistical terms; unfortunately, this expected change may also be caused by simple forgetting and "blurring," not solely due to an effect of psychotherapeutic interventions. This is especially true for the dream-word experiment. Therefore, a control group is needed to observe the "normal" time course in non-treated subjects. Above that, the experimental procedure should take into account forgetting and blurring in the follow-up sessions by appropriate subject instructions (see below), and the activation patterns remain constant over time. For this investigation, chronically depressed patients were recruited with whom an Operationalized-Psychodynamic-Diagnostics-Interview (OPD-Interview; OPD-Task-Force, 2008) concentrating on axis II (relational) and a dream-interview (see Figure 2 below) were conducted in a first diagnostic phase. From these two interviews, the stimuli for the fMRI-scanning are created individually for each patient because they are considered to be good triggers to elicit memory of an underlying conflict. Dream-Words are taken from a significant dream elicited in the dream interview and dysfunctional sentences taken from the OPD-Interview are formulated. Measurements are taken at three different time points revealing changes in activation-patterns occurring during the *course of therapy*. At T1, OPD-Sentences and Dream-Words were elicited and patients spent two nights in the sleep laboratory, where verbal Dream-Reports were collected in the second night after awakenings from REM211 to REM312 and in the morning. Finally the fMRI-Experiment was conducted using the OPD-Sentences and Dream-Words collected previously. At T2 and T3 EEG, Sleep Lab data and fMRI data were collected in the same manner using OPD-Sentences and Dream-Words from T1.

Participants

At present, 16 patients with recurrent major depressive disorders (Major Depression, Dysthymia, Double Depression for more than 24 months; Quick Inventory of Depressive Symptoms (QIDS) > 9 [scale range 0–27, clinical cut-off >

6]; Beck Depression Inventory (BDI) > 17 [scale range 0–63, clinical cut-off: > 9]; age: $M = 43$, range 23–58 years, $SD = 11.57$) take part in the FRED study. Patients of the FRED study were recruited at the Sigmund Freud Institute's outpatients department from the LAC Depression Study (Leuzinger-Bohleber, 2013) conducted there, diagnosed by trained clinicians using the Structured Clinical Interviews I and II for DMS-IV Diagnosis (German version; 1998). Exclusion criteria were other psychiatric conditions as main diagnosis, substance abuse, significant medical or neurological conditions (including medical causes of depression), psychotropic medication, and eye problems. All participants were right-handed. In both groups, depression severity and general symptoms of psychopathology were assessed using the Beck Depression Inventory (BDI, Hautzinger, Keller, & Kühner, 2006 [1995]) and the revised Symptom Check List (SCL-90-R, Franke & Derogatis, 2002), respectively. The control-group (13 females) consists of 18 healthy volunteers matched in age ($M = 34$, range 22–65 years, $SD = 14.59$). All participants gave written informed consent.

fMRI stimuli

Dream stimuli

To gather individualized and personally relevant stimuli relating to dreams, dream interviews were performed with each subject Thirty Dream-Words from personally significant dreams were extracted together with the subject, paying close attention that they reflect the narrated dreams as concisely as possible and as close to the dream experience as possible. The dream interviews were conducted by a trained clinician (TF) and audiotaped. The participants were asked to memorize these words one day prior to the fMRI-investigation. These 30 Dream-Words served as stimuli during the fMRI-session (dream experiment). The control condition comprised 30 accordant words taken out of a subjectively neutral "everyday life-story," which had no specific meaning for the individual patient and was taken out from a travel report in a newspaper article describing a camping vacation. They were matched in length and frequency of the words in the native language of the patient (Neutral-Words). The participant was instructed to memorize these words as well one day prior to fMRI-scanning. These 30 Neutral-Words served as stimuli during the fMRI-session (neutral condition). All words were presented in German.

Procedure

Four to six weeks prior to fMRI assessment, the participant was interviewed (SCID I+II, OPD), completed questionnaires (BDI, SCL-90-R) and gave written consent to participation. At the beginning of the fMRI session and prior to scanning, the subject was presented with his individual Dream-Words and asked whether these words adequately represented his significant dream. To control for state affectivity, the participant filled out the German version of the Positive and Negative Affect Schedule (PANAS) before entering the scanner. After scanning, a second PANAS was completed together with a questionnaire assessing on a 7-point Likert scale the extent to which the Dream-Words caused emotional arousal.

fMRI experiment

fMRI was performed using a 3.0 − Tesla head − scanner (Magnetom Allegra, SIEMENS, Erlangen, Germany) with a 4-channel-head coil applying an EPI mosaic sequence (FA = 90°, TE = 30 ms, matrix 64 × 64, interleaved acquisition, voxelsize 3 × 3 × 3 mm, 1.5 mm gap, 30 transverse slices covering the whole brain, T → C = −30°), obtaining a series (370 measurements) of blood-oxygenation-sensitive echoplanar image volumes every 2s.

Psychoanalytic dream material

Clinical case: Dream series from psychoanalytic sessions and from dream laboratory

BIOGRAPHY AND TRAUMA HISTORY[9]

The patient explained in the assessment interviews that he had been suffering from severe depression for the last 25 years, and that he came to our Institute because, after the last depressive breakdown, he had submitted an application for retirement pension. The doctor who assessed his application concluded that he did not require a pension, but an "intelligent psychoanalysis" − initially a response Mr. P. found highly insulting. He felt that he had not been taken seriously, especially his substantial physical symptoms: the unbearable pains covering his entire body, his acute eating disorders as well as his suicidal tendencies. Furthermore, the patient suffered from severe sleeping disorders. Often, he is unable to sleep at all. As a rule, he wakes up after one-and-a-half hours, or after three hours at the most. He feels physically exhausted and is barely able to concentrate his mind on anything.

Mr. P. had already undergone several unsuccessful attempts at therapy, including behavioral therapy, Gestalt Therapy, "body therapy" as well as several inpatient treatments in psychiatric and psychosomatic clinics. He is among the group of patients that for the most part seem unable to respond to psychotropic drugs, and whose relapses occur at ever-shorter intervals and with increasing intensity. After many consultations with various psychiatrists and neurologists, he then discovered that solely Lyrica[10] enabled him more or less to deal with his states of physical stress and his anxiety attacks.

The patient is an only child. One of the known details about his early history is that he was a "cry-baby". When he was four years old, Mr. P.'s mother fell seriously ill. W. was admitted to a convalescent home for children, evidently founded on authoritarian, inhumane educational principles reminiscent of National Socialist ethos. Just how traumatic an experience this stay in a home was is something that became transparent during psychoanalysis. Mr. P.'s first childhood memories revolve around the following event: he recalls how his father took him by the hand and led him out of the home. He also recalls how a girl had been forced to eat her own vomit.

Mr. P. experienced two further separations from his ill mother, but these incidents had proven less traumatic since he had been taken in by relatives.

In spite of the dissociative states following the traumatic separations and his social isolation, P. was a good pupil, who went on to complete his first apprenticeship training and later his university studies. During adolescence, he had a psychosomatic breakdown, which the parents diagnosed as a "crisis in growing up". At the age of 15 years, he met his first girlfriend. His condition improved. At the age of 22, he ended the relationship with his first girlfriend because he fell in love with another woman. Although the separation ran in his favor, he reacted very severely to it. Although he had also initiated the separation from his second girlfriend, he suffered for weeks due to the separation. After entering another relationship, he was dramatically overcome by a nervous breakdown during a party held by his new girlfriend: he had to be taken to hospital due to hyper-ventilation (panic attacks).

As already mentioned: Mr. P. had undergone several psychotherapies. Although all his therapies alleviated him, "neither of them cured him". His depressions became worse and worse until they became chronic.

Clinical material: Dream series elicited in psychoanalytic treatment[11]

CLINICAL DREAM 1: FIRST YEAR OF TREATMENT

> I catch sight of a man lying at the side of the road severely wounded – his intestines are spewing out, and everything is saturated in blood. . . . A helicopter appears. It is unclear as to whether the man is still being shot at, or whether one should go to his aid. Someone appears claiming that the man now has passed away. I notice that the man is still alive and he really does open his eyes and enquires; why is nobody helping me? The woman hands him a lid of a saucepan, which he should hold over his open wound . . . I then wake up riveted by panic. . . .
>
> (Leuzinger-Bohleber, 2012, p. 66/67)

CLINICAL DREAM 2: THIRD YEAR OF TREATMENT

> I am gazing at a group of people all smeared with clay and who are working together on the outer shell of a house. A cold wind blows – the work is torturous, arduous, and barely tolerable. And yet, in the dream I have a certain sense that the men will succeed: at some

point the house will be built and provide them with a warm home. I then turn to my wife and say: "You see, we can do it – one just has to stay together. . . .

(Leuzinger-Bohleber, 2012, p. 70/71)

Laboratory material: Dream series elicited in the dream laboratory[12]

LABORATORY DREAM 1 – T1 (END OF FIRST YEAR OF TREATMENT)

I am standing on a bridge over a dam. To my right and left are steep slopes – mountains (S1). There is a landslide. I see the slope and an entire house approaching me very fast, rapidly sliding rushing towards me (S2). I think to myself, that I will not be able to escape it (/C.P./). I am running (S3) and am amazed at how fast I can run (/C.P./). I succeed to save myself from the rapidly descending house (S3). I am in safety at the edge of this bridge (S4).

DREAM 2 – T1 (END OF FIRST YEAR OF TREATMENT)

There are more people in the room. I wear this cap. You three are here and somebody else, who will come up right after me. He has a lot of pretensions. It is morning and I wake up. I wear this cap and am hooked up to all those cables (S1). It is lively around me and you and the others are walking around and talk to each other. I pick up on you whispering and being annoyed at someone or making fun of him. The one that you are annoyed with is in the room as well, and he is supposed to put the cap on after me (S2). I remember that I have seen him once before in front of the door of my analyst (S3). He is here in the room and constantly poses pretensions. Everything should be the way he wants it. You are annoyed that you have to fulfil these wishes (S4). I think to myself: "Just take it easy" (/C.P./).

LABORATORY DREAM 3 – T2 (SECOND YEAR OF TREATMENT)

A Formula-1 race with Michael Schumacher (S1). Directly after the race he flies to Germany, in order to inaugurate a bridge (S2). Totally bonkers (/C.P./). He is in Germany and inaugurates the bridge (S3). He speaks with a few people sitting at a table. I am sitting at the table next to it and observe him and the others in debate (S4). How do I come up with something like this? (/C.P./)

LABORATORY DREAM 4 – T2 (SECOND YEAR OF TREATMENT)

I am on my way with my little son. Other children and adults are with us. A boy is there too, who has something against my son. It is summer. It is warm. We are walking along the banks of a river (S1). We want to buy a wagon or trailer (S2). The children are of different ages. One boy is already 11 or 12 years old. This boy is on edge, because the other children and also my son are so young and they cannot do what he wants them to do, because they are too small for this (S3). Then my mother appears. She sews a button back onto my shirt (S4). I don't know how this fits in (/C.P./). I say: "Just leave this stupid button alone." This unnerves me (S5). I am there to oversee everything. A woman is there too. She is the mother of that boy (S1).

178 Tamara Fischmann et al.

Data analysis

fMRI data analysis

The functional data was be analyzed as "event related" using the SPM99 soft-
ware from the Wellcome Department of Cognitive Neurology, London, UK,
running under Unix and Matlab 5.3 (Mathworks Inc., Sherborn, MA). An event
was defined by the beginning of the visual presentation of an action description.
All images were realigned (for motion correction), normalized into a standard
space (MNI template, Montreal Neurological Institute), and smoothed with
a 6-mm full-width-at-half-maximum Gaussian kernel. Low-frequency fluctuations were removed by setting a high-pass filter with 170 s cut-off, and a
low-pass filter was set to hemodynamic response function. Post hoc, the events
were assigned to their corresponding image acquisition, and these images were
then grouped under the appropriate experimental condition. For each subject, a
fixed-effect model (within the General Linear Model approach of SPM99) was
estimated, and the main condition effects of dreamwords>neutral words and
neutral words>dreamwords were calculated based only on events for which the
following response was correct. Intersubject variability was taken into account
by a subsequent random effects analysis of the resulting four t-contrast images
using a multisubject t-test model. Only activations significant at p<0.001 (cor-
rected for multi comparisons within a volume of 10 mm radius around the
center of each cluster) are reported.

Psychoanalytical-clinical dream analysis

Dreams were analyzed working with the dream associations in the psychoanalytical sessions (see e.g. Leuzinger-Bohleber, 2012, 2015).

Dream-coding-analysis (Moser & von Zeppelin)

The dream-coding-method of Moser and von Zeppelin (1996) is an evaluating
system used to analyse the dream material based on their model of cognitive-
affect regulation using formal criteria to investigate manifest dream-content
and its changing structures (for a more detailed description cf. Fischmann et al.,
2012).

For our purpose here, it suffices to know that according to Moser and von
Zeppelin the regulating processes of dream-organization are based on:

1   Positioning elements into the dream-world,
2   Monitoring the dream activity,
3   A working-memory containing (affective feedback-) information of each
    dream-situation and its consequences, and
4   Regulating procedures responsible for changes.

The coding system defines formal criteria and structures of a dream discernible within the manifest dream narrative elucidating affect-regulation processes of the dream: number of situations, type of places and social settings named in a dream (descriptions, attributes), objects occurring (descriptions, attributes), placement, movement, interactions of objects as well as the question of whether the dreamer himself was involved in interactions, or if he remains spectator.

As mentioned above, two principles of affect-regulation are assumed: (1) the security-principle and (2) the involvement-principle, which can be discriminated by the "positioning" of elements within the dream and through "interactions" taking place. Common to both principles is their ruling by negative and positive affects, i.e., anxiety is the motor for an enlargement of security also regulating involvement by for instance breaking off interactions and generating a new situation. It is assumed that problem-solving can take place and be tested only in interaction; therefore, the dream tends towards interaction.

It is assumed that the more elements used in a dream scene, the more possibilities are available for the dreamer to regulate his affects and contents processed in the dream. If the dream omits "interactions," security aspects are dominant.

Results

fMRI

The patient Mr. P. confronted with Dream-Words in contrast to neutral words (Dream-Words>neutral words) taken from the first year of treatment (T1) in comparison to those of year 2 (T2) showed differential activation of the Precuneus, the Prefrontal Cortex and the parietal lobe. Activations in these brain areas that are known to be significant to emotional processing of the self (experience of self-agency) largely disappeared in T2 as well as MFC activation an area postulated to serve as an online detector of information processing conflict (Botvinick, Cohen, & Carter, 2004) but also has a regulative control function for affective signals (Critchley, 2003; Matsumoto, Suzuki, & Tanaka, 2003; Posner & DiGirolamo, 1998; Roelofs, van Turennout, & Coles, 2006; Stuphorn & Schall, 2006, cf. Fig. 2).

Psychoanalytic dream evaluation

Clinical dream 1 reported here is a typical dream of a severely traumatized person where the patient himself is in a position of an observer: the dream subject is in an extreme life threatening situation, completely helpless, in unbearable pain and not being helped by anyone. In clinical dream 2 (two years later) the patient is the active dreamer, observing a situation which still is painful but with hope that "something can be done" in order to overcome a hopeless situation.

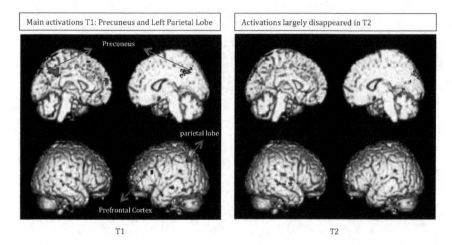

Figure 9.2 T1 and T2 comparison of Dream-Word-recognition in a single case

Dream-coding-analysis (Moser & von Zeppelin)

Laboratory Dream 1 (T1) after being subdivided in its elements and given a coding in the respective column of either the positioning field (PF), the field of trajectories (LTM) or the interaction field (IAF) reveals the following:

The first situation of this dream (S1) is coined by the security principle – many cognitive elements are simply being placed. But it also hosts a multitude of involvement potential as many attributes are being named for the elements placed. In the second situation (S2), a first attempt is made to deal with this potential – albeit rather limited (LTM) – but again increasing potentiality by adding another attribute (ATTR). As a result, the affectivity seems to increase to such an extent that the dream-scene has to be interrupted by a comment (/C.P./). In S3, the dreamer finally succeeds to invoke a *"successful"* interaction between the threatening cognitive element (CEU_3 (house)) and himself (SP). Initially, this leads to another interrupt: the dreamer is surprised by his capabilities and finally in S4 a cathartic self-changing interaction is conjured up: he is in safety.

In summary, the patient describes a threatening situation, which is initially determined by the security-principle. The relatively sophisticated description of the first scene bears potential, which the dreamer makes full use of in order to regulate the threatening affects. The wish to "bring himself to safety" is fulfilled in this dream.

Laboratory dream 2 (T1) shows characteristics of a typical "laboratory dream". The patient uses the research situation as an opportunity to regulate his anxieties to be "too pretentious". He projects this onto an object processor (OP) turning into an observer. Thus he successfully distances himself, which gives him the possibility to comprehend the events in more detail.

Table 9.3 Moser coding sheet of laboratory dream I (T I)

Sit.	PF	LTM	IAF
S I	SP PLACE (dam) CEU_1 (bridge) CEU_2 (mountains) ATTR (steep)		
S2	SP PLACE (slope) CEU_3 (house)	LTM CEU_2 I ATTR	
/C.P./			
S3	SP CEU_3 ATTR (rapidly sliding)		IR.C
/C.P./			
S4	SP CEU_1		IR.S

In the first situation (S1), there is a lot of potential to regulate affects – albeit still governed by the security principle. It includes a social setting (SOC SET), variable attributes (ATTR) and a lot of processors inviting action. By placing another patient (OP2) into the dream scene the dreamer (subject processor SP) gets the opportunity to take an observational stance, which leads to a movement (trajectory LTM) of the OP1 group of researchers in S2. S3 is regulated by the security principle and the potential existent in S2 (LTM) cannot be exploited in S3. In S4, finally this is achieved by an interaction just to disembogue in another interrupt. The affectivity of the situation increases to such an extent that it has to be interrupted: the dreamer cautions the object processor (OP2) or rather himself "to take it easy".

In laboratory dream 3 (T2), the dreamer again takes an observational stance. In contrast to the previous dream he succeeds in creating a connecting inter-action between two CEs, which is not interrupted but seamlessly leads into a displacement relation. Although this may still be considered to be a distancing maneuver from an affective event, it is not as marked as in the previous dream. The involvement principle is more distinct here than it had been previously. The interrupt at the end of the dream is not a rebuke as before, but rather expresses astonishment at what occupies his mind and a (conscious) approxima-tion to the underlying complex may be assumed.

The laboratory dream 4 (T2) is regulated from the beginning by the involve-ment principle, which alludes to an advanced therapeutic effect. In all successive situations more interactions appear: also connecting self-changing relations of subjects and objects. The self-processor (SP) himself is involved and does not have to retreat into an observing position anymore (no IR.D) – he faces his affects increasingly. After S4 triggers an interrupt, the dreamer (SP) interactively "fends this off" via verbal relation (V.R.). Thus we might assume that the dreamer progressively deals with the affects underlying the dream-complex in an interactive manner and is able to depict them in dream scenes. The affects are no longer isolated – which implies that previously isolated affects of the dream-complex can be integrated now.

In summary, the analysis shows that the patient's laboratory dreams from the end of his first year in therapy were still abundant with anxieties and yearning for security making him hesitant to get involved with others. Nevertheless, in these dreams he already showed potentials of what we might consider to be the result of the ongoing therapy, i.e., signs of involvement abilities, enabling him to make use of others by projecting his fears into them and testing if he could bear the rising anxieties involved in the actions he projected onto them while he still remained in a distant observer position. In the end, his fears of getting involved dominated, for he could not yet exploit these potentials. In the second year of analysis his dreams revealed his enhanced abilities to get involved (laboratory dream 4 is largely dominated by the involvement principle from the beginning) and were abundant with interactions with others portraying his increased ability to face his affects. Rising affectivity is now met; albeit still with an interrupt but followed by a dream scene of a different quality, he fends off his rising anxiety via a more aggressive response (V.R. S5 in laboratory dream 4) alluding to a progressive approach to the underlying (unconscious) conflict-laden dream-complex. Affects are no longer isolated but increasingly integrated into existing memory networks.

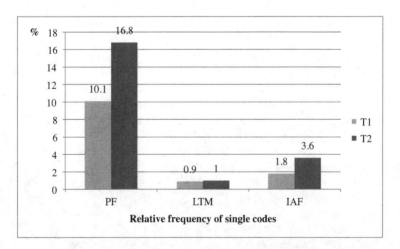

Figure 9.3 Relative frequency of single codes relativized by the average number of words

To illustrate these changes occurring from a more experimental perspective the following graph might deem to be helpful:

There is a clearly recognizable increase in potentials (PF) from T1 to T2, which can be exploited for interaction (IAF). The finding of an enhanced ability to get involved can be seen here by simply having a look at the manifest dreams.

Discussion

Via analysis of the manifest content of Mr. P's laboratory dream series, by applying a specific empirically validated method (Doell-Hentschker, 2008), we gained insights to his clinical improvement corresponding to the clinical analysis of changes in his manifest dreams as discussed by M. Leuzinger-Bohleber (2012), where she applied a specific technique (cf. Leuzinger-Bohleber, 1987, 1989, p.324), which is largely based on Moser's memory- and affect-regulation-models.

Comparing the clinical dreams from the beginning of psychoanalysis with those of the second year of analysis, she observed changes in the patterns of the relationships, where *the dream-subject shows better relationships with others* (e.g., people helping each other in the second reported dream). In the first dreams, the dream subject had mostly been alone: no one helped him and smoothed out his anxieties, panics and despair. *The range of actions of the dream-subject is increased* and *the emotional spectrum is enlarged* (in the dreams at the beginning of psychoanalysis we find only panic – in the third year of analysis, we also observe surprise, joy, satisfaction, humor and yet continuous anxieties and pain).

There is also a noted change in the dream atmosphere, with the *variety of affects as well as its increased intensities* and *manifest anxiety being less frequent*. The dreamer's *increased capability to perceive different and even contradictory emotions* become more and more visible. New feelings of anger, rage but also positive affections, tenderness and sexual attractions appear towards the second year of treatment. The dream subject is no longer a (distant) observer but plays an active part and is involved in intensive emotional interaction with others.

Furthermore, Leuzinger-Bohleber distinguished *clearer problem-solving strategies* (more successful than non-successful problem-solving) and a *broader range of different problem-solving strategies* from the manifest dreams. The dream-subject is no longer as flooded as in a traumatic situation in which he experiences extreme helplessness and lack of power. In his dreams he encounters objects willing to help and support him. This seems to be a very important indicator that the inner object world of the severely traumatized patient has changed (see Leuzinger-Bohleber, 2012, 2015).

The consistencies of the clinical and extra-clinical analyses are remarkable, which from a scientific perspective is of utmost relevance. But to be sure the clinical case study still provides greater psychodynamic relevant clinical and structural information, as the extra-clinical analysis suffices with the content of the manifest dreams and it has no further biographical data at hand with which results could be enhanced. The consistency in the finding on the other hand consolidated the reliability of the clinical case analysis, which substantiates the method of clinical case studies.

The fMRI results regarding changes in brain activation patterns when confronted with conflict-laden dream material (Dream-Words) elucidate the brain areas involved. These preliminary results point to the Precuneus and Left Parietal Lobe when conflict is still acute. The changes found clinically have thus found their neurobiological resonance and have been validated furthermore. This is further supported by the finding that the medial PFC – usually involved when conflict-laden information and control of affective signals is being processed – is no longer contrastingly active after one year of treatment.

Concluding remarks

By illustrating the differences between the clinical use of dreams as an indicator for changes in the inner (traumatic) object world in psychoanalyses and the systematic "scientific" investigation of laboratory dreams by the so-called Moser-method and by showing that these changes are also evident on a neurobiological level, these results give impressive evidence of how psychoanalytical treatment can be evaluated, enriching on an empirical, clinical and neurobiological base. The case report focused on the importance of the psychoanalytic context of dreams, the observation of transference and countertransference reactions, the associations of the patient and the analysand etc. necessary to unravel the unconscious meaning of the dream (Leuzinger-Bohleber, 2012). One great advantage of the psychoanalytical clinical "research" on dreams continues to be the understanding of the meaning of a dream in cooperation with the dreamer – the patient. His association, and conscious and unconscious reactions to a dream interpretation still are the criteria in order to evaluate the "truth" of the interpretation (see, e. g., Leuzinger-Bohleber, 1987, 1989, 2008). To make a long story short: the transformation of the unconscious world (like dreams) – and as products of it the maladaptive emotions, cognitions and behaviours ("symptoms") of the patient – still remain the final psychoanalytical criteria for a therapeutic "success" based on "true insights" of the patient in his unconscious functioning.

On the other hand, this kind of "truth" often remains fuzzy and subjective, at least in the eyes of the non-psychoanalytical, scientific community. Therefore, we have seized the unique possibility to analyse changes in the manifest dreams – gathered in a controlled, laboratory situation – by a theory driven, precise systematic coding system as the Moser method is further supported by its simultaneous neurobiological evidence. These analyses have a high reliability – and inter-subjectivity – and thus may convince independent observers or even critics.

Notes

1 This chapter is a modified version of former publications (see also: Fischmann, Russ, & Leuzinger-Bohleber, 2013, Fischmann et al., 2015a, 2015b).

2 Ulrich Moser and Ilka von Zeppelin are fully trained psychoanalysts who have been engaged in interdisciplinary research for decades. Ulrich Moser was professor for Clinical Psychology at the University of Zurich. Since the in the 1960s and 70s, he has been involved in modelling parts of psychoanalytic theories. By the means of computer simulation, he tested the logical and terminological consistency of psychoanalytic theories of defence and the generation of dreams. Based on this basic research on dreams, he developed his own model of the generation of dreaming as well as a coding system for investigating the manifest dreams. In this chapter, as well as in the chapter by Varvin, Fischmann, Jovic, Rosenbaum and Hau, the dream model and the coding system by Moser and v. Zeppelin are applied.

3 Another version of this paper was published by Fischmann, Russ, & Leuzinger-Bohleber (2013).

4 The LAC Study is an ongoing, large multicentric study comparing the outcomes of psychoanalytical and cognitive-behavioral longterm treatments of chronic depressed patients. Since 2007, over 400 of such patients have been recruited (see chapters 3; 5.1; Leuzinger-Bohleber et al., 2010, www.sigmund-freud-institut.de).

5 In September of 2007, we were very pleased to announce that the American foundation Hope for Depression had granted us financial support.

6 Funded by the Neuro-Psychoanalysis Society – HOPE (M. Solms, J. Panksepp et al.) and the Research Advisory Board of the IPA.

7 We are grateful to the BIC and MPIH (W. Singer, A. Stirn, M. Russ) and the Hanse-Neuro-Psychoanalysis-Study (A. Buchheim, H. Kächele, G. Roth, M. Cierpka et al.) and LAC-Depression Study for supporting us in an outstanding way.

8 In the ongoing large LAC depression-study we are comparing the short-term and long-term effects of long-term psychoanalytic and cognitive-behavioral psychotherapies. Up to this point, we have recruited around 380 chronically depressed patients in different research centres: Frankfurt a. M., Mainz, Berlin and Hamburg (participating research team and methods: see www.sigmund-freud-institut.de).

9 I have described the clinical and biographical background of this severely traumatized, chronically depressed patient extensively in other papers (Leuzinger-Bohleber, 2012, in print). From my clinical perspective, I illustrate how the manifest dreams as well as the dream work changed during psychoanalysis and also reports of the transformation of the inner (traumatic) object world. In this paper, we would like to contrast my clinical views with a more systematic investigation of the changes in the manifest dreams.

10 Lyrica (generic name: Pregabalin) is an anticonvulsant drug used for neurotic pain, also effective for generalized anxiety disorder (since 2007 approved for this use in the European Union).

11 Within the frame of this paper we cannot elaborate the psychoanalytical understanding of the transformations of the manifest dreams as well as the working with the dream associations in the psychoanalytical sessions (see, e.g., Leuzinger-Bohleber, 2012, 2015). We can communicate only a first impression of these changes of the dreams to the reader by two dreams, one from the first and one from the third year of treatment here. The first dream reported here is a typical dream of a severely traumatized person where the patient himself is in a position of an observer: the dream subject is in an extreme life threatening situation, completely helpless, in unbearable pain and not being helped by anyone. In the second dream, the patient is the active dreamer, observing a situation which still is painful but with hope that "something can be done" in order to overcome a hopeless situation.

12 A total of four dreams – two from the end of the first year of therapy and two elicited one year later – serve as material to be analyzed for changes within the course of therapy using the Moser method. Elements of the coding system are included in parentheses.

References

Abbass, A. A., Nowoweiski, S. J., Bernier, D., Tarzwell, R., & Beutel, M. E. (2014). Review of psychodynamic psychotherapy neuroimaging studies. *Psychotherapy and Psychosomatics*, *83*(3), 142–147.

Atmaca, M., Yildirim, H., Koc, M., Korkmaz, S., Ozler, S., & Erenkus, Z. (2011). Do defense styles of ego relate to volumes of orbito-frontal cortex in patients with obsessive-compulsive disorder? *Psychiatry Investigation*, *8*(2), 123–129.

Belmaker, R. H., & Agam, G. (2008). Major depressive disorder. *New England Journal of Medicine*, *358*, 55–68.

Beutel, M. E., Stark, R., Pan, H., Silbersweig, D., & Dietrich, S. (2010). Changes of brain activation pre-post short-term psychodynamic inpatient psychotherapy: An fMRI study of panic disorder patients. *Psychiatry Research: Neuroimaging*, *184*(2), 96–104.

Beutel, M. E., Stark, R., Pan, H., Silbersweig, D. A., & Dietrich, S. (2012). Langzeitergebnisse einer Funktionellen-Magnetresonanztomographie-Studie. *Psychotherapeut*, *57*(3), 227–233.

Böker, H., & Seifritz, E. (Eds.) (2012). *Psychotherapie und Neurowissenschaften*. Bern: Huber.

Botvinick, M. M., Cohen, J. D., & Carter, C. S. (2004). Conflict monitoring and anterior cingulate cortex: An update. *Trends in Cognitive Sciences*, *8*, 539–546.

Buchanan, T. W. (2007). Retrieval of emotional memories. *Psychological Bulletin*, *133*(5), 761.

Buchheim, A., Viviani, R., Kessler, H., Kächele, H., Cierpka, M., Roth, G., . . . & Taubner, S. (2012). Changes in prefrontal-limbic function in major depression after 15 months of long-term psychotherapy. *PLoS ONE*, *7*(3), e33745.

Caspi, A., Sugden, K., Moffitt, T. E., Taylor, A., Craig, I. W., Harrington, H., . . . & Poulton, R. (2003). Influence of life stress on depression: Moderation by a polymorphism in the 5-HTT gene. *Science*, *301*(5631), 386–389.

Critchley, H. (2003). Emotion and its disorders. *British Medical Bulletin*, *65*, 35–47.

de Greck, M., Bölter, A. F., Lehmann, L., Ulrich, C., Stockum, E., Enzi, B., . . . & Northoff, G. (2013). Changes in brain activity of somatoform disorder patients during emotional empathy after multimodal psychodynamic psychotherapy. *Frontiers in Human Neuroscience*, *7*, 410, 25–35.

Dewan, E. M. (1970). The programming (P) hypothesis for REM sleep. In E. Hartmann (Ed.), *Sleep and Dreaming* (pp. 295–307). Boston, MA: Little Brown.

Doell-Hentschker, S. (2008). *Die Veränderungen von Träumen in Psychoanalytischen Behandlungen: Affekttheorie, Affektregulierung und Traumkodierung*. Frankfurt am Main: Brandes & Apsel.

Fan, Y., Wonneberger, C., Enzi, B., de Greck, M., Ulrich, C., Tempelmann, C., . . . & Northoff, G. (2011). The narcissistic self and its psychological and neural correlates: An exploratory fMRI study. *Psychological Medicine*, *41*, 1641–1650.

Fischmann, T., Leuzinger-Bohleber, M., & Kaechele, H. (2012). Traumforschung in der psychoanalyse: Klinische Studien, Traumserien, extraklinische Forschung im Labor. *Psyche – Zeitschrift für Psychoanalyse und ihre Anwendungen*, *66*, 833–861.

Fischmann, T., Leuzinger-Bohleber, M., Schoett, M., Russ, M. (2015a). How to investigate transformations in psychoanalysis? Contrasting clinical and extra-clinical findings on changes of dreams in psychoanalysis with a severely traumatised, chronically depressed analysand. In M. Leuzinger-Bohleber (Ed.), *Finding the Body in the Mind: Embodied Memories, Trauma, and Depression*. London: Karnac Books.

Fischmann, T., Leuzinger-Bohleber, M., Schoett, M., Russ, M. (2015b). Traum und psychische Transformationsprozesse in Psychoanalysen: ein Dialog zwischen Psychoanalyse und Neurowissenschaften. In M. Leuzinger-Bohleber, T. Fischmann, H. Böker, G. Northoff,

M. Solms (Eds.), *Psychoanalyse und Neurowissenschaften. Chancen – Grenzen – Kontroversen.* Stuttgart: Kohlhammer.

Fischmann, T., Russ, M., Baehr, T., Stirn, A., & Leuzinger-Bohleber, M. (2012). Changes in dreams of chronic depressed patients: The Frankfurt fMRI/EEG study (FRED). *The Significance of Dreams: Bridging Clinical and Extraclinical Research in Psychonalysis, 6,* 157.

Fischmann, T., Russ, M. O., & Leuzinger-Bohleber, M. (2013). Trauma, dream, and psychic change in psychoanalyses: A dialog between psychoanalysis and the neurosciences. *Frontiers in Human Neuroscience, 7, 877.*Fosshage, J. (2007). The organizing functions of dreaming: Pivotal issues in understanding and working with dreams. *International Forum of Psychoanalysis, 16,* 213–221.

Franke, G. H., & Derogatis, L. R. (2002). *SCL-90-R: Symptom-Checkliste von LR Derogatis: Deutsche Version: Manual.* Weinheim: Beltz Test.

Gawrysiak, M. J., Swan, S. A., Nicholas, C., Rogers, B. P., Dougherty, J. H., & Hopko, D. R. (2013). Pragmatic psychodynamic psychotherapy for a patient with depression and breast cancer: Functional MRI evaluation of treatment effects. *American Journal of Psychotherapy, 67*(3), 237–255.

Gerber, A. J., & Peterson, B. S. (2006). Measuring transference phenomena with fMRI. *Journal of the American Psychoanalytic Association, 54*(4), 1319.

Hautzinger, M., Keller, F., & Kühner, C. (2006). *Beck Depressions-inventar (BDI-II).* Frankfurt: Harcourt Test Services.

Kandel, E. R. (2009). The biology of memory: A forty-year perspective. *Journal of Neuroscience, 29*(41), 12748–12756.

Kehyayan, A., Best, K., Schmeing, J. B., Axmacher, N., & Kessler, H. (2013). Neural activity during free association to conflict–related sentences. *Frontiers in Human Neuroscience, 7,* 705.

Kessler, H., Taubner, S., Buchheim, A., Münte, T. F., Stasch, M., Kächele, H., . . . & Wiswede, D. (2011). Individualized and clinically derived stimuli activate limbic structures in depression: An fMRI study. *PLoS ONE, 6*(1), e15712.

Legrand, D., & Ruby, P. (2009). What is self-specific? A theoretical investigation and a critical review of neuroimaging results. *Psychological Review, 116*(1), 252–282.

Leuzinger-Bohleber, M. (1987). *Veränderung kognitiver Prozesse in Psychoanalyse Bd. 1: Eine hypothesengenerierende Einzelfallstudie.* Berlin: Springer (PSZ-Drucke).

Leuzinger-Bohleber, M. (1989). *Veränderung kognitiver Prozesse in Psychoanalyse Bd. 2: Fünf aggregierte Einzelfallstudien.* Berlin: Springer (PSZ-Drucke).

Leuzinger-Bohleber, M. (2008). Biographical truths and their clinical consequences: Understanding "embodied memories" in a third psychoanalysis with a traumatized patient recovered from severe poliomyelitis. *The International Journal of Psychoanalysis, 89*(6), 1165–1187.

Leuzinger-Bohleber, M. (2012). Changes in dreams – From a psychoanalysis with a traumatised, chronic depressed patient. In P. Fonagy, H. Kächele, M. Leuzinger-Bohleber & D. Taylor (Eds.), *The Significance of Dreams: Bridging Clinical and Extraclinical Research in Psychoanalysis* (pp. 49–85). London: Karnac.

Leuzinger-Bohleber, M. (2013). Chronische Depression und Trauma. Konzeptuelle Uberlegungen zu ersten klinischen Ergebnissen der LAC-Depressionsstudie. In M. Leuzinger-Bohleber, U. Bahrke & A. Negele (Eds.), *Chronische Depression:Verstehen-Behandeln-Erforschen* (pp. 56–82). Gottingen: Vandenhoeck u. Ruprecht.

Leuzinger-Bohleber, M. (2015). Working with severely traumatized, chronically depressed analysands. *International Journal of Psychoanalysis, 96*(3), 611–636.

Leuzinger-Bohleber, M., Bahrke, U., Beutel, M., Deserno, H., Edinger, J., Fiedler, G., . . . & Will, A. (2010). Psychoanalytische und kognitiv-verhaltenstherapeutische Langzeitthera- pien bei chronischer Depression: Die LAC-Depressionsstudie. *Psyche, 64*(9–10), 782–832.

Maguire, E. A., Henson, R. N., Mummery, C. J., & Frith, C. D. (2001). Activity in prefrontal cortex, not hippocampus, varies parametrically with the increasing remoteness of memo- ries. *Neuroreport, 12*(3), 441–444.

Matsumoto, K., Suzuki, W., & Tanaka, K. (2003). Neural correlates of goalbased motor selec- tion in the prefrontal cortex. *Science, 301*, 229–232.

Moser, U., & von Zeppelin, I. (1996). *Der geträumte Traum.* Stuttgart: Kohlhammer.

Northoff, G., & Hayes, D. J. (2011). Is our self nothing but reward? *Biological Psychiatry, 69*, 1019–1025.

OPD Task Force (Eds.) (2008). *Operationalized psychodynamic diagnosis OPD-2: Manual of diag- nosis and treatment planning.* Cambridge, MA/Göttingen: Hogrefe Publishing.

Posner, M. L., & DiGirolamo, G. J. (1998). Executive attention: Conflict, target detection, and cognitive control. In R. Parasuraman (Ed.), *The Attentive Brain* (pp. 401–423). Cam- bridge: MIT Press.

Risch, N., Herrell, R., Lehner, T., Liang, K., Eaves, L., Hoh, J., . . . & Merikangas, K. R. (2009). Interaction between the serotonin transporter gene (5-HTTLPR), stressful life events, and risk of depression: A meta-analysis. *Journal of the American Medical Association, 301*(23), 2462–2471.

Roelofs, A., van Turennout, M., & Coles, M. G. H. (2006). Anterior cingulate cortex activ- ity can be independent of response conflict in stroop-like tasks. *Proceedings of the National Academy of Sciences, 103*, 13884–13889.

Schmeing, J. B., Kehyayan, A., Kessler, H., Do Lam, A. T., Fell, J., Schmidt, A. C., & Axmacher, N. (2013). Can the neural basis of repression be studied in the MRI scanner? new insights from two free association paradigms. *PLoS ONE, 8*(4), e62358.

Siegel, P., & Peterson, B. S. (2012). Demonstrating psychodynamic conflict with a neuro- psychoanalytic experimental paradigm. *Neuropsychoanalysis: An Interdisciplinary Journal for Psychoanalysis and the Neurosciences, 14*(2), 219–228.

Solms, M., & Panksepp, J. (2012). The "Id" knows more than the "Ego" admits: Neuropsy- choanalytic and primal consciousness perspectives on the interface between affective and cognitive neuroscience. *Brain Sciences, 2*(4), 147–175.

Stickgold, R., Hobson, J., Fosse, R., & Fosse, M. (2001). Sleep, learning, and dreams: Off-line memory reprocessing. *Science, 294*(5544), 1052.

Stuphorn, V., & Schall, J. D. (2006). Executive control of countermanding saccades by the supplementary eye field. *Nature Neuroscience, 9*(7), 925–931.

Chapter 10

Non-verbal memories of trauma in early childhood

Conscious or unconscious?

Theodore J. Gaensbauer

DENVER

Based on interviews of a four-year-old who experienced a traumatic loss at twenty-two months of age, this chapter will discuss verbal and non-verbal memories of early trauma in the context of traditional views of consciousness. Historically, based on the phenomena of "infantile amnesia," i.e., the fact that adults generally do not have memories of events occurring prior to age three to four years, it was long assumed that infants and toddlers would not remember traumatic events (Freud, 1905; Gaensbauer, 1995; 2002; Hayne & Jack, 2011). Countering this assumption, research over the past several decades utilizing methods of memory assessment not dependent on verbal communication has clearly demonstrated that young children, including children in the preverbal period, have much greater memory capacities than was previously appreciated (Meltzoff, 1995; Bauer, 1997; Rovee-Collier & Gerhardstein, 1997). This research has called into question the supposition that the preverbal period is pre-representational in nature and has greatly altered our understanding of the impact of trauma occurring early in life (Gaensbauer, 1985; Gaensbauer, 1995). For example, clinical research studies have documented that the capacity to experience PTSD symptoms that involve non-verbal memory is present by the second half of the first year of life, if not earlier (Scheeringa & Gaensbauer, 1999). Examples of such symptoms include affective reactions to triggers, avoidance of stimuli associated with a trauma, behavioral and play reenactments, meaningful pointing or gesturing, altered gaze patterns, and concrete or symbolically based internal representations that shape the child's expectations and responses to everyday events (Gaensbauer, 1995; 2002; Paley & Alpert, 2003; Coates & Gaensbauer, 2009)

Although the question of whether young children have memories of early events is no longer an issue, the degree to which the children are consciously aware that their non-verbal expressions reflect actual memories remains a subject of ongoing discussion. Traditionally, memories have been classified into two major categories: declarative/explicit memories that the individual consciously recognizes as memories of a past event and that can be verbally "declared" and procedural/implicit memories that involve behavioral and affective responses that have become automatic and appear to be activated without conscious intent (Zola-Morgan & Squire, 1993; Squire, 2004). Within this traditional classification, non-verbal memories from early childhood have generally been considered to be implicit in nature, occurring outside of conscious awareness. Indeed, procedural/implicit memory has also been referred to as "early memory," whereas declarative/explicit memory has been referred to as "later memory" (Siegel, 1995).

Studies of memory retention in early childhood have found that, with rare exceptions, children are not able to verbally describe events that occurred prior to the onset of language fluency (Simcock & Hayne, 2002; Nelson & Fivush, 2004; Peterson et al., 2005; Bauer, 2007). Since outcome measures utilized as evidence of memory in the preverbal period, such as classical and operant conditioning, preferential gaze patterns, facial and behavioral expressions of emotion, and deferred imitation, involve expressive modalities typically associated with procedural memories, the non-verbal memories of infants and toddlers have generally been seen as implicit in nature. Many developmental researchers have concluded that the capacities for language and symbolic representation that emerge around the age of two are prerequisites for a conscious sense of self. This new level of self-awareness is thought to be crucial for the development of autobiographical memory, the conscious awareness on the child's part that an event has occurred in the past (Howe & Courage, 1997; Howe et al., 2003; Nelson & Fivush, 2004).

Though there is no question that the verbal reporting of memories at age two and older can be categorized as explicit and conscious, the assumption that non-verbal memories are implicit and outside of conscious awareness deserves examination for several reasons. The first is the fact that the neural mechanisms underlying deferred imitation and visual paired-comparisons, hallmark measures of memory in preverbal children, likely involve the same neural networks that mediate declarative or explicit memory in adults (McDonough et al., 1995; Manns et al., 2000; Bauer, 2013). A second neuropsychological consideration is the fact that, even after the onset of language fluency, young children will continue to process and internally represent events through non-verbally based neural mechanisms. Children experience and internalize events through multiple modalities, as cognitive, affective, and the full range of sensory motor networks are activated in a holistic manner (Meltzoff, 1990; Fivush, 1998; Gaensbauer, 2004; 2011). The triggering of any specific memory can involve activation of any or all of the neural pathways that were activated when the memories were initially laid down. As a result, non-verbal memory networks have the potential to be triggered as part of any memory retrieval and presumably would be available to consciousness.

In short, even after language fluency is achieved, children will not be utilizing language as the sole, or even primary, vehicle for understanding what is going on around them (Simcock & Hayne, 2003). For example, verbal explanations of upcoming events that are not accompanied by some sort of concrete, non-verbally based demonstration of what is being described are unlikely to be fully understood by young children, even if they are verbally fluent. Telling the child that "Your mother is going away on a trip for work and will be back on Saturday," or more seriously as reflected in the case to be described below, "Your mother died and went to Heaven," will not automatically conjure up for the child exactly what these events involve. For these reasons, concrete, non-verbal modalities such as drawings, play, or demonstrations in action can be crucial in helping children to understand what is happening in their environment (Benham & Slotnik, 2006; Gaensbauer & Kelsay, 2008).

In short, questions about the relationship between verbal and non-verbal memories in early childhood and, more specifically, how non-verbal memories of trauma should be classified remain open. To illustrate the degree to which the various forms of memory can defy easy categorization, I will describe and discuss the range of memory expressions that emerged in the course of a forensic evaluation of a traumatized child.

Case description

Conditions of the evaluation: Emilio was seen for four videotaped sessions as part of a forensic evaluation that took place when he was four years of age. Two years earlier he and his mother had been involved in an automobile accident in which his mother was killed. In addition to evaluating the emotional and developmental impact of the trauma he experienced, I was required to give crucial attention to issues of memory. For Emelio to have legal standing in the civil case that was being pursued by his family, it had to be demonstrated that he had specific memories of the accident. Because it was important that I not be seen as leading him or planting memories, I was not able to provide the kinds of cues and scaffolding that help young children share what they know. At the same time, the conditions of the evaluation allowed Emilio to communicate his memories spontaneously in forms that were largely determined by him.

Background: Emilio was twenty-two months of age when he witnessed his mother's death. He was in the back seat of the car his mother was driving when their car was broadsided by a car driven by an intoxicated man who ran a red light. Immediate witnesses who helped pull Emilio from the car observed his mother turned back toward Emilio, her face bloated and turning blue. She was gurgling and choking from the blood and fluid that was filling her airway. Emilio was screaming, "Mommy! Mommy!" Broken glass was everywhere and Emilio was bleeding profusely from a cut artery on his forehead. He had superficial cuts around his head and neck from small pieces of embedded glass and suffered small abrasions over other parts of his body. Otherwise, he was without serious injury. He was taken by ambulance to a hospital where his abrasions were cleaned and the cut on his forehead sutured. The sutures were removed one week later and ointment was regularly applied to the scar over the next year. His mother was taken by ambulance to a different hospital, where she died of her injuries.

Emilio's parents had lived with the maternal grandparents prior to the accident, so Emilio was surrounded by loving adults and a supportive extended family. The effects of losing his mother were thus somewhat ameliorated by the availability of these other important attachment figures, although he showed ongoing intense separation anxiety and other fears after the accident, as well as ongoing moments of sadness. However, he did not have significant PTSD symptoms; he had no problems being in a car or driving past the intersection where the accident occurred. He did not report nightmares or flashbacks and sudden loud noises were the only obvious accident-related trigger of anxiety.

After the accident, Emilio was told that his mother had been too sick and that she had died and gone to heaven. He was present at the funeral and burial, but was kept at the back of the room during the funeral and behind the other people at the burial site. His family operated on the assumption that he wouldn't really see or understand what was happening. Prior to the funeral service, Emilio was allowed to walk around the room where at least for some period of time his mother was lying in an open casket. The family assumed that because he was so small and close to the ground he would not be able to actually see his mother in the casket.

At the time of the accident, Emilio's had just begun to talk in simple sentences. His language fluidity expanded dramatically after his second birthday. From the time of the accident going forward, his family reported that they had not talked to him about the accident or what specifically happened to his mother. His father felt strongly that Emilio should not be reminded of the traumatic experience and should have only positive memories of his mother. The other members of the family respected this wish. Family members did, however, talk a great deal about his mother's love for him and the happy experiences he and his mother had shared. They were also very attuned to Emilio's emotional needs and provided comfort during times when he was anxious or sad. Although aware that these feelings were likely related to the loss of his mother, they did not ask about any specific thoughts or memories he might be having at these times. There were two instances of very clear explicit recall reported. The first occurred within six months of the accident, as Emilio and his father were driving through the intersection where the accident occurred and Emilio announced, "This is where the drunk man hit my mother." Remarkably, the second occurred three years after the accident, when Emilio was at the courthouse with his aunt during the criminal trial of the drunk driver. Seeing the man across the lobby, Emilio told his aunt, "the man was sitting on the curb with his head down" as he demonstrated by crouching and holding his head in his hands. Otherwise, there had been no spontaneous reporting of any memories and, as mentioned, his family had not discussed the accident with him.

Initial sessions: From the beginning, Emilio's preoccupation with death was evident. Entering the playroom for the first session, he immediately went to the playhouse, found a boy doll who, he told me, was scared because a monster was going to kill him. Soon after, having removed a number of toys and doll furniture from a toy box and placed them on a table, he began poking me in the forehead with one of the toys (as will be noted, poking me in the forehead was a recurrent event throughout all four sessions). When I asked what was happening, he told me I was going to die because a bad guy "put fire on you." Not too long after this interaction, he found an adult female doll in the playhouse and stood it on the table next to me. He then pushed the doll over face first on the table and told me, "She died." A short time later he found another female doll in the playhouse and both informed me and demonstrated that "she fell off the roof." He then stood the doll on a lego "car" that consisted of a flat piece of plastic with wheels and brought it over to the table. Sustaining the automobile element, he saw a toy car on the table and pushed it back and forth several times with one hand while holding the doll with the other. He then gently laid the doll in a toy bathtub sitting on the table and said to me, "She died. She got very sick and died." With a very serious expression, he then laid the bathtub upside down on the table with the female doll underneath the tub. It had every appearance of a coffin. As he looked at the turned over bathtub and was quiet for a moment, I asked him what the family was going to do now that she was dead. He responded, "They're going to look all over the town for her." As he said this, he lifted up the bathtub, looked briefly at the doll, and then covered the doll again with the bathtub. I asked how the family will feel if they can't find her and he replied, "They'll die too."

In a subsequent session, as he was repeatedly putting his hand or a toy to my forehead, I commented that I had a "big cut" on my forehead and asked him what I should do. He said he would put a bandage on it and proceeded to pretend to do so. I then asked him if he had ever had a cut on his face. He said "No, but I had one on my hand but no blood came out of it. It got there all by itself." As he was saying this he held his right hand over his left hand and made up and down rhythmic, waving motions over the left that conveyed a picture of something spurting. The action sequence vividly portrayed what one could readily imagine he experienced, namely seeing blood coming in waves over his hand without realizing that the blood was coming from the arterial cut on his forehead.

Following up a short time later, I again asked him if he had ever had a cut on his face and he again said "No." However, as if these associations (consciously or unconsciously) led him to the accident, he then spontaneously asked me "Do you know how my mom died?" He then verbally described how there was a guy who drank alcohol and there was a red light and he didn't stop and he crashed into his mom's car and that was how she died. He then went on to say "but then I went to the hospital. That's when I was a baby." He then excitedly told me that "I had no diapers on! They fell off and right here I was naked!" as he spread his legs and pointed to his groin. Although the verbal description of how his mother died was very accurate, the language sounded much more like something he would have been told than something he would have come up with himself. His father and grandparents reported that this was the way the accident had been explained to him. The description and behavioral demonstration of losing his diaper and having his genitals exposed seemed more spontaneous and animated, although again it was very difficult to know if he was reporting a memory of his own or acting out an event he had been told about and thought was very funny. The fact that he lost his diaper had also been talked about, and his family reported that Emilio enjoyed telling others about it.

In contrast to these verbal descriptions that were likely based on what he had been told by adults, shortly after this discussion there were examples of non-verbal memories of his experience that I believe were extremely unlikely to have been influenced by others. Following up on his description of the accident, I observed that he had been in the car and asked him if he could tell me what happened. He said "Something bad but I don't remember." Then, replicating his own experience of being struck by shattered glass, he began poking me all over my hands, arms, and face in a very animated, almost driven, way. As I matched his animation by exclaiming that I had "cuts all over," he sat back in his chair, arched his head back, held his hands to his throat, and proceeded over the next 30 to 40 seconds to make very loud choking sounds, as if he was desperately gasping for air. It was difficult to know how much conscious intention played a role in this dramatic reenactment of having cuts all over one's body and what I immediately inferred to be an imitation of his mother's dying breaths. However, both reenactments were in direct response to my question about what happened in the car, and I had a strong feeling that at some level he was purposefully communicating something to me that he could not readily access in words. When I commented that he was acting as if he couldn't breathe and that it was "scary," he repeated the words "I can't breathe." He then ended the discussion by putting all the toys back in the toy box.

Final session: Having provided the opportunity in the previous three sessions for memories to emerge spontaneously, during our final session I became somewhat more active. Recreating the scene just before the accident, I put a mother doll and baby doll in a toy car on the floor, placed another car next to it, and asked Emilio if he could show me what happened. After moving the cars around randomly, he ran the other car into the car representing his and his mother's car from behind (not the way they actually collided) and said "and now the mommy goes to heaven." As he was holding the boy doll from the car, I asked him what he did when the car crashed. He said he had to go to the doctor because he had a "scratch." I brought out a hospital bed and several medically dressed dolls and he put the boy doll in the hospital bed. I asked how he got to the hospital and he said, "I think the Doctor had to drive me." When I asked him where his "scratch" was he shrugged his shoulders and once again said he didn't remember. These repeated verbal denials of knowledge about his "scratch" were remarkable, given the facts that he had poked at my forehead repeatedly in the previous three sessions, had had sutures for his "scratch," and had had ointment placed on his forehead daily for the next year. When I asked if he could show me what the doctor did, he began to put all the dolls back in the toy box and said "I want to play something else."

At this point in the evaluation, I persisted in trying to get more information about what he may have remembered, starting again by asking him to show me the crash. This time, however, I put the cars in the right-angle positions relative to each other that they were in prior to the accident and asked him, "Was the other car coming like this?" He said, "I think it was." As the play situation more accurately reflected the actual scene, he became more animated and affectively engaged than he had during his previous demonstration. He took the drunk driver car, said it was "super fast!" and crashed it into the side of the mother and baby doll car with great force and a loud crash. Because of the importance of the question of what he specifically remembered, I asked again if he saw what happened to his mother. He didn't respond but picked up the Fisher Price wooden doll that was representing the boy in the car, looked at it closely and said, "It's a sad face." I said, "I bet you were sad when the car crashed and his Mommy went to Heaven" and asked again if he saw what happened to his Mommy. He repeatedly said "I only saw her when she was stopping but then when she died I didn't see her." Trying to make it more specific, I asked him if he saw her in the car and he said 'Yeah." I asked him if he could tell me what he saw. His response was "Uh . . . I saw . . . ya, ya, ya, ya, yeh, yeh . . . .(repeating)." As he repeated these "ya ya" sounds, his voice became increasingly coarse and guttural until the sounds turned into the gasping, choking sounds described above. He then ended the play by moving to the other side of the playroom.

Another example of the compartmentalization yet fluidity between verbal and non-verbal memories in regard to the cut on his forehead occurred later in this session. He was once again using a toy to poke at my forehead where I had a "scratch." Shifting the play into reality, I asked, "Can I see where your scratch is?" as I reached my hand over to brush hair away from his forehead where his scar actually was. Clearly knowing what I was asking, he moved his head so that I could see his scar more directly and started to point at the site. At the same time all this was happening, I again asked, "Do you have a scratch?" His verbal response was again "Nope. Nope." Since he had indicated by his behavior that he knew what I was referring to, I then asked him if he knew where he got his "scratch." He shrugged his shoulders and began playing with some toys. I persisted, saying "this cut right there" as I reached out again to expose his scar. This gesture served as an affectively meaningful stimulus trigger sufficient to evoke a breakthrough verbalization. He abruptly pulled away, saying, "You made me scared." I asked him what made him scared and he said, "Your talking." I asked "Was it scary when I asked you how you got your cut?" He responded "Yep." We both knew exactly what about my question had scared him.

A final example of the compartmentalization of verbal and non-verbal traumatic representations was seen toward the end of this last session. I asked Emilio if there were any other things that made him scared, and he told me he would hide under his bed because he was scared of his mirror. He was afraid that a bad guy would come through the mirror and steal him. Being struck with the image of the mirror, I asked him what would happen if the bad guy came through the mirror and, more specifically, would he break the mirror. He didn't pick up on the breaking part but instead repeated his fears that the bad guy would come back and try to steal him again and that he would "beat the guy's butt." I then made my question more explicit. Noting that mirrors were made of glass I asked him what happens when glass breaks. He responded in a dramatic tone, "That would be *baaad*! It would get in your eye and ear and your tummy and *blooood* would come out of you!" I asked him "Have you ever seen glass break?" Although clearly aware from his own experience what can happen when glass breaks, as evidenced by his previous response, his response to my question was a very definitive, "Never. Never ever!" The fear of someone coming through the glass and stealing him recapitulated another aspect of the traumatic accident, that of being taken from the shattered car by a man who was on the scene.

Discussion

In the vignettes, one can see multiple ways in which Emilio internalized the traumatic accident and death of his mother. Verbal descriptions included telling me how the accident happened and his mother went to heaven, how he lost his underpants at the hospital, how he went to the hospital because he had a scratch and the doctor had to drive him, and how the drunk driver looked at the scene. Non-verbal memories took several different forms including: internal representations contributing both to generalized anxiety about death and being killed and specific fears such as glass breaking and a man stealing him; play themes involving adult females dying; reenactment of his mother's burial accompanied by a description of how it feels not to have meaningful closure; repeated episodes of poking my forehead that in turn triggered many associations with the accident; and the dramatic demonstration of his mother's dying breaths.

As referred to in the introduction, it is noteworthy that, even at a time when Emilio's verbal skills were quite good, in the course of our sessions, non-verbal manifestations of memory both occurred more frequently and seemed more emotionally meaningful. The extended verbal descriptions about how the accident happened and how he lost his underpants at the hospital were told without any negative affect and in language that seemed more a recitation of what he might have been told than a story put into his own words. Although the pause that accompanied his verbal description of going to the hospital reflected a more serious mood, it was likely also influenced by the fact that we were re-enacting the hospital scene in play and he was looking directly at the boy doll lying in the hospital bed. In contrast to the relative lack of the expectable affects accompanying his verbal descriptions, he showed much more emotion when carrying out his non-verbal enactments. Examples would be his vigorous poking demonstration of being hit all over his [my] face and body; his dramatic loud choking; his plaintive observation of the boy doll with the sad face as he contemplated the hospital play scene after the accident; and the vigor with which he crashed the two toy cars when they were placed in their actual pre-accident position. Perhaps the best evidence of their affective impact was the fact that it was after non-verbal enactments that he was most likely to shut down or change the subject.

Interrelationships between Emilio's verbal and non-verbal memories were quite variable. At times, the two forms seemed compartmentalized and independent of each other. At other times, they seemed closely intertwined, although in unpredictable ways. There were very few instances where verbal and non-verbal memories were integrated into a coherent narrative, the clearest example being when he described with both words and gestures how the blood that covered his hand had arrived there mysteriously in a pulsating manner. More commonly, it seemed that one form of memory expression would trigger the other. An example of a verbal communication that triggered a non-verbal memory occurred when I asked him specific questions about what he saw in the car. The answers came in the non-verbal form of vigorous poking of my face and upper body and the choking sounds that captured his mother's dying breaths. An example of a non-verbal memory triggering a verbal expression occurred when he told me that my reaching for his forehead had scared him because it reminded him of where he got his cut. A more complicated back and forth sequence occurred when his non-verbal act of making a cut on my forehead triggered my verbal question of whether he ever had a cut on his forehead. This in turn triggered his asking me if I knew how his mother died. The fluid and porous boundaries between his verbal and nonverbal expressions in these instances made it very difficult to draw a line between what would be considered conscious, what would be considered preconscious, and what would be considered unconscious.

Most striking were those moments when Emilio's verbal and non-verbal memories seemed not only compartmentalized but in direct contradiction. One example would be his repeated denials of having a cut on his forehead despite demonstrating in his actions that he was very aware of his "scratch" and where it came from. A second would be his confident denial of ever being exposed to breaking glass immediately after describing very dramatically and in resonance with his own experience what happens when glass does break. These contradictions suggested a significant dissociation between the two forms of memory. Although such dissociation is commonly attributed to psychological defenses against traumatic experiencing, this explanation is not fully satisfactory for a number of reasons. Avoidance of exploration of his actual experiences was seen in both verbal and non-verbal spheres, with verbal denials occurring not only in affectively difficult moments, but also when there was little evidence of any stress. The expression of any particular memory, verbal or non-verbal, seemed quite unpredictable, as if determined more by the particular stimulus conditions that happened to trigger them at that particular moment than by defensive operations. The instance where he purposefully cooperated non-verbally with my request to see his scratch at the same time that he verbally denied its existence suggested something more complicated than a structured defense mechanism blocking conscious awareness, particularly since he so readily moved from the non-verbal element of the exchange to a verbal acknowledgment of his scar and where he had gotten it. Finally, when he carried out behavioral enactments in response to my questioning about what he observed, such as the choking noises, it was much more as if he didn't have or didn't need words to describe what he saw than that he was defended against a verbal description.

Looking beyond defensive operations, I believe that this compartmentalization yet porousness in boundaries between verbal and non-verbal memory expression can be explained by developmental changes occurring in early childhood. Particularly significant is the transition from primarily non-verbal learning in the preverbal period to primarily verbal mediated learning once language fluidity is achieved, a transition associated with significant neural reorganization involving hippocampal and prefrontal maturation and a shift away from right hemisphere domination as the left hemisphere comes increasingly on line (Nelson, 1995; Schore, 2003; Bauer, 2013). Language-based ways of knowing that will become the primary basis for organizing the communication of experiences henceforward into adulthood will be introduced. However, as noted in the introduction, this transition will not take place overnight and the neural networks mediating this more advanced and qualitatively different level of information processing will be far from mature even when language skills appear quite good. In essence, even after language onset, the child will, for an extended period of time, be utilizing two potentially unintegrated modalities for processing information.

Given that the two systems do not start out fully integrated, a significant amount of disjuncture is to be expected, especially for events occurring prior to the onset of language fluidity. Nor is the kind of disjuncture or dissociation described here exclusive to traumatic experience. Given the fundamental modularity of brain organization, initial dissociations can be seen in almost every aspect of children's mental and behavioral development (Fischer & Granott, 1995; Lyons-Ruth, 1999). To a large extent, the internal schema upon which learning and/or the development of skills depend will initially be established in modular fashion independently of each other, based on the stimuli that generate them These initial modules or representational schemata may remain isolated and go forward along distinct developmental pathways or they may become integrated over time, depending on the child's subsequent experiences (Fischer & Granott, 1995). In Emilio's case, though he had a degree of language fluidity at the time of the accident, it appears that affective and sensory-motor networks remained primary modalities through which he represented the traumatic experience. In part because of the painful nature of the memories, in part because he was not supported in expressing his memories, and in part because of the developmental disjuncture between verbal and non-verbal modes of processing described above, Emilio's non-verbal memories remained relatively dissociated from his verbal world.

Given that his traumatic memories were primarily non-verbal, one can see how opportunities to "play it out" would be not only the most useful vehicle for gaining access to Emilio's inner world, but also the most effective way to help him develop an overarching narrative in regard to traumatic events, one that could incorporate the opportunities for integrative understanding that language could afford him (Gaensbauer, 2004). Because of the forensic nature of our meetings, I was not able to provide this kind of support. However, one can see numerous opportunities where more elaborated play, accompanied by verbal scaffolding, would have been very helpful to him in the service of narrative understanding. I would suggest that in this endeavor one would not be trying to make unconscious memories conscious or implicit memories explicit. Rather, one would be facilitating the integration of non-verbal memories into a verbal framework.

Coming back to the basic question of whether non-verbal communications or reenactments in early childhood should be considered products of conscious awareness or should be considered implicit or unconsciously manifested, one is confronted with the issue of definition. What constitutes consciousness in the young child? As discussed earlier, conscious awareness and the capacity for autobiographical memory have been considered by many to be synonymous with the development around two years of age of the verbal self. By definition, though, such a conceptualization rules out the possibility that, prior to this age, a child reenacting a traumatic event would be aware that their behavior is referencing something that happened to them in the past. Yet preverbal children react purposefully and very adaptively to any number of situations based on non-verbally mediated memories of previous experiences in a similar situation. Such adaptive behavior certainly suggests the conscious utilization of an internal representation that is based at some level of awareness on the part of the child that "I have been in this situation before."

Developmental differences notwithstanding, cases such as Emilio's suggest that non-verbal expressions of memory in early childhood can be viewed in the same light as one might see them in an older child. When a sexually molested five-year-old is asked to show how she was touched by her babysitter and the child demonstrates by putting the hand of an adult doll in the genital area of a child doll, one considers that in a non-verbal way the child is conveying a conscious memory of an event that happened in the past. A twenty-six-month-old girl who witnessed domestic violence up to the age of eleven months before she was placed in foster care is given a male and female doll and immediately begins to violently bang the dolls together. Could this not similarly be considered a manifestation of a conscious reenactment of a memory as opposed to an unconscious, conditioned reenactment, particularly when the child proceeds to make a verbal reference to what she observed (Gaensbauer, 2004)? To take another example among many, a three-year-old who suffered a severe IV infiltration of his hand and arm at fifteen months responded to a play scene of a boy doll in a hospital bed by placing a mother doll in a chair at the foot of the bed (where she had sat during his hospitalization). He also put a toy crutch along the boy doll's leg in a way (as his mother explained) that likely represented the splint on his leg that protected the intravenous line in his ankle. In a subsequent session, in the process of making a tracing of his hand to use as a comparison with how swollen his hand was in the hospital, he grabbed the pen and began aggressively poking the sides of all of his fingers. This act clearly referenced the over forty needle punctures in his fingers and hands he had received in the hospital to allow fluid to escape (Gaensbauer, 1997). In these reenactments that took place in the context of hospital play, were these automatic responses out of conscious awareness or was the child consciously aware that the reenactments referenced specific experiences that had happened to him in the past? When I asked Emilio what he saw in the car and he poked me all over and imitated his mother's choking sounds, was he unconsciously manifesting a conditioned response or was he consciously aware that he was communicating a memory? Or as he moved back and forth between verbalizations and non-verbal enactments, at what points was he consciously remembering an aspect of his trauma and at what points was he unaware of the source of what he was communicating?

These questions have no easy answers. In a previous paper, I proposed that as a result of biologically based capacities for the mirroring of behavioral and affective stimuli they have observed, young children can be driven to reenact traumatic experiences automatically outside of conscious awareness (Gaensbauer, 2011). At the same time, I have reported on a number of cases, such as the three-year-old just described, where the child's reenactments of a preverbal experience seemed quite purposeful (Gaensbauer, 1997; 2002; 2004). Based on Emilio's memory expressions and these previous case reports, my answer to the question of whether non-verbal traumatic memories in a young child are to be considered conscious or unconscious is that it depends on the situation. It could be either. I would suggest that the issue of whether a traumatic memory is internalized and expressed verbally or non-verbally in a young child is separate from the question of whether its expression is conscious or unconscious. I would also suggest that consciously experienced non-verbal memories, be they traumatic or non-traumatic, play a critical role in children's management of stressful events. Very young children, even in the preverbal period, demonstrate a strong sense of agency and purpose, i.e., conscious intent, as they respond adaptively to stimuli associated with previous stressful experiences.

References

Bauer, P. J. (1997). Development of memory in early childhood. In N. Cowan (Ed.). *The development of memory in childhood*. Hove East Sussex, UK: Psychology Press, pp. 83–112.

Bauer, P. J. (2007). *Remembering the times of our lives: Memory in infancy and beyond*. New Jersey: Earlbaum.

Bauer, P. J. (2013). Event memory: Neural, cognitive and social influences on early development. In M. Legerstee, D. W. Haley, & M. H. Bornstein (Eds.). *The infant mind: Origins of the social brain.* New York: The Guilford Press, pp. 146–166.

Benham, A. L. & Slotnik, C. F. (2006). Play therapy: Integrating clinical and developmental Perspectives. In J. Luby (Ed.). *Handbook of preschool mental health: Development, disorders, and treatment,* New York: Guilford Press, pp. 331–371.

Coates, S. & Gaensbauer, T. J. (2009). Event trauma in early childhood: Symptoms, assessment, intervention. *Child and Adolescent Psychiatric Clinics of North America,* 18, 611–626.

Fischer, K. & Granott, N. (1995). Beyond one-dimensional change: Parallel, concurrent, socially distributed processes in learning and development. *Human Development,* 38, 302–314.

Fivush, R. (1998). Children's recollections of traumatic and nontraumatic events. *Development and Psychopathology,* 10, 699–716.

Freud, S. (1905 [1953]). Three essays on the theory of sexuality. In J. Strachey (Ed.). *The standard edition of the complete psychological works of Sigmund Freud* (vol. 7). London: Hogarth Press, pp. 125–248.

Gaensbauer, T. J. (1985). The relevance of infant research for psychoanalysis. *Psychoanalytic Inquiry,* 5, 517–530.

Gaensbauer, T. J. (1995). Trauma in the preverbal period: Symptoms, memories, and developmental impact. *The Psychoanalytic Study of the Child,* 50, 122–149.

Gaensbauer, T. J. (1997). Traumatic stress disorder. In A. Lieberman, S. Wieder, & E. Fenichel (Eds.). *DC: 0–3 casebook: A guide to the use of zero to three's "diagnostic classification of mental health and developmental disorders of infancy and early childhood" in assessment and treatment planning.* Washington, DC: Zero To Three: National Center for Infants, Toddlers and Families, pp. 31–46.

Gaensbauer, T. J. (2002). Representations of trauma in infancy: Clinical and theoretical implications for the understanding of early memory. *Infant Mental Health Journal,* 23, 259–277.

Gaensbauer, T. J. (2004). Telling their stories: Representation and reenactment of traumatic experiences occurring in the first year of life. In: S. Tortora (Ed.). The multisensory world of the infant. *Journal of Zero to Three: National Center for Infants, Toddlers, and Families,* 25(5), 25–31.

Gaensbauer, T. J. (2011). Embodied simulation, mirror neurons, and the reenactment of trauma in early childhood. *Neuropsychoanalysis,* 13(1), 91–107.

Gaensbauer, T. J. & Kelsay, K. (2008). Situational and story stem scaffolding in psychodynamic play therapy with very young children. In C. Shaefer, P. Kelly-Zion, J. McCormick, & A. Ohnogi (Eds.). *Play therapy for very young children.* Lanham, MD: Rowman and Littlefield, pp. 173–198.

Hayne, H. & Jack, F. (2011). Childhood amnesia. *Willey Interdisciplinary Reviews: Cognitive Science,* 2, 136–145.

Howe, M. L. & Courage M. L. (1997). The emergence and early development of autobiographical memory. *Psychological Review,* 1904(3), 499–523.

Howe, M. L., Courage, M. L., & Edison, S. C. (2003). When autobiographical memory begins. *Developmental Review,* 23, 471–494.

Lyons-Ruth, K. (1999). The two-person unconscious: Intersubjective dialogue, enactive relational representation, and the emergence of new forms of relational organization. *Psychoanalytic Inquiry,* 19, 576–617.

Manns, J. R., Stark, C. E. L., & Squire, L. R. (2000). The visual paired-comparison task as a measure of declarative memory. *Proceedings of the National Academy of Sciences,* 97(22), 12375–12379.

McDonough, L., Mandler, J. M., McKee, R. D., & Squire, L. R. (1995). The deferred imitation task as a nonverbal measure of declarative memory. *Proceedings of the National Academy of Science*, 92, 7580–7584.

Meltzoff, A. N. (1990). The implications of cross-modal matching and imitation on the development of representation and memory in infants. In A. Diamond (Ed.). *The development and neural bases of higher cognitive functions: Annals of the New York Academy of Sciences* (vol. 608). New York: New York Academy of Sciences, pp. 1–37.

Meltzoff, A. (1995). What infant memory tells us about infantile amnesia: Long-term recall and deferred imitation. *Journal of Experimental Child Psychology*, 59, 497–515.

Nelson, C. (1995). The ontogeny of human memory: A cognitive neuroscience perspective. *Developmental Psychology*, 31, 723–738.

Nelson, K. & Fivush, R. (2004). The emergence of autobiographical memory: A social cultural developmental theory. *Psychological Review*, 111(2), 486–511.

Paley, J. & Alpert, J. (2003). Memory of infant trauma. *Psychoanalytic Psychology*, 20, 329–347.

Peterson, C., Grant, V., & Boland, L. (2005). Childhood amnesia in children and adolescents: Their earliest memories. *Memory*, 13, 622–637.

Rovee-Collier, C. & Gerhardstein, P. (1997). The development of infant memory. In N. Cowen (Ed.). *The development of memory in childhood*. Hove East Sussex, UK: Psychology Press, pp. 5–40.

Scheeringa, M. S. & Gaensbauer, T. J. (1999). Posttraumatic stress disorder. In C. Zeanah (Ed.). *Handbook of infant mental health, 2nd edition*. New York: Guilford Press, pp. 369–381.

Schore, A. N. (2003). *Affect regulation and the origin of the self*. Mahwah, NJ: Erlbaum.

Siegel, D. (1995). Memory, trauma, and psychotherapy: A cognitive sciences view. *Journal of Psychotherapy and Practice and Research*, 4, 93–122.

Simcock, G. & Hayne, H. (2002). Breaking the barrier? Children fail to translate their preverbal memories into language. *Psychological Science*, 13, 225–231.

Simcock, G. & Hayne, H. (2003). Age-related changes in verbal and non-verbal memory during early childhood. *Developmental Psychology*, 39(5), 805–814.

Squire, L. R. (2004). Memory systems of the brain: A brief history and current perspective. *Neurobiology of Learning and Memory*, 82, 171–177.

Zola-Morgan, S. & Squire, L. R. (1993). Neuroanatomy of memory. *Annual Review of Neuroscience*, 16, 547–563.

Part IV

Conclusions

Chapter 11

Concluding remarks and future perspectives

Robert M. Galatzer-Levy

CHICAGO

The 2014 Sandler Conference, The unconscious: A bridge between psycho-analysis and cognitive science researchers and clinicians in dialogue, was one of those rare conferences that lived up to its title. Not only were the papers and dialogue of extraordinary quality, but the sense of excitement of a group of colleagues moving toward a joint venture filled the two-and-a-half days of meetings. As such a conference should, this meeting stimulated intensely personal intellectual and emotional reactions in me. My closing remarks were intended not so much to summarize or critique the presentations, but rather to describe some of what the conference had stimulated for me. In what follows, I have tried to retrain these spontaneous responses as my main focus while providing enough scholarly apparatus that the reader can follow up on ideas that may be unfamiliar and invite deeper exploration.

Between 1896 and 1905 Freud published a series of masterful studies that lay the foundation of psychoanalysis by clearly demonstrating that mental processes that are actively barred from awareness result in symptoms, dreams, parapraxes including memory lapses, jokes and creative acts in the arts (Freud 1896, Freud 1900, Freud 1901, Freud 1905, Freud 1905). He carefully described these unconscious mental processes and showed the central ways in which they differ from conscious mentation.

Earlier in his career, Freud had attempted to integrate his psychological findings with the rapidly emerging neuroscience of his day (Freud 1891, Freud 1895), an effort he explicitly abandoned in chapter 7 of *The Interpretation of Dreams* in favor of a purely psychological theory. Nonetheless, his neuroscience thinking clearly shaped Freud's metapsychology (Pribram and Gill 1976) as generally biological thought continued to inform Freud's theorizing throughout his career (Sulloway 1979). But generally during this same period during which Freud lay the foundations of the study of the unconscious, he realized that an explanation of these phenomena in terms of the newly emerging neuroscience of his time was beyond the capacities of the field and opted instead for a purely psychological theory, one which found the bases of unconscious phenomena in the realm of human meanings and motives.

The subsequent 110 years saw Freud's theories extended to include phenomena like creativity and social structures, elaboration of elements of the theory in varied and sometimes contradictory directions, and enlarging to include an ever-widening range of meanings and motives central to human psychology.

Freud's thinking about unconscious mental processes seems to have begun with the assumption that normally mental processes approximate rationality, following the rules of logic and rigorously maintaining the distinction between sign and signified. Implicitly, Freud saw non-rational thinking as defective, primitive or childish. He had little tolerance, much less appreciation, for romantic attitudes and treated any indication of them in himself and others as a matter for ironic attack.[1] Rational decision-making requires the specification of measurable goals. Given Freud's biological orientation, it is not surprising that Freud took physiological well-being and reproductive success as the natural measure of the success of mental processes. His recognition that social function is necessary to such well-being led to the theory of mind forever in conflict between social demands and physiological pleasures, yet still a mind forever engaged in a rational struggle between these two goals (Freud 1927). Almost all psychoanalytic thinking has continued along lines set out by Freud's non-rational mental processes, first primarily in terms of processes that were almost entirely barred from awareness and later in terms of processes (like splitting and denial) which included conscious awareness of their content but protected against the consequences of consciousness by separating conscious elements from interacting with one another.

During the same century that psychoanalysts continued to harvest fruits of Freud's planting through ever-deepening and richer studies of the processes he had discovered, investigators from many other fields came to the study of related problems and developed conceptualizations that at least bordered on the question of unconscious mental processes.

First came the instantiation of processes that had formerly been thought to be purely mental in computational machinery. Freud's contemporary, Gottlob Frege, recognized that all logical processes could be set down as sequences of symbols, like those of arithmetic, and that the rules for manipulating these symbols constitute what we call logic (Frege 1893). Logic, like arithmetic, could be reduced to a set of rules for operating on symbols. Alan Turing understood that, if logic could be specified in this way, it could be implemented on a purely mechanical device, an idea that he first developed conceptually and then practically (Hodges 1983). Although attempts were made to reduce the remarkable significance of this development, for example, accusing computers of being "purely mechanical," it became ever more obvious that the computers could do more and more of the things thought to be the province of humans alone. Increasingly rich theories of computation emerged and with them an ever-increasing appreciation that brain function could be modeled using concepts and practices from computer science (Dietrich, Fodor et al. 2009). In fact, it became clear that the once prized goal of rationality was better achieved by computer machinery than human beings, a narcissistic blow that generated whole genres of science fiction discourse and academic controversy.

As the theory and practice of computation was elaborated, so, too, richer possibilities became open to it – possibilities that reflected efforts that came close to addressing the problem of existential meaning, a search which Kierkegaard (Kierkegaard 1997), vol. 5, p. 5, and many others had declared beyond the bounds of rationality and, hence, implicitly beyond the capacities of a machine governed exclusively by rational processes.

Most computers are carefully designed to process information logically and using methods that give highly predictable results, for the very good reason that they are most valued as part of twentieth-century technology. Devices designed to ensure that a rocket lands on the moon should not waste their resources on aesthetic, mythological, or existential ideas, in the way humans do. Furthermore, since computers must be programmed they have been designed with logical architectures that make it easy to know the consequences of a particular step in a program. Thus, until very recently, computers operated through a set series of sequential steps and were carefully designed to avoid the complexities that arise from abandoning such organization. Yet it is in these areas of complexity and the failures of straight forward rationality, where we process information in massively parallel and intertwined fashion or in other ways that allow for the emergence for surprising novel ideas and feelings that could not have been readily anticipated from their components that make them up or lead to them, that our most significant psychological experiences appear.

Imagine Oedipus the Simple computer confronted with the dilemma, "I desire to engage in sex with my mother but I fear my father will castrate me if I attempt it." Desire and fear are easily represented in the computer world by assigning numeric values to them in an overall hedonic state and deciding how to act on the basis of the sum of these hedonic values. If the sum exceeds some preset number, Oedipus tries to engage his mother sexually; if not, he abstains. Oedipus the Complex, another computer, is faced with the same dilemma but he is at the same time engaged in many other computations, such as deciding whether the words Mama, Madonna, and Marilyn are equivalent, and at the same time working on the problem of what to do about the cattle whose ownership he and his seven siblings might reasonably claim, as well as a few thousand other problems. His designer, who reveals herself under the name Evolution, had long ago learned a principle that was later discovered by computer scientists and called "NP computability" (Fortnow 2013) had not attempted to have Oedipus figure out a single strategy for all these problems that led to a hedonic maximum because the computation quickly took far too long for any physical computer. Instead, the designer set Oedipus the Complex to work on a large number of problems simultaneously with these various computations in contact with one another through a network. While Oedipus did not come up with perfect solutions, i.e., solutions that found the maximal hedonic pleasure, he started to do things that were surprising and seemed off. He tried to have sex with Madelyn instead of his mother, which actually worked out pretty well, but occasionally he came up with things that were really surprising, solutions that emerged from the very complexity of what he was computing (Holland 1998, Galatzer-Levy 2002). Every once in a while he came up with something astounding, like civilization (Freud 1927, Freud 1930).

As computers with fundamentally different architectures, particularly computers designed based on networks of parallel processors have been developed, many of the practical limitations of older computer designs are being overcome and machines that can do ever more of the tasks that seemed uniquely human are emerging. See, e.g., (Easley and Kleinberg 2010). What I am thinking about here is the way in which networks come ever closer in many respects to Freud's hermeneutics and subsequent developments, like French structuralism, have gradually given an approximation of theories of meaning within a computational framework. It is from studies that integrate models from computation and neurosciences that specific promising theories of the particulars of information processing in the mind-brain are emerging. For example, at this meeting, Karl Friston presented a beautiful model of how decision-making using the mathematical probability concept called a Markov blanket may be instantiated within the nervous system. It is a particularly interesting example of the field of computational neuroscience, a field dedicated for studying how the abstract ideas of computational theory can be applied to actual nervous systems. Other ideas derived from computer science and mathematics promise to enrich psychoanalytic thinking and particularly areas where psychoanalysis and brain science converge. For example, the study of fractal geometry is highly suggestive for making sense of phenomena like the selective permeability and boundaries that exists between various aspects of mental functions and interpersonal relations.

During the latter part of the twentieth century, the idea of a computational theory of brain function became an ever more practical reality. Theories of how and where brain functions occur emerged and were tested. Although I suspect that the tendency to conceptualize brain functions in terms of anatomical structures, which continues from a neurological tradition of brain localization, probably misses out on both a more dynamic picture and a more global picture of brain function, it is clear that current developments come ever closer to making Freud's discarded dream of an adequate computational picture of brain function to explain the psychology that he discovered a real possibility.[2]

During the same time frame, purely psychological conceptualizations of nonconscious mental processes in fields like cognitive psychology, social psychology and behavioral economics have sought to explain human behavior based on information processing that goes on outside of awareness. Were it not for the huge narcissistic investment that makes people in general overestimate the importance of their conscious experience and the way they conduct themselves and, in particular, leads people like ourselves who are highly invested in thinking as a means of coping with the world to overestimate both the power and significance of reason in daily life, it would be obvious that most of what human beings do occurs without conscious attention to the activity, and, in fact, day-to-day living would become quite impossible were we to attend to every muscle movement, shift in gaze, or even the connection between thoughts and fantasies that pass through our minds. Our implicit knowledge of how to do things and our habitual performance of various tasks takes up most of our active doing. How all this relates to the Freudian unconscious remains unclear except that it has a much greater part of the explanation for ordinary action than intuition suggests. The major aspect of the choice between what Kahneman (Kahneman 2013) finally came to refer to as "thinking fast" and "thinking slow" clearly boils down to questions of computational efficiency and the time available for decision-making. Our beloved theory of motivated avoidance of awareness as an exclusive explanation of why things are outside awareness needs to give way to an appreciation of the evolutionary value of being able to think fast enough to get through life.[3] The exploration of the relationship of these two forms of unawareness is an obvious topic for clinical investigation. Conscious thought is intrinsically slow, probably because its rules are more complex and the associative networks involved are more extensive than those involved in many types of non-conscious mental functioning.

The study of the psychological impact of trauma opens views of yet another area in which major understanding of mental function that transforms consciousness occurs. In addition to its enormous practical importance, from a purely scientific point of view, study of the mental processes involved in trauma provide a rich picture of the possibilities for the management of extreme distress through alterations in the nature of consciousness itself. Phenomena like dissociation, disavowal and denial commonly seen in trauma, while maintaining distressing content available to consciousness in a descriptive sense, alter consciousness in a way that is in many ways functionally equivalent to repression. Under the influence of these processes, mental contents are separated in a manner that ordinarily does not occur in consciousness but would appear to be a central aspect of unconscious mental processes. The study of the emotional states of post-traumatic mental function thus gives us an additional window into the operation of unconscious mental processes.

These five developments, that is the elaboration of the psychoanalytic theory of unconscious mental function, the development of a richer picture of computation generally, the increasingly richer picture of brain function, the much elaborated study of non-conscious mental functioning and studies of the impact of trauma on consciousness all call for a re-examination of concepts and phenomena referred to as unconscious mental functioning.

During the two-and-a-half days of the conference, we were treated to a wonderful smorgasbord of ideas about where we are and where we might go in terms of the development of thinking about unconscious mental functioning.

One thing that has become absolutely clear is that if we are to talk among ourselves as analysts and, even more, if we are to talk with students of other disciplines, it is essential to find ways to develop shared vocabularies that are sufficiently unambiguous to communicate important views, including differences in views, so that real ideas are not lost because we are using homonyms to refer to quite different matters. Eliding motivated limitations of awareness secondary to potential anxiety with limitation in awareness resulting from mental actions being habitual, i.e., actions that are kept out of awareness because consciousness would be an impediment to their performance, simply leads to confusion. Similarly referring to inborn psychological structures postulated in some psychoanalytic theories by the same terms as painful narratives that are barred from awareness unnecessarily complicates discourse. I think there is a universal agreement that a confusion of tongues serves no one well and that clarification, rather than debate over the choice of words, will prove most fruitful. Psychoanalysts would do well, for example, to avoid using expressions like "the unconscious" to refer to repressed mental content, since this usage tends to suggest a claim that is certainly not now credible, if it ever was, that the absence of psychological material from consciousness results from defense against anxieties aroused by the material that is outside of awareness.

But the studies described in this conference have gone far beyond conceptual clarification. Some of the ideas we have discussed basically turn Freudian thinking on its head. For example, Freud's implicit assumption that consciousness is an ordinary accompaniment of mental life is replaced with the idea that consciousness is a likely rare mental process occurring primarily in times of difficulty as a means of slow thinking involved with careful testing of hypothetical models of the environment rather than the ordinary stuff of acting in the world. Since the most salient part of the world for human beings involves interactions with other human beings, Freud's idea that the major computational effort must be devoted to the maintenance of physiological homeostasis comes squarely into question, as the maintenance of social connection may be both a more important and more challenging computational problem.

There are inevitably many important topics that could not be touched on in the brief time we had available for the conference. But I think there is one topic that is tremendously challenging and central to the field that has hardly received mention. This is the question of why conscious mental functioning includes the subjective experience of being, in an important sense, aware of a process that we believe to be thinking. Mark Solms concept of a conscious id, as valuable as it is, seems to leave this central element of the subjective dimension of consciousness untouched.

At the risk of simply adding to the already too vast and so far not very fruitful literature about the subjective experiences referred to as consciousness, I would like to suggest that we explore the possibility that the subjective element of consciousness emerges when mental processes take themselves as the object of examination. The Turing test, designed to answer the question of whether artificial intelligence, in the sense of a nonhuman entity having the same sort of intelligence as a human, examines whether an interrogator, separated from the physicality of the object of interrogation can differentiate that object from a person (Turing 1950). After it became apparent that computers could become as good as or better than people at solving purely cognitive problems, like playing chess, the obvious subject of interrogation became whether the computer was conscious. In order to answer questions like "Do you like the color blue?" or "How do you like to spend your time?" (whether truthfully or not) the object of interrogation, must have the ability to formulate nontrivial answers concerning its own functioning, i.e., genuine self-consciousness. Self-consciousness might be mimicked by an entity that had a database of appropriate self-reports about the kinds of things a conscious entity would say in response to questions. What would differentiate a non-conscious from a conscious entity would be its capacity to make responses that were based on its observation of its own functioning. This suggests that the core of consciousness is self-observation. Self-observation is the kind of complex reflexive process that results in emergent phenomena, so the possibility that consciousness is such an emergent phenomenon from self-observation is worthy of exploration.

For all my enthusiasm about various theories derived from computer science on brain science and psychoanalysis, I think we should be cautious about the degree to which we require these theories to correspond with the observed phenomenon. Are the ideas consistent with observations? For example, I particularly like the idea that consciousness is a special mode of processing involved in testing the relationship between internal hypotheses and the external world. As Rudolfo Llinás (Llinás 2001) pointed out long ago, the capacity for prediction is the core element of the evolutionary advantage of having the nervous system able to integrate and mediate between sensation and action. As our worm ancestors pushed through the muck, attempting to ingest something that would provide them with enough energy to go on pushing through it, it became essential that they be able to make accurate predictions about what they would find as they moved forward so that they might change course in search of nutriment and avoidance of danger. As a result, the caudable nerve plexis gradually evolved to be able to perform both more complex computations and to have specialized organs that could provide sense data about the external environment, e.g., olfactory sensors and eyes. This seems to me like a very solid argument based in multiple observations about why the central nervous system evolved as it did. Whether consciousness and fantasy are then best thought of as steps in the solution of current problems or better thought of as possibly serving other functions remains an open question. For example, they might well serve as simulations of a range of potential environmental problems in a manner that optimally stresses the nervous system to develop means of solving those problems not yet directly encountered, rather like the way in which lifting weights increases muscle strength that may ultimately be used for other purposes (Doidge 2007).

Finally, I would like to observe the extent to which fundamentally mathematical concepts, not always recognized as such, have been central to almost all of the presentations we have heard. Here I am using mathematics in the sense that Bion (Bion 1962, Bion 1963, Bion 1983) did when he recognized that from the richness of psychological situations it was often possible to abstract features whose formal manipulation leads to a richer understanding of the phenomena. Since the brain is a complex system in the sense that involves huge numbers of feedback loops, the mathematics involved is inevitably nonlinear and carries with it all the features that one expects of nonlinear system (for a guide to this enormous field see Galatzer-Levy (Galatzer-Levy 2009). One aspect of nonlinear dynamical systems theory concerns the nature of the predictions that are possible for nonlinear systems. For linear systems (or systems that are close enough to linear so that useful computations can be made as if the system were linear), predictions can be made in the form of precise descriptions of the system at a specified times. For example, Kepler could predict that Mars would be in such and such a location in the sky at such and such a time. The accuracy of these predictions is taken as good evidence of the truth of the underlying hypothesis that led to the prediction. For nonlinear systems by their very nature, predictions to particular quantities and data points are never possible because in nonlinear systems the slightest change in initial conditions can often lead to entirely different directions for the system's development. Instead, what can be predicted in nonlinear systems are patterns of action and movement of processes in spaces whose dimensions reflect the subject under study (e.g., in psychoanalysis, a space reflecting the dimensions of mental functions). Predictions for nonlinear systems are to patterns of motion (or, if you prefer, patterns of change), which are called attractors, rather than predicting the particular location of the system at a given moment. We might predict, for example, that an individual will be obsessively struggling to make decisions over extended periods of time but not what the content of his thinking will be at a particular moment. This is *not* because of a failure to gather sufficient information about the individual in question but rather because it is an inherent feature of nonlinear systems that predication to details cannot be made. This Sandler conference was organized to initiate a program of investigation into unconscious mental processes. The members of the IPA Research Committee believe the program can be profoundly fruitful and exciting over the coming years. As the structure of the program suggests, we share the idea that the topic requires convergent study from a variety of angles ranging from clinical psychoanalysis to neuroimaging to mathematical exploration. Some elements of the conference explored broad frameworks of study, while others gave detailed instances of investigation. The major goal of the conference was to introduce ourselves into the potentially creative muddle that constitutes our present understanding of unconscious mental process. At least for me, and I suspect for many of you, the conference was a spectacularly successful engagement in that undertaking.

Notes

1 Freud's attitude toward Romanticism is, on another level, more complex. He often turns to the Romantics and other non-scientific sources, especially when trying to understand non-logical thought. For example, in trying to describe the concrete thinking of some patients in erotic transferences, he writes that they "are accessible only to the logic of soup, with dumplings for arguments" (Freud 1915, p. 168, (mis)quoting the Romantic poet Heine in an effort to vividly capture the nature of the mental process).

2 The spectacular strides in neuroimaging in recent decades and the resulting refinements in correlations of brain anatomy and function have tended to obscure the limitations of these methods of study. In particular, current neuroimaging techniques cannot provide information about either localization or time course of mental events on a level that corresponds to the mental processes that most interest psychoanalysis. At the same time, these exciting developments tend to call attention away from formulations of brain function in terms of the brain as a dynamical system, an approach which is, in the long run, more consistent with general understandings of complex systems such as neural networks.

3 The psychology of the overvaluation of reason and the valorization of conscious mental process, so evident in Freud's writing, is in need of far more extensive study than it has received. It is clearly in part a historical response to the emergence of technologies founded in rational thought as well as a terror of the power of irrationality associated with the great wars of the twentieth century. But there is a great deal yet to be explored here. Some of the sociological-historical study of the topic is particularly suggestive (Erickson 2013).

References

Bion, W. R. (1962). *Learning from experience.* New York, Basic Books Pub. Co.

Bion, W. R. (1963). *Elements of psycho-analysis.* New York, Basic Books Pub. Co.

Bion, W. R. (1983). *Transformations.* New York, J. Aronson: Distributed by Scribner.

Dietrich, D., et al. (2009). *Simulating the mind: A technical neuropsychoanalytic approach.* New York, Springer.

Doidge, N. (2007). *The brain that changes itself: Stories of personal triumph from the frontiers of brain science.* New York, Viking.

Easley, D. & Kleinberg, J. (2010). *Networks, crowds, and markets: Reasoning about a highly connected world.* New York, Cambridge.

Erickson, P., et al. (2013). *How reason almost lost its mind: The strange career of cold war rationality.* Chicago, University of Chicago Press.

Fortnow, L. (2013). *The golden ticket P, NP and the search for the impossible.* Princeton, NJ, Princeton University Press.

Frege, G. (1893). *Grundgesetze der Arithmetik: begriffsschriftlich abgeleitet.* Jena, Pohle.

Freud, S. (1891). *On aphasia; critical study.* London, Imago.

Freud, S. (1895). Project for a scientific psychology. In J. Strachey (Ed.). *The standard edition of the complete psychological works of Sigmund Freud.* London, Hogarth Press: 295–387.

Freud, S. (1896). The aetiology of hysteria. In J. Strachey (Ed.). *The standard edition of the complete psychological works of Sigmund Freud.* London, Hogarth Press: 191–221.

Freud, S. (1900). The interpretation of dreams. In J. Strachey (Ed.). *The standard edition of the complete psychological works of Sigmund Freud.* London, Hogarth Press.

Freud, S. (1901). The psychopathology of everyday life. In J. Strachey (Ed.). *The standard edition of the complete psychological works of Sigmund Freud.* London, Hogarth Press.

Freud, S. (1905). Fragment of an analysis of a case of hysteria. In J. Strachey (Ed.). *The standard edition of the complete psychological works of Sigmund Freud.* London, Hogarth Press.

Freud, S. (1905). Jokes and their relation to the unconscious. In J. Strachey (Ed.). *The standard edition of the complete psychological works of Sigmund Freud*. London, Hogard Press.

Freud, S. (1915). Observations on transference-love: Further recommendations on the technique of psychoanalysis II. In J. Strachey (Ed.). *The standard edition of the complete psychological works of Sigmund Freud*. London, Hogarth press: 158–171.

Freud, S. (1927). Civilization and its discontents. In J. Strachey (Ed.). *The standard edition of the complete psychological works of Sigmund Freud*. London, Hogarth Press: 57–146.

Freud, S. (1930). Civilization and its discontents. In J. Strachey (Ed.). *The standard edition of the complete psychological works of Sigmund Freud*. London, Hogarth Press: 64–148.

Galatzer-Levy, R. (2002). Emergence. *Psychoanalytic Inquiry*, **22**: 708–727.

Galatzer-Levy, R. (2009). Finding Your Way Through Chaos, Fractals and Other Exotic Mathematical Objects: A Guide for the Perplexed. *Journal of the American Psychoanalytic Association*, **57**: 1227–1249.

Hodges, A. (1983). *Alan turing: The enigma*. New York, Simon & Schuster.

Holland, J. (1998). *Emergence: From chaos to order*. New York, Perseus.

Kahneman, D. (2013). *Thinking, fast and slow*. New York, Farrar, Straus and Giroux.

Kierkegaard, S. (1997). *Journals and papers*. Charlottesville, VA, InteLex Past Masters.

Llinás, R. (2001). *I of the vortex: From neurons to self*. Cambridge, MA, MIT Press.

Pribram, K. & Gill, M. (1976). *Freud's "project" reassessed*. New York, Basic Books.

Sulloway, S. (1979). *Freud, biologist of the mind: Beyond the psychoanalytic legend*. New York, Basic Books.

Turing, A. (1950). Computing Machinery and Intelligence. *Mind*, **59**: 433–460.

Index